Hands-On Financial Modeling with Excel for Microsoft 365

Second Edition

Build your own practical financial models for effective forecasting, valuation, trading, and growth analysis

Shmuel Oluwa

BIRMINGHAM—MUMBAI

Hands-On Financial Modeling with Excel for Microsoft 365

Second Edition

Publishing Product Manager: Devika Battike
Senior Editor: Nazia Shaikh
Content Development Editor: Sean Lobo
Technical Editor: Rahul Limbachiya
Copy Editor: Safis Editing
Project Coordinator: Aparna Ravikumar Nair
Proofreader: Safis Editing
Indexer: Rekha Nair
Production Designer: Sinhayna Bais
Marketing Coordinator: Priyanka Mhatre

First published: July 2019

Second edition: June 2022

Production reference: 1200522

Published by Packt Publishing Ltd.
Livery Place
35 Livery Street
Birmingham
B3 2PB, UK.

ISBN 978-1-80323-114-3

www.packt.com

Contributors

About the author

Shmuel Oluwa is a financial executive and seasoned instructor of over 25 years in a number of finance-related fields, with a passion for imparting knowledge. He has developed considerable skills in the use of Microsoft Excel and has organized training courses in business Excel, financial modeling with Excel, forensics and fraud detection with Excel, Excel as an investigative tool, accounting for non-accountants, and credit analysis with Excel, amongst others. He has given classes in Nigeria, Angola, Kenya, and Tanzania but his online community of students covers several continents. Shmuel divides his time between London and Lagos with his pharmacist wife. He is fluent in three languages: English, Yoruba, and Hebrew.

About the reviewer

Jane Sarah Lat is a results-oriented and commercially astute finance professional with 12+ years in financial management and analysis. She has a background working in finance for blue-chip multinational organizations. Jane is a **Certified Management Accountant (CMA)** and received her **Graduate Diploma of Chartered Accounting (GradDipCA)** from the **Chartered Accountants Australia and New Zealand (CA ANZ)**. Driven by her passion to continuously upskill with analytic capabilities, she became a Microsoft Certified Data Analyst Associate and TIBCO Certified Professional on Spotfire. Jane holds a Bachelor of Science in accountancy from the University of Santo Tomas in the Philippines graduating magna cum laude.

Table of Contents

Part 2 – The Use of Excel Features and Functions for Financial Modeling

3

Formulas and Functions – Completing Modeling Tasks with a Single Formula

4

Referencing Framework in Excel

5
An Introduction to Power Query

Part 3 – Building an Integrated 3-Statement Financial Model with Valuation by DCF

6
Understanding Project and Building Assumptions

7
Asset and Debt Schedules

8
Preparing a Cash Flow Statement

9
Ratio Analysis

10
Valuation

11

Model Testing for Reasonableness and Accuracy

Part 4 – Case Study

12

Case Study 1 – Building a Model to Extract a Balance Sheet and Profit and Loss from a Trial Balance

13

Case Study 2 – Creating a Model for Capital Budgeting

Preface

Financial modeling is an essential tool for financial decision-making. Today, as professional disciplines continue to overlap, the discipline of financial modeling continues to take center stage. Anyone who works with data needs a structured way to capture, analyze, and display information in order to assist the decision-making process.

Financial modeling meets these requirements by creating integrated mathematical models that can be modified and updated with just a few keystrokes.

Virtually all decisions converge to monetary considerations that will ultimately benefit from mathematical representation in a financial model. This is why financial modeling is so popular with students and seasoned professionals alike.

In this book, with the benefit of years of feedback from students across the globe, I have tried to present concepts and methods in a clear and uncluttered fashion using several illustrations that will take you step by step through various procedures. I have also introduced different case studies and examples of financial models to illustrate the diversity of the subject.

After reading this book, you will be able to approach any financial decision-making situation with confidence. You will understand the importance of preparing a template, isolating assumptions, growth drivers, and integrating your model to facilitate modification and analysis.

Who this book is for

This book is for students and professionals with an interest in financial analysis, data analysis, accountancy, and valuation, and anyone involved in the financial decision-making process.

What this book covers

Chapter 1, An Introduction to Financial Modeling and Excel, examines various definitions of financial modeling and discusses the basic components of a financial model. It also looks at the limitations of Excel and explains why Excel is still the ideal tool for financial modeling.

Chapter 2, Steps for Building a Financial Model, takes you through the process of building a discounted cash flow financial model, from discussions with the client to ratio analysis and valuation. It adopts a step-by-step approach, with each step explained in detail.

Chapter 3, Formulas and Functions – Completing Modeling Tasks with a Single Formula, explains the use of formulas and functions in Excel with examples of lookup functions, utility functions, pivot tables, and charts. It also looks at a number of new functions introduced in Excel for Microsoft 365.

Chapter 4, The Referencing Framework in Excel, takes a detailed look at the referencing framework in Excel. It explains how this important concept helps to speed up your work as a modeler, providing welcome relief from the boredom and grind of repetitive calculations that are synonymous with modeling.

Chapter 5, An Introduction to Power Query, as the title says, introduces this game-changing feature of Excel that addresses a vital function in financial modeling: getting and transforming data from a wide range of sources. The chapter is reinforced with the inclusion of two real-world case studies.

Chapter 6, Understanding Project and Building Assumptions, takes you through discussions with management/clients, building assumptions, and identifying growth drivers.

Chapter 7, Asset and Debt Schedules, takes you through the preparation of these essential schedules and connecting them with the balance sheet and profit and loss account.

Chapter 8, Preparing a Cash Flow Statement, emphasizes the importance of cash in financial analysis and valuation, with elements of this statement explained in detail.

Chapter 9, Ratio Analysis, talks about the importance of ratio analysis to investment analysts by exposing trends and relationships not immediately noticeable in the financial statements.

Chapter 10, Valuation, brings the discounted cash flow model to an end with descriptions of absolute and relative methods of valuation.

Chapter 11, Model Testing for Reasonableness and Accuracy, attempts to mitigate the uncertainty inherent in financial models with sensitivity and scenario analyses.

Chapter 12, Case Study 1 - *Building a Model to Extract a Balance Sheet and Profit and Loss from a Trial Balance*, speaks to accountants and auditors who carry out this task frequently. This process is automated with a model that can be updated from year to year with just a few keystrokes.

Chapter 13, Case Study 2 - *Creating a Model for Capital Budgeting*, explains the importance of capital budgeting and, with the help of a comprehensive case study, builds a model that you can adapt and use.

To get the most out of this book

The book assumes a basic knowledge of Excel. A basic understanding of accounting terms is also useful but not essential.

Software/hardware covered in the book	Operating system requirements
Excel for Microsoft 365	Windows, macOS, or Linux
ECMAScript 11	

You will need a Microsoft 365 subscription to have access to the new Excel functions referred to throughout the book. This book assumes minimal knowledge of mathematics, accounting, and statistics. Where concepts in this discipline arise, I have endeavored to explain the topics in simple terms and use examples and illustrations to ensure a thorough understanding of the concepts.

If you are using the digital version of this book, we advise you to type the code yourself or access the code from the book's GitHub repository (a link is available in the next section). Doing so will help you avoid any potential errors related to the copying and pasting of code.

Download the color images

We also provide a PDF file that has color images of the screenshots and diagrams used in this book. You can download it here: `https://static.packt-cdn.com/downloads/9781803231143_ColorImages.pdf`.

Conventions used

There are a number of text conventions used throughout this book.

`Code in text`: Indicates code words in text, database table names, folder names, filenames, file extensions, pathnames, dummy URLs, user input, and Twitter handles. Here is an example: "Mount the downloaded `WebStorm-10*.dmg` disk image file as another disk in your system."

A block of code is set as follows:

```
html, body, #map {
  height: 100%;
  margin: 0;
  padding: 0
}
```

When we wish to draw your attention to a particular part of a code block, the relevant lines or items are set in bold:

```
[default]
exten => s,1,Dial(Zap/1|30)
exten => s,2,Voicemail(u100)
exten => s,102,Voicemail(b100)
exten => i,1,Voicemail(s0)
```

Any command-line input or output is written as follows:

```
$ mkdir css
$ cd css
```

Bold: Indicates a new term, an important word, or words that you see onscreen. For instance, words in menus or dialog boxes appear in **bold**. Here is an example: "Select **System info** from the **Administration** panel."

> **Tips or Important Notes**
> Appear like this.

Get in touch

Feedback from our readers is always welcome.

General feedback: If you have questions about any aspect of this book, email us at customercare@packtpub.com and mention the book title in the subject of your message.

Errata: Although we have taken every care to ensure the accuracy of our content, mistakes do happen. If you have found a mistake in this book, we would be grateful if you would report this to us. Please visit www.packtpub.com/support/errata and fill in the form.

Piracy: If you come across any illegal copies of our works in any form on the internet, we would be grateful if you would provide us with the location address or website name. Please contact us at copyright@packt.com with a link to the material.

If you are interested in becoming an author: If there is a topic that you have expertise in and you are interested in either writing or contributing to a book, please visit authors.packtpub.com.

Share Your Thoughts

Once you've read *Hands-On Financial Modeling with Excel for Microsoft 365*, we'd love to hear your thoughts! Scan the QR code below to go straight to the Amazon review page for this book and share your feedback.

https://packt.link/r/1-803-23114-9

Your review is important to us and the tech community and will help us make sure we're delivering excellent quality content.

Part 1 – Financial Modeling Overview

Understand the meaning of financial modeling with Excel, including an overview of the steps to follow when building an integrated financial model.

This part includes the following chapters:

- *Chapter 1, An Introduction to Financial Modeling and Excel*
- *Chapter 2, Steps for Building a Financial Model*

1
An Introduction to Financial Modeling and Excel

If you asked five professionals the meaning of financial modeling, you would probably get five different answers. The truth is that they would all be correct in their own context. This is inevitable since the boundaries for the use of financial modeling continue to be stretched almost daily, and new users want to define the discipline from their own perspective.

To provide some clarity, in this chapter, we will learn some popular definitions and basic ingredients of a financial model and what my favorite definitions are. You will also learn about the different tools for financial modeling that currently exist in the industry, as well as those features of Excel that make it the ideal tool to use in order to handle the various needs of a financial model.

By the end of the chapter, you should be able to hold your own in any discussion about basic financial modeling.

We will cover the following topics:

- The main ingredients of a financial model
- Understanding mathematical models
- Definitions of financial models
- Types of financial models
- Limitations of Excel as a tool for financial modeling
- Excel—the ideal tool

The main ingredients of a financial model

First of all, there needs to be a situation or problem that requires you to make a **financial decision**. Your decision will depend on the outcome of two or more alternative scenarios as described in the following subsections.

Financial decisions can be divided into three main types:

- Investment
- Financing
- Distributions or dividends

Investment

We will now look at some reasons for investment decisions:

- **Purchasing new equipment**: You may already have the capacity and know-how to make or build the equipment in-house. There may also be similar equipment already in place. Considerations will thus be whether to make, buy, sell, keep, or trade in the existing equipment.

- **Business expansion decisions**: This could mean taking on new products, opening up a new branch, or expanding an existing branch. The considerations would be to compare the following:

  A.   The cost of the investment: Isolate all costs specific to the investment, for example, construction, additional manpower, added running costs, adverse effects on existing business, marketing costs, and so on.

B.   The benefit gained from the investment: We could gain additional sales. There will be a boost in other sales as a result of the new investment, along with other quantifiable benefits. Regarding the **return on investment (ROI)**, a positive ROI would indicate that the investment is a good one.

Financing

Financing decisions primarily revolve around whether to obtain finance from personal funds or external sources:

- **Individual**: For example, if you decided to get a loan to purchase a car, you would need to decide how much you wanted to put down as your deposit so that the bank would lend you the difference. The considerations would be as follows:

  - **Interest rates**: The higher the interest rate, the less you would seek to finance externally.

  - **Tenor of the loan**: The longer the tenor, the lower the monthly repayments, but the longer you remain indebted to the bank.

  - **How much you can afford to contribute**: This will establish the least amount you will require from the bank, no matter what interest rate they are offering.

  - **Amount of monthly repayments**: How much you will be required to pay monthly to repay the loan.

- **Company**: A company would need to decide whether to seek finance from internal sources (approach shareholders for additional equity) or external sources (obtain bank funding). We can see the considerations in the following list:

  - **Cost of finance**: The cost of finance can be easily obtained with the interest and related charges. These finance charges will have to be paid whether or not the company is making a profit. Equity finance is cheaper since the company does not have to pay dividends every year, also the amount paid is at the discretion of the directors.

  - **Availability of finance**: It's generally difficult to squeeze more money out of shareholders unless perhaps there has been a run of good results and decent dividends. So, the company may have no other choice than external finance.

  - **The risk inherent in the source**: With external finance, there is always the risk that the company may find itself unable to meet the repayments as they fall due. This exposes the company to all the consequences of defaulting, including security risk and embarrassment among other things.

- **The desired debt-to-equity ratio**: The management of a company will want to maintain a debt-to-equity ratio that is commensurate with their risk appetite. Risk takers will be comfortable with a ratio of more than 1:1, while risk-averse management would prefer a ratio of 1:1 or less.

Dividends

Distributions or **dividend decisions** are made when there are surplus funds. The decision would be whether to distribute all the surplus, part of the surplus, or none at all. We can see the considerations in the following list:

- **The expectations of the shareholders**: Shareholders provide cheap funds and are generally patient. However, shareholders want to be assured that their investment is worthwhile. This is generally manifested by profits, growth, and in particular, dividends, which have an immediate effect on their finances. The funds are considered cheap because payment of dividends is not mandatory but at the discretion of the directors.

- **The need to retain surplus for future growth**: It is the duty of the directors to temper the urge to succumb to pressure to declare as many dividends as possible, with the necessity to retain at least part of the surplus for future growth and contingencies.

- **The desire to maintain a good dividend policy**: A good dividend policy is necessary to retain the confidence of existing shareholders and to attract potential investors.

You should now have a better understanding of financial decision making. Let's now look at mathematical models that are created to facilitate financial decision making.

Understanding mathematical models

In the scheme of things, the best or optimum solution is usually measured in monetary terms. This could be the option that generates the highest returns, the cheapest option, the option that carries an acceptable level of risk, or the most environmentally friendly option, but is usually a mixture of all these features.

Inevitably, there is inherent uncertainty in the situation, which makes it necessary to make assumptions based on past results. The most appropriate way to capture all the variables inherent in the situation or problem is to create a mathematical model. The model will establish relationships between the variables and assumptions that serve as input to the model. This model will include a series of calculations to evaluate the input information and to clarify and present the various alternatives and their consequences. This model is referred to as a financial model.

Definitions of financial models

Wikipedia considers a financial model to be a mathematical model that represents the performance of a financial asset, project, or other investment in abstract form.

Corporate Finance Institute believes that a financial model facilitates the forecasting of future financial performance by utilizing certain variables to estimate the outcome of specific financial decisions.

BusinessDictionary agrees with the notion of a mathematical model in that it comprises sets of equations. The model analyzes how an entity will react to different economic situations with a focus on the outcome of financial decisions. It goes on to list some of the statements and schedules you would expect to find in a financial model. Additionally, the publication considers that a model could estimate the financial impact of a company's policies and restrictions put in place by investors and lenders. It goes on to give the example of a cash budget as a simple financial model.

eFinance Management considers a financial model to be a tool with which the financial analyst attempts to predict the earnings and performance of future years. It considers the completed model to be a mathematical representation of business transactions. The publication names Excel as the primary tool for modeling.

Here's my personal definition:

A mathematical model created to resolve a financial decision making situation. The model facilitates decision making by presenting preferred courses of action and their consequences, based on the results of the calculations performed by the model.

This definition mentions *financial decision making* and a *mathematical model*. It goes on to explain the relationship between them, which is to *facilitate decision making*. Importantly, it notes that the model presents *preferred courses of action* from which the decision maker can make a choice, taking into consideration the *consequences* of each option.

Types of financial models

There are several different types of financial models. The model type depends on its purpose and target audience. Generally speaking, you can create a financial model when you want to value or project something, or a mixture of the two.

The following models are examples that seek to calculate values.

The 3-Statement model

The 3-Statement model is the starting point for most valuation models and here's what it includes:

- **Balance sheet** (or statement of financial position): This is a statement of assets (which are resources owned by the company that have economic value, and that are usually used to generate income for the company, such as plants, machinery, and inventory), liabilities (which are obligations of the company, such as accounts payable and bank loans), and owner's equity (which is a measure of the owner's investment in the company).

The following is an example of a balance sheet showing assets, liabilities, and equity. Note how the accounting equation plays out with total assets minus current liabilities being *equal* to equity plus non-current liabilities:

	Wuzobia Global Limited								
	Balance Check	TRUE	TRUE	TRUE	TRUE	TRUE	TRUE	TRUE	TRUE
	(Unless otherwise specified, all finance) Units	Y01A	Y02A	Y03A	Y04F	Y05F	Y06F	Y07F	Y08F
	ASSUMPTIONS								
	BALANCE SHEET								
	ASSETS								
	Non current assets								
	Property, plant and equipment	90,000	80,000	70,000	240,000	210,000	180,000	150,000	120,000
	Investments	12,197	11,549	18,106	58,106	58,106	58,106	58,106	58,106
	Total non current assets	102,197	91,549	88,106	298,106	268,106	238,106	208,106	178,106
	Current assets								
	Inventories	15,545	18,007	21,731	14,530	21,860	14,659	21,390	14,790
	Trade and other receivables	20,864	31,568	35,901	33,812	39,063	37,117	42,519	40,730
	Cash and cash equivalents	7,459	17,252	9,265	65,106	67,707	98,408	121,224	172,905
	Total current assets	43,868	66,827	66,897	113,447	128,630	150,184	185,734	228,425
	Current liabilities								
	Trade and other payables	12,530	16,054	15,831	14,072	15,938	14,179	16,045	14,287
	Overdraft	-	-	-	-	-	-	-	-
	Total current liabilites	12,530	16,054	15,831	14,072	15,938	14,179	16,045	14,287
	Net current assets	31,338	50,773	51,066	99,375	112,693	136,005	169,689	214,138
	Total Assets less current liasbilities	133,535	142,322	139,172	397,481	380,799	374,111	377,795	392,244
	Non current liabilities								
	Unsecured loans	40,000	35,000	30,000	275,000	245,000	215,000	185,000	155,000
	Other non current liabilities	5,000	5,000	5,000	5,000	5,000	5,000	5,000	5,000
	Total non current liabilities	45,000	40,000	35,000	280,000	250,000	220,000	190,000	160,000
	Equity								
	Share capital	70,000	70,000	70,000	70,000	70,000	70,000	70,000	70,000
	Retained earnings	18,535	32,322	34,172	47,481	60,799	84,111	117,795	162,244
	Total equity	88,535	102,322	104,172	117,481	130,799	154,111	187,795	232,244
	Total equity and non current liabiliti	133,535	142,322	139,172	397,481	380,799	374,111	377,795	392,244

Figure 1.1 – Balance sheet (statement of financial position)

- **Income statement** (or statement of comprehensive income): This is a statement that summarizes the performance of a company by comparing the income it has generated within a specified period to the expenses it has incurred in realizing that income over the same period to arrive at a profit (as in this case) or loss:

Balance Check	TRUE	TRUE	TRUE	TRUE	TRUE	TRUE	TRUE	TRUE
(Unless otherwise specified, all finance Units	Y01A	Y02A	Y03A	Y04F	Y05F	Y06F	Y07F	Y08F
PROFIT & LOSS								
Revenue	260,810	272,241	245,009	297,938	311,453	325,582	340,351	355,791
Cost of sales	177,782	184,703	179,052	179,690	180,331	180,974	181,619	182,267
GROSS PROFIT	83,028	87,538	65,957	118,247	131,122	144,608	158,732	173,524
Sales and marketing expenses	9,204	10,521	11,099	11,210	11,719	12,250	12,806	13,387
General and administration expenses	25,145	26,402	21,752	26,786	28,001	29,271	30,599	31,987
Depreciation	10,000	10,000	10,000	30,000	30,000	30,000	30,000	30,000
Other expenses	5,675	13,342	4,394	8,559	8,948	9,353	9,778	10,221
OPERATING PROFIT	33,004	27,273	18,712	41,692	52,455	63,733	75,549	87,929
Other income	3,333	2,183	2,156	2,156	2,156	2,156	2,156	2,156
Interest	2,000	3,750	3,250	15,250	26,000	23,000	20,000	17,000
Other Finance cost	9,265	9,644	9,848	9,586	9,586	9,586	9,586	9,586
PROFIT BEFORE TAX	25,072	16,062	7,770	19,013	19,025	33,303	48,120	63,499
Income tax expense	6,537	2,275	5,320	5,704	5,708	9,991	14,436	19,050
PROFIT AFTER TAX	18,535	13,787	1,850	13,309	13,318	23,312	33,684	44,449

Figure 1.2 – Income statement (statement of comprehensive income)

- **Cash flow statement**: This is a statement that identifies inflow and outflow of cash to and from various sources, operations, and transactions during the period under review. The net cash inflow should equal the movement in cash and cash equivalents shown on the balance sheet during the period under review.

The following screenshot shows an example of a cash flow statement:

	Balance Check		TRUE	TRUE	TRUE	TRUE	TRUE	TRUE	TRUE	TRUE
	(Unless otherwise specified, all financials an Units	YO1A	YO2A	YO3A	YO4F	YO5F	YO6F	YO7F	YO8F
113	CASH FLOW STATEMENT									
115	**Cashflow from Operating Activities**									
116	PAT		13,787	1,850	13,309	13,318	23,312	33,684	44,449
117	Add: Depreciation		10,000	10,000	30,000	30,000	30,000	30,000	30,000
118	Add: Interest Expense		3,750	3,250	15,250	26,000	23,000	20,000	17,000
120	**Net Change in Working Capital**									
121	Add: Increase in Accounts payable		3,524	(223)	(1,759)	1,865	(1,758)	1,866	(1,758)
122	Less: Increase in Inventory		(2,462)	(3,724)	7,201	(7,331)	7,201	(7,331)	7,201
123	Less: Increase in Account Receivables		(10,704)	(4,333)	2,089	(5,252)	1,946	(5,402)	1,789
124	Net Change in Working Capital		(9,642)	(8,280)	7,532	(10,717)	7,389	(10,867)	7,232
126	**Cashflow from Operations**		17,895	6,820	66,091	58,600	83,701	72,816	98,681
128	**Cashflow from Investment Activities**									
129	Less: Capex		-	-	(200,000)	-	-	-	-
130	Add: Proceeds from Disposal of Assets									
131	Less: Increase in WIP									
132	Less: Increase in Investments		648	(6,557)	(40,000)	-	-	-	-
133	Cashflow from Investment Activities		648	(6,557)	(240,000)	-	-	-	-
135	**Cashflow from Financing Activities**									
136	Add: New Equity Raised									
137	Add: New Unsecured Loans Raised		-	-	250,000	-	-	-	-
138	Less: Unsecured Loans Repaid		(5,000)	(5,000)	(5,000)	(30,000)	(30,000)	(30,000)	(30,000)
139	Less: Dividends Paid									
140	Less: Interest Expense		(3,750)	(3,250)	(15,250)	(26,000)	(23,000)	(20,000)	(17,000)
141	Cashflow from Financing Activities		(8,750)	(8,250)	229,750	(56,000)	(53,000)	(50,000)	(47,000)
143	**Net Cashflow**		9,793	(7,987)	55,841	2,600	30,701	22,816	51,681
145	**Cash Balance**									
146	Opening Balance		7,459	17,252	9,265	65,106	67,707	98,408	121,224
147	Net Cashflow		9,793	(7,987)	55,841	2,600	30,701	22,816	51,681
148	Closing Balance		17,252	9,265	65,106	67,707	98,408	121,224	172,905

Figure 1.3 – Cash flow statement

The mathematics of the 3-Statement model starts with historical data. In other words, the income statement, the balance sheet, and the cash flow statement for the previous 3 to 5 years will be entered into Excel. A set of assumptions will be made and used to drive the financial results, as displayed in the three statements, over the next 3 to 5 years. This will be illustrated in more detail later in the book and will become clearer.

The discounted cash flow model

The **discounted cash flow** (DCF) model is considered by most experts to be the most accurate for valuing a company. Essentially, the method considers the value of a company to be the sum of all the future cash flow the company can generate. In practice, the cash is adjusted for various obligations to arrive at the free cash flow. The method also considers the time value of money, a concept with which we will become much more familiar in *Chapter 10, Valuation*.

The DCF method applies a valuation model to the 3-Statement model mentioned in the *The 3-Statement model* section. Later, we will encounter and explain fully the technical parameters included in this valuation model.

The comparative companies model

This model relies on the theory that similar companies will have similar multiples. **Multiples** are, for example, comparing the value of the company or enterprise (**enterprise value** or **EV**) to its earnings. There are different levels of earnings, such as the following:

- **Earnings before interest, tax, depreciation, and amortization (EBITDA)**
- **Earnings before interest and tax (EBIT)**
- **Profit before tax (PBT)**
- **Profit after tax (PAT)**

A number of multiples can be generated and used to arrive at a range of EVs for the company. The comparative method is simplistic and highly subjective, especially in the choice of comparable companies; however, it is favored among analysts, as it provides a quick way of arriving at a rough estimate of a company's value.

Again, this method relies on the 3-Statement model as a starting point. You then identify three to five similar companies with the quoted EVs.

In selecting similar companies (a peer group), the criteria to consider will include the nature of the business, size in terms of assets and/or turnover, geographical location, and more.

We then use the EVs and selected multiples of these companies to arrive at an EV for the target company. These are the steps to follow:

1. Calculate the multiples for each of the companies (such as *EV/EBITDA*, *EV/SALES*, and *P/E* ratio (also known as price-earnings ratio).

2. Then calculate the **mean** and **median** of the multiples of the peer group of companies.

   The median is often preferred over the mean, as it corrects the effect of outliers. Outliers are those individual items within a sample that are significantly larger or smaller than the other items and will thus tend to skew the mean one way or the other.

3. Then adopt the median multiplier for your target company and substitute the earnings, for example, EBITDA, calculated in the 3-Statement model in the following equation:

$$Multiple = EV/EBITDA$$

4. When you rearrange the formula, you arrive at the EV for the target company:

$$EV = Multiple \times EBITDA$$

The merger and acquisition model

When two companies seek to merge, or one seeks to acquire the other, investment analysts build a **mergers and acquisitions (M&A)** model. Valuation models are first built for the individual companies separately, then a model is built for the combined post-merger entity, and the earnings per share for all three are calculated. The **earnings per share (EPS)** is an indicator of a company's profitability. It is calculated as net income divided by the number of shares.

The purpose of the model is to determine the effect of the merger on the acquiring company's EPS. If there is an increase in post-merger EPS, then the merger is said to be accretive, otherwise, it is dilutive.

The leveraged buyout model

In a leveraged buyout situation, company A acquires company B for a combination of cash (equity) and loan (debt). The debt portion tends to be significant. Company A then runs company B, servicing the debt, and then sells company B after 3 to 5 years. The **leveraged buyout (LBO)** model will calculate a value for company B as well as the likely return on the eventual sale of the company.

All these are examples of models created to value something. We will now look at models that project something.

Loan repayment schedule

When you approach your bank for a car loan, your accounts officer takes you through the structure of the loan including loan amount, interest rate, monthly repayments, and sometimes, how much you can afford to put down as a deposit.

The following table arranges these assumptions in a logical manner so as to easily accommodate any changes in the assumptions and immediately display the effect on the final output:

Amortization Table

Assumptions				
Cost of Asset	20,000,000			
Customer's Contribn	10%	< | >		
Loan Amount	18,000,000			
Interest Rate (Annual)	10%	< | >		
Tenor (Years)	10	< | >		
Payment periods per year	12			
Interest Rate (Periodic)	0.83%			
Total periods	120			
Periodic Repayment (PMT)	=PMT(C11,C12,C7)			

Periods	PMT	Interest Paid	Principal Reduction	Balance
0				18,000,000.00
1	237,871.33	150,000.00	87,871.33	17,912,128.67
2	237,871.33	149,267.74	88,603.59	17,823,525.09
3	237,871.33	148,529.38	89,341.95	17,734,183.14
4	237,871.33	147,784.86	90,086.47	17,644,096.67
5	237,871.33	147,034.14	90,837.19	17,553,259.48
6	237,871.33	146,277.16	91,594.16	17,461,665.32
7	237,871.33	145,513.88	92,357.45	17,369,307.87
8	237,871.33	144,744.23	93,127.09	17,276,180.77
9	237,871.33	143,968.17	93,903.15	17,182,277.62
10	237,871.33	143,185.65	94,685.68	17,087,591.94
11	237,871.33	142,396.60	95,474.73	16,992,117.21
12	237,871.33	141,600.98	96,270.35	16,895,846.86
13	237,871.33	140,798.72	97,072.60	16,798,774.26
14	237,871.33	139,989.79	97,881.54	16,700,892.72
15	237,871.33	139,174.11	98,697.22	16,602,195.50
16	237,871.33	138,351.63	99,519.70	16,502,675.80
17	237,871.33	137,522.30	100,349.03	16,402,326.78
18	237,871.33	136,686.06	101,185.27	16,301,141.51
19	237,871.33	135,842.85	102,028.48	16,199,113.03
20	237,871.33	134,992.61	102,878.72	16,096,234.31
21	237,871.33	134,135.29	103,736.04	15,992,498.27
22	237,871.33	133,270.82	104,600.51	15,887,897.76
23	237,871.33	132,399.15	105,472.18	15,782,425.58
24	237,871.33	131,520.21	106,351.11	15,676,074.47
25	237,871.33	130,633.95	107,237.37	15,568,837.10
26	237,871.33	129,740.31	108,131.02	15,460,706.08
27	237,871.33	128,839.22	109,032.11	15,351,673.97
28	237,871.33	127,930.62	109,940.71	15,241,733.26

Figure 1.4 – Amortization table

The loan repayment schedule model illustrated in the preceding screenshot consists of a section that contains all our assumptions, and another section with the repayment schedule, which is integrated with the assumptions in such a way that any change in the assumptions will automatically update the schedule without further intervention from the user.

The monthly repayment is calculated using Excel's **PMT** function. The tenor is 10 years, but repayments are monthly (12 repayments per year), giving a total number of repayments of *(nper) of 12 × 10 = 120*. Note that the annual interest rate will have to be converted to a rate per period, which is *10%/12 (rate/periods)*, to give *0.83%* per month in our example. The *PV* is the loan amount. We also need to keep in mind that the actual loan amount is the cost of the asset minus the customer's deposit.

Selection scroll bars have been added to the model so that the customer's deposit (10%–25%), interest rate (18%–21%), and tenor (5–10 years) can be easily varied and the results immediately observed since the parameters will recalculate automatically.

The preceding screenshot shows the kind of amortization table banks use in order to turn around customers' options so quickly.

The budget model

A **budget model** is a financial plan of cash inflows and outflows of a company. It builds scenarios of required or standard results for turnover, purchases, assets, debt, and more. It can then compare the actual result with the budget or forecast and make decisions based on the results. Budget models are typically monthly or quarterly and focus heavily on the profit and loss account.

Other types of models

Other types of financial models include the following:

- **Initial public offer model**: A financial model created to support a company's initial public offering prepared to attract investors.

- **Sum of the parts model**: In this method of valuation, the different divisions or segments of a company are assessed separately. The value of the company is the aggregate of all the parts.

- **Consolidation model**: This is created by taking the results of several business units or divisions and combining them into one model.

- **Options pricing mode**: This is a model for mathematically arriving at a theoretical price for an option.

Hopefully, you will now appreciate the diverse range of models that exist and the challenges a modeler will have to ensure that their models are clear, comprehensive, and error-free.

A lot of emphasis must be placed on using the right tool and having a thorough grasp of that tool.

Limitations of Excel as a tool for financial modeling

Excel has always been recognized as the go-to software for financial modeling. However, there are significant shortcomings in Excel that have made the serious modeler look for alternatives, in particular in the case of complex models. The following are some of the disadvantages of Excel that dedicated financial modeling software seeks to correct:

- **Large datasets**: Excel struggles with very large data. After most actions, Excel recalculates all formulas included in your model. For most users, this happens so quickly that you don't even notice. However, with large amounts of data and complex formulas, delays in recalculation become quite noticeable and can be very frustrating. Alternative software can handle huge multidimensional datasets that include complex formulas.

- **Data extraction**: In the course of your modeling, you will need to extract data from the internet and other sources. For example, financial statements from a company's website, exchange rates from multiple sources, and more. This data comes in different formats with varying degrees of structure. Excel does a relatively good job of extracting data from these sources. However, it has to be done manually, and thus it is tedious and limited by the skill set of the user. **Oracle BI**, **Tableau**, and **SAS** are built, among other things, to automate the extraction and analysis of data. (This deficit has been mitigated in Office 365 with the use of Power Query, now integrated as part of Excel. See *Chapter 5*, *An Introduction to Power Query*.)

- **Risk management**: A very important part of financial analysis is risk management. Let's look at some examples of risk management here:

  A.   **Human error**: Here, we talk about the risk associated with the consequences of human error. With Excel, exposure to human error is significant and unavoidable. Most alternative modeling software is built with error prevention as a prime consideration. As many of the procedures are automated, this reduces the possibility of human error to a bare minimum.

  B.   **Error in assumptions**: When building your model, you need to make a number of assumptions since you are making an educated guess as to what might happen in the future. As essential as these assumptions are, they are necessarily subjective. Different modelers faced with the same set of circumstances may come up with different sets of assumptions leading to quite different outcomes. This is why it is always necessary to test the accuracy of your model by substituting a range of alternative values for key assumptions and to observe how this affects the model.

This procedure of substituting alternative values for some assumptions, referred to as sensitivity and scenario analyses, is an essential part of modeling. These analyses can be done in Excel, but they are always limited in scope and are done manually. Alternative software can easily utilize **Monte Carlo** simulation for different variables or sets of variables to supply a range of likely results as well as the probability that they will occur. Monte Carlo simulation is a mathematical technique that substitutes a range of values for various assumptions, and then runs calculations over and over again. The procedure can involve tens of thousands of calculations until it eventually produces a distribution of possible outcomes. The distribution indicates the chance or probability of individual results happening. *Chapter 11, Model Testing for Reasonableness and Accuracy*, includes a simple example of Monte Carlo simulation.

Excel – the ideal tool

In spite of all the shortcomings of Excel, and the very impressive results from alternative modeling software, Excel continues to be the preferred tool for financial modeling.

The reasons for this are easy to see:

- *Already on your computer*: You probably already have Excel installed on your computer. The alternative modeling software tends to be proprietary and has to be installed on your computer manually.

- *Familiar software*: About 80% of users already have a working knowledge of Excel. The alternative modeling software will usually have a significant learning curve in order to get used to unfamiliar procedures.

- *No extra cost*: You will most likely already have a subscription to Microsoft Office including Excel. The cost of installing new, specialized software and teaching potential users how to use the software tends to be high and continuous. Each new batch of users has to undergo training on the alternative software at an additional cost.

- *Flexibility*: The alternative modeling software is usually built to handle certain specific sets of conditions so that while they are structured and accurate under those specific circumstances, they are rigid and cannot be modified to handle cases that differ significantly from the default conditions. Excel is flexible and can be adapted to different purposes.

- *Portability*: Models prepared with alternative software cannot be readily shared with other users, or outside of an organization since the other party must have the same software in order to make sense of the model. Excel is the same from user to user, right across geographical boundaries.

- *Compatibility*: Excel communicates very well with other software. Almost all software can produce output, in one form or another, that can be understood by Excel. Similarly, Excel can produce output in formats that lots of different software can read. In other words, there is compatibility whether you wish to import or export data.

- *Superior learning experience*: Building a model from scratch with Excel gives the user a great learning experience. You gain a better understanding of the project and of the entity being modeled. You also learn about the connection and relationship between different parts of the model.

- *Understanding data*: No other software mimics human understanding the way Excel does. Excel understands that there are 60 seconds in a minute, 60 minutes in an hour, 24 hours in a day, and so on, to weeks, months, and years. Excel knows the days of the week, months of the year, and their abbreviations, for example, Wed for Wednesday, Aug for August, and 03 for March! Excel even knows which months have 30 days, which months have 31 days, which years have 28 days in February, and which are leap years and have 29 days. It can differentiate between numbers and text. It also knows that you can add, subtract, multiply, and divide numbers, and we can arrange text in alphabetical order. On the foundation of this human-like understanding of these parameters, Excel has built an amazing array of features and functions that allow the user to extract almost unimaginable detail from an array of data. Some of these are highlighted in *Chapter 5*, *An Introduction to Power Query*.

- *Navigation*: Models can very quickly become very large, and with Excel's capacity, most models will be limited only by your imagination and appetite. This can make your model unwieldy and difficult to navigate. Excel is wealthy in navigation tools and shortcuts; it makes the process less stressful and even enjoyable. The following are examples of just a few of the navigation tools:

    C. *Ctrl + PageUp/PageDown*: These keys allow you to quickly move from one worksheet to the next. *Ctrl + PageDown* jumps to the next worksheet and *Ctrl + PageUp* jumps to the previous worksheet.

    D. *Ctrl + Arrow Key* ($\rightarrow \downarrow \leftarrow \uparrow$): If the active cell (the cell you're in) is blank, then pressing *Ctrl + Arrow Key* will cause the cursor to jump to the first populated cell in the direction of the cursor. If the active cell is populated, then pressing *Ctrl + Arrow Key* will cause the cursor to jump to the last populated cell before a blank cell in the direction of the cursor.

Summary

You should now have a better idea of what constitutes a financial model. You should also understand the shortcomings of Excel, why some alternative tools are sometimes used, but also why Excel continues to be the favored tool for financial modeling.

In the next chapter, we will learn about and understand the various steps involved in creating a model.

2
Steps for Building a Financial Model

The process of building a financial model can be broken down into several distinct stages. Most of these stages can run concurrently with others, while some can't start until others are concluded. This chapter introduces you to the steps required for building a model, with explanatory notes on the nature of each of the steps.

Any project you wish to undertake should begin with gaining an accurate understanding of what the project is all about. If you start off in the wrong direction, one of three things will happen:

- Partway through the project, you'll realize that this is not what the client wants, and you'll then have to start all over again.

- You'll end up convincing the client to accept a project that was never intended.

- You'll persist with the wrong project, and it'll end up being rejected.

So much depends on this stage that it typically takes up about 75% of your total modeling time.

In this chapter, we will cover the following topics:

- Discussions with management

- Building assumptions

- Building a template for your model
- Uploading historical financial data
- Projecting the balance sheet and profit and loss account
- Additional schedules and projections
- Cash flow statement
- Preparing Ratio analysis
- Valuation

Discussions with management

This is where you determine or confirm the scope and target of your model. Management is also the primary source of information about future plans and trends.

Usually, it's not possible to get all of the details at the first time of asking. You should, therefore, be prepared to go back to the section heads and ask the same, or similar, questions from a position of better understanding.

The following paragraphs describe the steps to take to ensure that you get the most out of your discussions with management, as well as where to concentrate your attention.

Gauging management expectations

While discussing with management, you need to get a clear understanding of their expectations from the assignment and what they hope will be achieved.

If all that is required is a projected cash flow, then a full-blown valuation model would be a waste of time and resources, and you probably wouldn't get paid for the extra work. We will take a detailed look at the all-important cash flow statement and different valuation models later in this book.

Knowing your client's business

It is essential that you know the client's business thoroughly. You need to know the industry of the business and identify any peculiarities due to geographical location, as well as those specific to the client. You should also gain some knowledge of the trends in the industry, and who the client's competitors are. If the client operates in a specialized industry, you need to consider consulting with someone who is an expert in that field. Whenever there is uncertainty, corroborative evidence is one of the best forms of assurance that you are doing the right thing.

Department heads

It is the department heads that will contribute the most toward building assumptions about future growth and expected trends. They have been in their respective areas of expertise for years and have come to understand the business better than most. As a result, you should place reliance on their responses.

You should, therefore, be in a position to assess how competent they are to give credible insight into the company's plans.

Once we have commenced discussions with management, we can start to identify and articulate our assumptions. This can run concurrently with your discussions once you have determined the nature, scope, and purpose of the assignment.

Building assumptions

Financial modeling is all about projecting results or behavior into the future.

To do this, you will need to build up a set of assumptions to bridge the gap between actual performance and future results. Although you will need to project every single item in the model, your assumptions will focus on items that will have a material effect on the final results. Other non-material items can be projected as, say, a percentage of turnover (for revenue items) or a best-judgment figure (for balance sheet items).

Your assumptions will need to consider whether items will increase, decrease, or stay the same. How you calculate the projected change is referred to as the **growth driver**. For example, for revenue items, it could be inflation, year-on-year growth, or some other indicator.

In the course of the assignment, you may need to make new assumptions and/or modify others. A great way to make your model easier and faster to navigate and update is to standardize and simplify your model by creating a template.

Building a template for your model

It is always important to be systematic in the way you build and maintain your model. Even if only you will make use of the model, whenever you have cause to revisit the model after a period of time, you do not want to have to wade through various schedules and worksheets to find what you need.

This is even more important if your model is going to be used by someone else.

A good way to ensure that your model is easy to follow and use is to build a template (a standard format) with some simple rules guiding how data is to be input and presented. In general, you will require at least six columns of figures, three each of historical and projected years, and another three or four columns for descriptive information. The template should enhance navigation and be easy to follow. The first major decision is whether to adopt a single-worksheet or multiple-worksheet approach.

In the following sections, we will learn about some of the features of both approaches, including pros and cons and tips to make your model easy to follow, such as color-coding.

Multiple-worksheet approach

In a multiple-worksheet approach, each worksheet is dedicated to one statement. So, you have assumptions, balance sheet, profit and loss, cash flow statements, and so on, all on separate worksheets. This means that you will end up with 10 or more worksheets. The following screenshot gives an indication of the multiple tabs required in this approach:

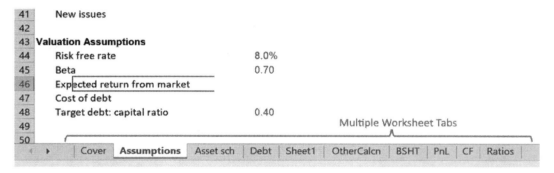

Figure 2.1 – Multiple tabs under the multiple-worksheet approach

When you dedicate one worksheet to one statement only, for example, the balance sheet, you know that everything on the balance sheet worksheet relates to the balance sheet alone. There is no ambiguous content on the worksheet. If you then need to modify or query the content of that worksheet, you can do so without having to consider whether or not you are affecting a statement other than the balance sheet.

In order to facilitate efficient navigation through your model, you should ensure that each year is in the same column on each worksheet. So, if the Y05F year is in the J column on the balance sheet worksheet, it should be in the J column on the profit and loss, cash flow, and all other worksheets.

Single-worksheet approach

In order to follow this approach, you must ensure that you maintain a standard layout for all statements right from the onset. Any changes to column width or attempts to insert or delete columns will affect all statements since they are stacked one on top of the other. An important part of this approach is the grouping of each statement. Excel allows you to group rows so that they can be collapsed and hidden or expanded and revealed by clicking the – or + signs that are displayed alongside the row labels when the group is created. The following screenshot is an example of the single-worksheet approach:

Wazobia Global Limited

Balance Check		TRUE	TRUE	TRUE	TRUE	TRUE
(Unless otherwise specified, all finai	Units	Y01A	Y02A	Y03A	Y04A	Y05A
Accumulated Depreciation						
Opening Balance		–	10,000	20,000	30,000	60,000
Add: Depreciation during current year		10,000	10,000	10,000	30,000	30,000
Closing Balance		**10,000**	**20,000**	**30,000**	**60,000**	**90,000**
Net Book Value		90,000	80,000	70,000	240,000	210,000
DEBT SCHEDULE						
Unsecured Loans						
Opening		–	40,000	35,000	30,000	275,000
Additions		40,000	–	–	250,000	–
Repayments On 40M	8 yrs		5,000	5,000	5,000	5,000
Repayments On 250M	10 yrs					
Closing	0	40,000	35,000	30,000	275,000	270,000
Interest rate		10%	10%	10%	10%	10%
Interest		2,000	3,750	3,250	15,250	27,250
SOCI - OTHER CALCN						
Equity						
Opening		70,000	70,000	70,000	70,000	70,000
Additions		–	–	–	–	–
Closing		70,000	70,000	70,000	70,000	70,000
Retained earnings						
Opening		–	18,535	32,322	74,172	87,481
Result for the year - PAT		18,535	13,787	41,850	13,309	12,443
Closing		18,535	32,322	74,172	87,481	99,924
RATIOS						
Profitability Ratios						
EBIT Margin		10%	7%	4%	11%	14%
PBT Margin		10%	6%	3%	6%	6%
PAT Margin		7%	5%	1%	4%	4%

Cover	**Financial Model**	Valuation	⊕		

Figure 2.2 – An example of a vertical layout financial model

There are vertical lines down the left border, just before the row numbers. The length of each vertical line covers the range of rows included in that particular group. The collapse or expand button is displayed at the end of the line, just after the last row of the group. It appears as a – sign when the group is expanded. Clicking the – sign will collapse the group and turn the sign to a + sign. Click the + sign if you wish to expand the group.

You will create the groups so that, when you collapse a statement, the title of that statement will remain visible, as shown in the following screenshot:

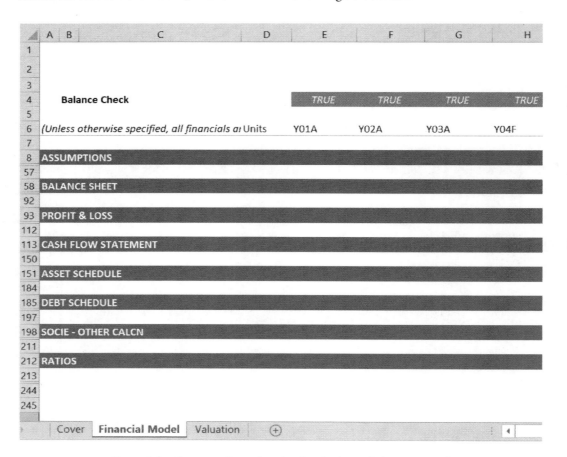

Figure 2.3 – Groups collapsed under the single-worksheet approach

In the preceding screenshot, you will notice that, with the schedules collapsed, row **8** is followed by row **38**. The rows in between contain the **ASSUMPTIONS** schedule, which is hidden when the grouped rows are collapsed. By pressing the + sign beside the row **38** label, the group will be expanded to expose the full schedule. *Figure 2.3* is an example of how your groups should look when arranged properly.

Next, we will look at the column layout. With navigation issues at the back of your mind, reduce the width of the first two columns, **A** and **B**, and expand column **C**, as shown in *Figure 2.4*.

Column **A** will be used for the first level of titles, column **B** for the second level of titles, and column **C** for the description or details that would require a wider column.

The following screenshot shows how your model template should look:

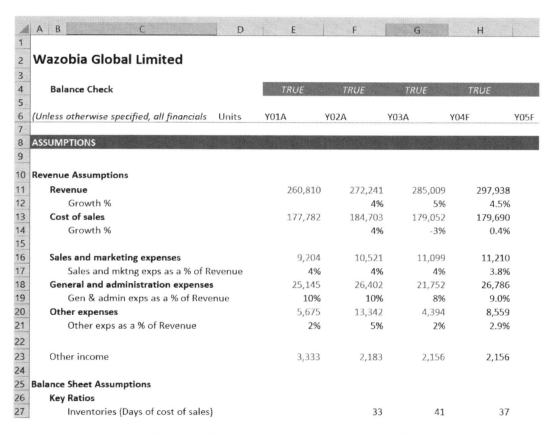

			Units	Y01A	Y02A	Y03A	Y04F	Y05F
Wazobia Global Limited								
Balance Check				TRUE	TRUE	TRUE	TRUE	
(Unless otherwise specified, all financials			Units	Y01A	Y02A	Y03A	Y04F	Y05F
ASSUMPTIONS								
Revenue Assumptions								
	Revenue			260,810	272,241	285,009	297,938	
	Growth %				4%	5%	4.5%	
	Cost of sales			177,782	184,703	179,052	179,690	
	Growth %				4%	-3%	0.4%	
	Sales and marketing expenses			9,204	10,521	11,099	11,210	
	Sales and mktng exps as a % of Revenue			4%	4%	4%	3.8%	
	General and administration expenses			25,145	26,402	21,752	26,786	
	Gen & admin exps as a % of Revenue			10%	10%	8%	9.0%	
	Other expenses			5,675	13,342	4,394	8,559	
	Other exps as a % of Revenue			2%	5%	2%	2.9%	
	Other income			3,333	2,183	2,156	2,156	
Balance Sheet Assumptions								
	Key Ratios							
	Inventories (Days of cost of sales)				33	41	37	

Figure 2.4 – Template extract for a financial model

This arrangement gives a cascading effect and facilitates quick navigation between headings of the same level, using Excel keyboard shortcuts. For example, with the cursor on **ASSUMPTIONS**, cell **A8**, pressing *Ctrl* + the down arrow (↓) will cause the cursor to jump down to cell **A25**, **Balance Sheet Assumptions**. Column **D** will be for the **Units** and column **E** for the first year of historical financial data. As mentioned earlier in this chapter, the years should retain the same column on every worksheet in the multiple worksheet approach. With the single-worksheet approach, this is not an issue as the statements are stacked one on top of another:

- **Color-coding**: This is a method used to differentiate between typed-in (hardcoded) cells that may be changed and revised, and those cells that contain formulas. Hardcoded cells should be in blue font, with calculated cells retaining the default black color. This will be very helpful when troubleshooting or when there is the need to amend original assumptions. You will be able to identify the input cells very quickly, which are the only cells that may require modifying.

- **Freeze panes**: With this option, you will be able to leave titles and column headings visible when you scroll down below their usual level of visibility. You should freeze panes so that **Balance Check** and **Years** will remain visible in the frozen rows of the balance sheet.

- **Rounding off**: The significance of rounding off becomes apparent when you have to populate 10 columns with annual financials. Screen space gets filled up very quickly, making it necessary to scroll to the right in order to view some of the data.

As much as possible, you should round off your figures so that all of the years fit within one screen width.

Hopefully, you now see how a standard approach and template can make your modeling faster and more efficient.

Uploading historical financial data

Once you have the template in place, the next step is to obtain historical financials. With historical data, we are interested in the balance sheet, profit and loss account, and cash flow statement. It is common, in the course of preparing financial statements, to have a number of initial drafts that may have content that will be superseded when the final statements are agreed upon. Ensure that the financials you are given are the final audited financial statements.

The more information you have, the more accurate your projections will be; however, you must not get carried away, as too much information will make the model unnecessarily cumbersome. Generally, historical data is limited to 5 years, with another 5 years of projected financials. Try to get soft copies of the historical financials in Excel readable format, as this will significantly reduce the amount of time you will need to spend converting into your template format.

Inevitably, you will need to tidy up the data to bring formatting and arrangement in line with your model template and resolve other anomalies. The actual figures from the historical financials will not change as you create your model; however, more often than not, you would have obtained the financials from a source that works with different preferences and priorities to yours. Moreover, the financials were not prepared with you and your financial model in mind. Imported data is, therefore, riddled with formatting or presentation anomalies that make it difficult, and sometimes impossible, to utilize some Excel tools and shortcuts. This makes it necessary to retype some or all of the financials.

The following screenshot is the **ACCENTURE PLC** balance sheet published on **August 31, 2016**, extracted from the Accenture website (`https://www.accenture.com/_acnmedia/PDF-35/Accenture-2016-Shareholder-Letter10-K006.pdf`). It illustrates how even the most accomplished financials will need to be adjusted to suit your template:

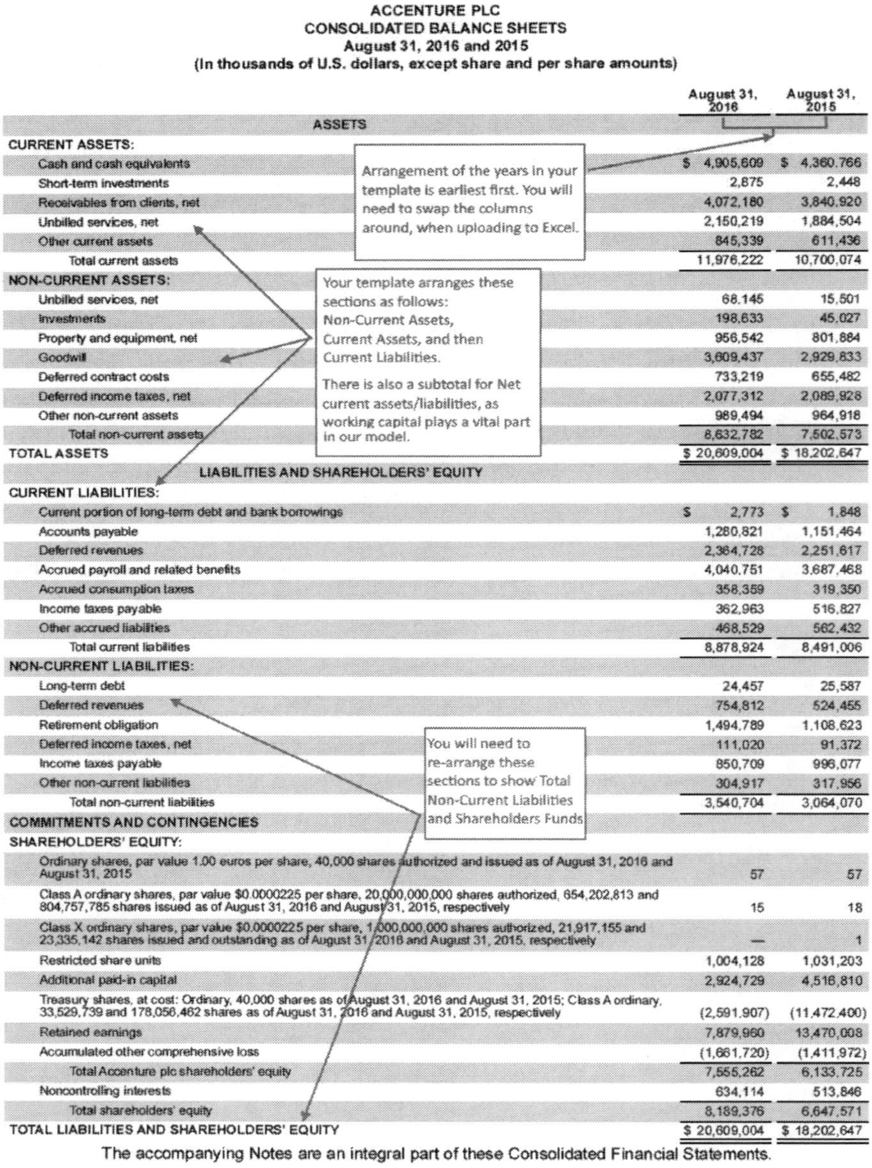

ACCENTURE PLC
CONSOLIDATED BALANCE SHEETS
August 31, 2016 and 2015
(In thousands of U.S. dollars, except share and per share amounts)

	August 31, 2016	August 31, 2015
ASSETS		
CURRENT ASSETS:		
Cash and cash equivalents	$ 4,905,609	$ 4,360,766
Short-term investments	2,875	2,448
Receivables from clients, net	4,072,180	3,840,920
Unbilled services, net	2,150,219	1,884,504
Other current assets	845,339	611,436
Total current assets	11,976,222	10,700,074
NON-CURRENT ASSETS:		
Unbilled services, net	68,145	15,501
Investments	198,633	45,027
Property and equipment, net	956,542	801,884
Goodwill	3,609,437	2,929,833
Deferred contract costs	733,219	655,482
Deferred income taxes, net	2,077,312	2,089,928
Other non-current assets	989,494	964,918
Total non-current assets	8,632,782	7,502,573
TOTAL ASSETS	$ 20,609,004	$ 18,202,647
LIABILITIES AND SHAREHOLDERS' EQUITY		
CURRENT LIABILITIES:		
Current portion of long-term debt and bank borrowings	$ 2,773	$ 1,848
Accounts payable	1,280,821	1,151,464
Deferred revenues	2,364,728	2,251,617
Accrued payroll and related benefits	4,040,751	3,687,468
Accrued consumption taxes	358,359	319,350
Income taxes payable	362,963	516,827
Other accrued liabilities	468,529	562,432
Total current liabilities	8,878,924	8,491,006
NON-CURRENT LIABILITIES:		
Long-term debt	24,457	25,587
Deferred revenues	754,812	524,455
Retirement obligation	1,494,789	1,108,623
Deferred income taxes, net	111,020	91,372
Income taxes payable	850,709	996,077
Other non-current liabilities	304,917	317,956
Total non-current liabilities	3,540,704	3,064,070
COMMITMENTS AND CONTINGENCIES		
SHAREHOLDERS' EQUITY:		
Ordinary shares, par value 1.00 euros per share, 40,000 shares authorized and issued as of August 31, 2016 and August 31, 2015	57	57
Class A ordinary shares, par value $0.0000225 per share, 20,000,000,000 shares authorized, 654,202,813 and 604,757,785 shares issued as of August 31, 2016 and August 31, 2015, respectively	15	18
Class X ordinary shares, par value $0.0000225 per share, 1,000,000,000 shares authorized, 21,917,155 and 23,335,142 shares issued and outstanding as of August 31, 2016 and August 31, 2015, respectively	—	1
Restricted share units	1,004,128	1,031,203
Additional paid-in capital	2,924,729	4,516,810
Treasury shares, at cost: Ordinary, 40,000 shares as of August 31, 2016 and August 31, 2015; Class A ordinary, 33,529,739 and 178,056,462 shares as of August 31, 2016 and August 31, 2015, respectively	(2,591,907)	(11,472,400)
Retained earnings	7,879,960	13,470,008
Accumulated other comprehensive loss	(1,661,720)	(1,411,972)
Total Accenture plc shareholders' equity	7,555,262	6,133,725
Noncontrolling interests	634,114	513,846
Total shareholders' equity	8,189,376	6,647,571
TOTAL LIABILITIES AND SHAREHOLDERS' EQUITY	$ 20,609,004	$ 18,202,647

The accompanying Notes are an integral part of these Consolidated Financial Statements.

Figure 2.5 – Accenture accounts for 2015 and 2016

The screenshot shows uploaded data for the 2016 accounts of Accenture Plc. It gives us figures for 2 years, 2015 and 2016. Since we need 5 years' historical financial statements, we will need to download two more sets of accounts, for the years ending August 31, 2014 (which will include the 2013 figures) and 2012, so that we have the accounts for the years 2012 to 2016. This means that you will have to repeat all of the corrections and adjustments on the other two sets of accounts. After correcting for formatting and presentation in the historical accounts, you should convert the historical financials into your template with the earliest year in column **E** followed by the next four years in subsequent columns. You should ensure that the balance check for these historical years is **TRUE**, which will give you confidence that the historical figures have been completely and accurately imported. The balance check is an automated check to visually display whether or not the balance sheet is in balance, that *net assets* equals *shareholders' funds*. The following screenshot illustrates how the balance check shows that the balance sheets are in balance and how it should be visible from anywhere in the model:

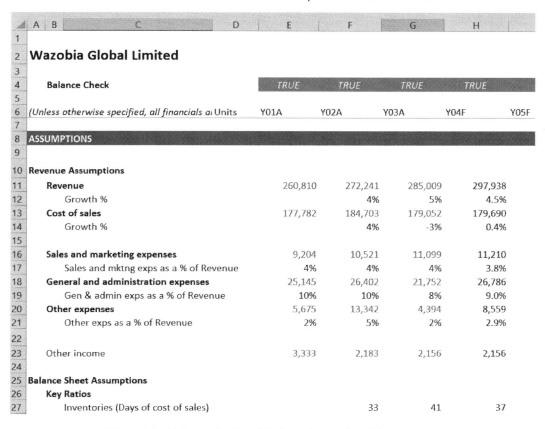

		E	F	G	H
2	**Wazobia Global Limited**				
4	Balance Check	*TRUE*	*TRUE*	*TRUE*	*TRUE*
6	(Unless otherwise specified, all financials ai Units	Y01A	Y02A	Y03A	Y04F	Y05F
8	ASSUMPTIONS				
10	Revenue Assumptions				
11	Revenue	260,810	272,241	285,009	297,938
12	Growth %		4%	5%	4.5%
13	Cost of sales	177,782	184,703	179,052	179,690
14	Growth %		4%	-3%	0.4%
16	Sales and marketing expenses	9,204	10,521	11,099	11,210
17	Sales and mktng exps as a % of Revenue	4%	4%	4%	3.8%
18	General and administration expenses	25,145	26,402	21,752	26,786
19	Gen & admin exps as a % of Revenue	10%	10%	8%	9.0%
20	Other expenses	5,675	13,342	4,394	8,559
21	Other exps as a % of Revenue	2%	5%	2%	2.9%
23	Other income	3,333	2,183	2,156	2,156
25	Balance Sheet Assumptions				
26	Key Ratios				
27	Inventories (Days of cost of sales)		33	41	37

Figure 2.6 – Balance check visible from the profit and loss account

Rows **1** to **6** will be frozen at the top of the page so that they will remain visible no matter how far down the worksheet you scroll.

Projecting the balance sheet and profit and loss account

In order to project the financials, you will need to determine the growth drivers for the balance sheet and profit and loss account. Growth drivers are those parameters that best capture the movement in individual items over the years. The nature of the item and your expertise will determine which parameter you select as an appropriate growth driver. An example of a growth driver for turnover is the year-on-year growth or inflation.

You should know that the balance sheet growth drivers are not as straightforward as with the profit and loss. We will cover this in detail in *Chapter 6, Understanding Project and Building Assumptions*.

Once the historical growth drivers have been calculated, you will need to project them over the next 5 years. You will be guided by your notes on the discussions with management and, in particular, the section heads for their suggestions on how growth is likely to behave in the next 5 years. An example may be a steady annual increase at the historical **compounded annual growth rate (CAGR)** for the previous 5 years. The CAGR will be explained in detail in *Chapter 6, Understanding Project and Building Assumptions*.

Once you have done that, apply the driver for the first projected year, Y06F, to the actual turnover of the previous year, Y05A, which is the final year of historical data, to arrive at the projected turnover for Y06F and so on, as seen in the following screenshot:

(Unless otherwise specified, all financials Units	Y01A	Y02A	Y03A	Y04F	Y05F	Y06F
ASSUMPTIONS						
Revenue Assumptions						
Revenue	260,810	272,241	285,009	297,938	311,453	=I11*(1+J12)
Growth %		4%	5%	4.5%	4.5%	4.5%
Cost of sales	177,782	184,703	179,052	179,690	180,331	180,974

Figure 2.7 – Buildup of turnover

Follow this procedure for each of the following years, for each item, to build up the balance sheet and profit and loss account.

Additional schedules and projections

At this stage, it would have come to your attention that **Balance Check** for the projected years is now red and **FALSE**. This is because our balance sheet and profit and loss account are not yet complete.

We have projected growth for most items, but there are some items that require specific treatment, such as CapEx, depreciation, loans, and interest.

ASSET SCHEDULE is prepared to capture the movement in property, plant, and machinery. The following screenshot shows the full **Capex** and **Depreciation Schedule** values:

Wazobia Global Limited

Balance Check		TRUE	TRUE	TRUE	TRUE	TRUE	TRUE	TRUE	TRUE
(Unless otherwise specified, all financials are in N '000, Units		Y01A	Y02A	Y03A	Y04A	Y05A	Y06F	Y07F	Y08F
ASSET SCHEDULE									
Depreciation Method	SLM								
Asset Life	Years	10	10	10	10			10	10
Disposal of Assets	N Mn	-	-	-	-			-	-
Capex	N Mn	100,000	-	-	200,000	-	-	-	-
Depreciation Schedule									
Y01A		10,000	10,000	10,000	10,000	10,000	10,000	10,000	10,000
Y02A									
Y03A									
Y04F					20,000	20,000	20,000	20,000	20,000
Y05F									
Y06F									
Y07F									
Y08F									
Total Depreciation		10,000	10,000	10,000	30,000	30,000	30,000	30,000	30,000
Gross Block									
Opening Balance		-	100,000	100,000	100,000	300,000	300,000	300,000	300,000
Add: Capex		100,000	-	-	200,000	-	-	-	-
Less: Assets Sold/ Disposed		-	-	-	-	-	-	-	-
Closing Balance		100,000	100,000	100,000	300,000	300,000	300,000	300,000	300,000
Accumulated Depreciation									
Opening Balance		-	10,000	20,000	30,000	60,000	90,000	120,000	150,000
Add: Depreciation during current year		10,000	10,000	10,000	30,000	30,000	30,000	30,000	30,000
Closing Balance		10,000	20,000	30,000	60,000	90,000	120,000	150,000	180,000
Net Book Value		90,000	80,000	70,000	240,000	210,000	180,000	150,000	120,000

Figure 2.8 – ASSET SCHEDULE

The company's plans for **CapEx** over the duration of the model will be reflected here. Historical **CapEx** and disposal of assets will be shown under the years during which the expenditure or sale took place. The schedule will also take into account the cost of the assets and useful life and depreciation rates and methods. Assets with different depreciation rates will be treated separately.

The ultimate destination of this schedule is the end-of-year total cost of fixed assets, the accumulated depreciation charge. This will be arrived at using the *BASE* method. These balances are taken to the balance sheet. Another important output of this schedule is the total depreciation for the year that is taken to the profit and loss account.

DEBT SCHEDULE is prepared to map the movement in secured and unsecured loans. Here, again, using the *BASE* method, we arrive at the closing balances that are taken to the balance sheet. The schedule is also used to calculate the interest charge for the year, which is taken to the profit and loss account. The following screenshot is an illustration of the debt schedule and other schedules used to update the balance sheet and profit and loss account:

Wazobia Global Limited

Balance Check		TRUE	TRUE	TRUE	TRUE	TRUE	TRUE	TRUE	TRUE
(Unless otherwise specified	Units	Y01A	Y02A	Y03A	Y04A	Y05A	Y06F	Y07F	Y08F
DEBT SCHEDULE									
Unsecured Loans									
Opening		-	40,000	35,000	30,000	2,75,000	2,70,000	2,65,000	2,60,000
Additions		40,000	-	-	2,50,000	-	-	-	-
Repayments On 40M	8 yrs		5,000	5,000	5,000	5,000	5,000	5,000	5,000
Repayments On 250M	10 yrs								
Closing	0	40,000	35,000	30,000	2,75,000	2,70,000	2,65,000	2,60,000	2,55,000
Interest rate		10%	10%	10%	10%	10%	10%	10%	10%
Interest		2,000	3,750	3,250	15,250	27,250	26,750	26,250	25,750
SOCI - OTHER CALCN									
Equity									
Opening		70,000	70,000	70,000	70,000	70,000	70,000	70,000	70,000
Additions		-	-	-	-	-	-	-	-
Closing		70,000	70,000	70,000	70,000	70,000	70,000	70,000	70,000
Retained earnings									
Opening		-	18,535	32,322	74,172	87,481	99,924	1,20,160	1,48,560
Result for the year - PAT		18,535	13,787	41,850	13,309	12,443	20,236	28,401	36,955
Closing		18,535	32,322	74,172	87,481	99,924	1,20,160	1,48,560	1,85,515
RATIOS									

Figure 2.9 – Debt schedule and SOCI

Equity is represented by share capital and accumulated reserves that have not been distributed. Additions to share capital will be reflected here, as well as movement in reserves as a result of profit or loss for the year, and dividends and other distributions. The final balances of share capital and reserves are taken to the balance sheet.

At this stage, our profit and loss accounts for the projected years are now completely populated; however, our balance check is still showing a red **FALSE**, indicating that there is something missing from the balance sheet. The value for **Cash** will be derived from the cash flow statement.

Cash flow statement

Unlike other items, it is not possible to project cash. The cash balance is a fallout from all transactions carried out during the period under review.

This fact is captured in the cash flow statement, which considers the inflows and outflows of cash. The net result is then applied to the opening cash balance to arrive at the closing cash balance at the period end. The following screenshot shows a completed cash flow statement, which ends with a closing balance for cash that is taken to the balance sheet:

Wazobia Global Limited

Balance Check		TRUE	TRUE	TRUE	TRUE	TRUE	TRUE	TRUE	TRUE
(Unless otherwise specified,	Units	Y01A	Y02A	Y03A	Y04A	Y05A	Y06F	Y07F	Y08F
CASH FLOW STATEMENT									
Cashflow from Operating Activities									
PAT		13,787	41,850	13,309	12,443	20,236	28,401	36,955
Add: Depreciation		10,000	10,000	30,000	30,000	30,000	30,000	30,000
Add: Interest Expense		3,750	3,250	15,250	27,250	26,750	26,250	25,750
Net Change in Working Capital									
Add: Increase in Accounts payable		3,524	(223)	(1,759)	-	1,610	(1,397)	1,611
Less: Increase in Inventory		(2,462)	(3,724)	7,201	0	(5,745)	5,496	(5,747)
Less: Increase in Account Receivables		(10,704)	(4,333)	7,847	-	(10,972)	7,929	(11,110)
Net Change in Working Capital		(9,642)	(8,280)	13,290	0	(15,107)	12,028	(15,245)
Cashflow from Operations		17,895	46,820	71,849	69,693	61,879	96,678	77,460
Cashflow from Investment Activities									
Less: Capex		-	-	(2,00,000)	-	-	-	-
Add: Proceeds from Disposal of Assets					-	-		
Less: Increase in WIP					-	-		
Less: Increase in Investments		648	(46,557)	(5,000)	5,000	-	-	-
Cashflow from Investment Activities		648	(46,557)	(2,05,000)	5,000	-	-	-
Cashflow from Financing Activities									
Add: New Equity Raised									
Add: New Unsecured Loans Raised		-	-	2,50,000			-	
Less: Unsecured Loans Repaid		(5,000)	(5,000)	(5,000)	(5,000)	(5,000)	(5,000)	(5,000)
Less: Dividends Paid									
Less: Interest Expense		(3,750)	(3,250)	(15,250)	(27,250)	(26,750)	(26,250)	(25,750)
Cashflow from Financing Activities		(8,750)	(8,250)	2,29,750	(32,250)	(31,750)	(31,250)	(30,750)
Net Cashflow		9,793	(7,987)	96,599	42,443	30,129	65,428	46,710
Cash Balance									
Opening Balance		7,459	17,252	9,265	1,05,864	1,48,306	1,78,435	2,43,864
Net Cashflow		9,793	(7,987)	96,599	42,443	30,129	65,428	46,710
Closing Balance		17,252	9,265	1,05,864	1,48,306	1,78,435	2,43,864	2,90,573

Figure 2.10 – Cash flow statement

When the closing cash balance is taken to the balance sheet, the balance check for the projected years should now show **TRUE** on a green background, giving some assurance that calculations up till that point are correct.

The cash flow statement is one of the most important statements for a company. To most investment analysts, cash is king.

You may wonder why you need another statement that looks similar to a rearranged balance sheet. Remember that the accounts are prepared on the accrual basis of accounting. This means that part of the turnover shown in the profit and loss account may not yet have been converted into cash. For example, at the year-end, some customers may not yet have paid for goods purchased from you on credit. Similarly, expenses are recorded when incurred even though you may not yet have paid for them; for example, expenses such as electricity or goods you have purchased on credit are usually paid in arrears.

The cash flow statement is constructed to extract cash inflows and outflows from the balance sheet and profit and loss account. The statement shows, separately, cash flow from operations, cash flow from investing activities, and cash flow from financing activities. You would expect cash generated from operations to be regularly greater than net income. If the reverse is the case, you would want to know why there is a delay in converting income into cash. The **Cashflow from Investment Activities** section shows the movement in long-term assets, such as long-term investments and property, plant, and equipment.

Fresh loans and repayment of existing loans, as well as movement in share capital, will be reflected under **Cashflow from Financing Activities**. In order to maintain a healthy dividend policy, repay loans, and have funds for expansion, a company needs to consistently generate more cash than it utilizes.

Now that we have concluded the three-statement model, we turn our attention to assessing the health of the company.

Preparing ratio analysis

With the preparation of a cash flow statement, we now have the core content of a set of financial statements. These financial statements, now referred to as a *statement of financial position*, *statement of comprehensive income*, and *cash flow statement*, along with explanatory notes and schedules, are distributed to shareholders of the company and government. It is also these financial statements that are available to other interest groups, such as investors and holders of the debt capital of the company.

The financial statements provide a significant amount of information about the company and its results for the period under review; however, on their own, they are not adequate for decision-making. Ratio analysis provides an in-depth look at the details behind the figures. The following screenshot is an example of a set of ratio analyses:

	Balance Check	TRUE	TRUE	TRUE	TRUE	TRUE	TRUE	TRUE	TRUE
	(Unless otherwise specified, all financial Units	Y01A	Y02A	Y03A	Y04F	Y05F	Y06F	Y07F	Y08F
	RATIOS								
	Profitability Ratios								
	EBIT Margin	10%	7%	4%	11%	14%	17%	20%	23%
	PBT Margin	10%	6%	3%	6%	6%	10%	14%	18%
	PAT Margin	7%	5%	1%	4%	4%	7%	10%	12%
	Growth Rate								
	Revenue		4%	-10%	22%	5%	5%	5%	5%
	EBIT		-27%	-44%	211%	31%	25%	21%	18%
	PBT		-36%	-52%	145%	0%	75%	44%	32%
	PAT		-26%	-87%	619%	0%	75%	44%	32%
	As % of Sales								
	Cost of sales	68%	68%	73%	60%	58%	56%	53%	51%
	Sales and marketing expenses	4%	4%	5%	4%	4%	4%	4%	4%
	General and administration expenses	10%	10%	9%	9%	9%	9%	9%	9%
	Other expenses	2%	5%	2%	3%	3%	3%	3%	3%
	Liquidity Ratios								
	Quick Ratio	2.3	3.0	2.9	7.0	6.7	9.6	10.2	15.0
	Rate of Returns								
	ROAE		14%	2%	12%	11%	16%	20%	21%
	ROACE		10%	1%	5%	3%	6%	9%	12%
	ROAA		9%	1%	4%	3%	5%	7%	9%
	Leverage Ratios								
	Debt/ Equity	51%	39%	34%	238%	191%	143%	101%	69%
	Debt/ EBITDA	1.21	1.34	1.67	4.36	3.33	2.55	1.94	
	Interest Coverage	13.5	5.3	3.4	2.2	1.7	2.4	3.4	4.7

Figure 2.11 – Ratio analysis

By looking at the relationship between strategic pairs of figures from the accounts, ratio analysis can provide insights about the profitability, liquidity, efficiency, and debt management of a company for the year, as well as over a period of time. The ratios in the preceding screenshot are by no means exhaustive. There is a vast array of ratios to choose from and different modelers will have their own preferred set of ratios.

However, what is important is that you should be able to interpret whichever ratios you choose to include in such a way as to provide qualitative assistance to the decision-making process.

Valuation

There are two main approaches to valuation, which are as follows:

- **Relative approach**: In this approach, you have the following methods:

  - **The comparative company method of valuation**: This method obtains the value of a business by looking at the value of similar businesses and their trading multiples, the most common of which is **enterprise value (EV)** and **earnings before interest, tax, depreciation, and amortization (EBITDA)**, where EV is divided by EBITDA.

  - **The precedent transaction method**: Here, you compare the business to other similar businesses in the industry that have recently been sold or acquired. Again, you can use multiples to derive a value for your business or company.

- **Absolute approach**: This approach estimates all future free cash flows of the company and discounts it back to today. It is called the **discounted cash flow (DCF)** method. Essentially, the approach considers that the worth of a company can be equated to the amount of cash it can generate after considering the following:

  - Free cash flow

  - Time value of money

  - Discount factor

  - Cost of capital

  - Weighted average cost of capital

  - Terminal growth rate

  - Terminal value

These technical concepts will be explained in greater detail in *Chapter 10, Valuation*.

The DCF method usually results in the highest value for the entity but is widely considered to be the most accurate.

In order to give meaning to the different results obtained for the value of the company, you would then plot them all to obtain a range of values that can be interpreted in a number of ways.

Typically, the company will be said to be undervalued if it is quoted at a price lower than the lowest value calculated, and overvalued if it is quoted at a price higher than the highest value calculated. Where a single value is required, the mean of all of the calculated values can be taken.

Summary

In this chapter, we looked at the steps to be followed in building a financial model. We gained an understanding of why it is necessary to have a systematic approach. We went through the steps from discussions with management through to calculating a valuation of the enterprise and the shares of the company, understanding the purpose and importance of each step.

In the next chapter, we will look at how we can use Excel formulas and functions to speed up our work and make modeling a more rewarding experience.

Part 2 –
The Use of Excel
Features and Functions
for Financial Modeling

In this part, you will learn about the tools and features of Excel that are regularly used in financial modeling. These will be explained in enough detail to enable you to start using them confidently.

This part includes the following chapters:

- *Chapter 3, Formulas and Functions – Completing Modeling Tasks with a Single Formula*
- *Chapter 4, The Referencing Framework in Excel*
- *Chapter 5, An Introduction to Power Query*

3
Formulas and Functions – Completing Modeling Tasks with a Single Formula

One of the first things that makes **Excel** more than a glorified electronic calculator is its use of functions and formulas. This feature allows Excel to combine a number of mathematical tasks—some of which can be quite complex—into a single function.

In this chapter, you will learn how to use formulas and will understand a selection of the most widely used functions.

The following topics will be covered in this chapter:

- Understanding functions and formulas
- Working with lookup functions
- Utility functions
- Pivot tables and charts
- Pitfalls to avoid
- New functions in Excel 365

Understanding functions and formulas

In order to enter either a formula or a function, you must first type =. A **formula** is a statement that includes one or more operands (+, -, /, *, and ^), such as =34+7 or =A3-G5 (this formula subtracts the contents of cell G5 from the contents of cell A3). A function can also be included as part of a formula, such as =SUM(B3:B7)*A3. This formula will add the contents of cells B3 to B7 and multiply the result by the contents of cell A3.

A **function** is a command that contains a series of instructions for Excel to carry out. A function contains one or more arguments, inviting the user to specify the input cell or range of cells on which the instructions are to be carried out, for example, MATCH(A5, F4:F23,false).

A function can include a formula as part of an argument, such as =IF(A4*B4>C4,D4,E4).

However, the distinction between them is often ignored and the term *formula* is used to indicate either a formula or function.

To enter a formula, we start with the = sign followed by the name of a function and then open brackets. While creating the formula, an on-screen guide is displayed just below the text of the formula, showing the arguments to be specified. Each argument is separated from the next with a comma, and the first argument appears in bold font as it is the active argument. Once you have specified the input for an argument, press the comma (,) key. The bold highlight moves on to the next argument as that is now the active argument. When all inputs have been specified, we close the brackets and press *Enter* to end the formula.

Working with lookup functions

Lookup functions are some of the most widely used functions in Excel. Generally, the intention is to fetch a value from one dataset (the source) to another dataset (the target).

Let's first understand what a proper Excel dataset is.

The first row of a dataset is the header row that contains the names of all the fields. As you can see in the illustration in *Figure 3.1*, the header row of the sales report includes the following fields: `Date`, `Product`, `Product Code`, `Salesperson`, and so on. Each column in the dataset represents a field, and each row represents a record. Finally, no entire row or entire column in the dataset must be empty, and there must be at least one empty row below the dataset, at least one empty column to the right, one empty row above (unless the dataset begins from row `1`), and one empty column to the left (unless the dataset begins from column `A`) of the dataset.

For example, say you have two datasets: a sales report that includes data for various products sold within a specified period, and a `Products Database` table that contains the product name, code, and unit cost.

The following screenshot is a sample sales report showing daily sales, including `Product`, `Product Code`, `Salesperson`, and other details:

	A	B	C	D	E	F	G	H	I	J	K
1											
2		Sales Report									
3											
4		Date	Product	Product Code	Salesperson	Units Sold	Unit Price	Sales	Unit Cost	Cost of Sales	Profit
5		01/11/2018	Desktop PC	BN001	Mobola	30	78,000	2,340,000			
6		02/11/2018	Desk Fan	PVC03	Iyabo	36	19,200	691,200			
7		03/11/2018	Printer	BN003	Dupe	27	54,000	1,458,000			
8		04/11/2018	Microwave	SK003	Mobola	44	32,400	1,425,600			
9		06/11/2018	Standing Fan	PVC02	Deji	26	21,600	561,600			
10		07/11/2018	Desktop PC	BN001	Deji	35	78,000	2,730,000			
11		08/11/2018	Cooker	SK002	Lara	42	66,000	2,772,000			
12		09/11/2018	Cooker	SK002	Tunde	48	66,000	3,168,000			
13		10/11/2018	Desk Fan	PVC03	Mobola	43	19,200	825,600			
14		11/11/2018	Printer	BN003	Dupe	31	54,000	1,674,000			
15		13/11/2018	Standing Fan	PVC02	Mobola	25	21,600	540,000			
16		14/11/2018	Desktop PC	BN001	Mobola	43	78,000	3,354,000			
17		15/11/2018	Washing Machine	SK001	Dupe	50	84,000	4,200,000			
18		16/11/2018	Laptop	BN002	Iyabo	36	84,000	3,024,000			
19		17/11/2018	Standing Fan	PVC02	Lara	33	21,600	712,800			
20		18/11/2018	Hoover	PVC01	Dupe	34	30,000	1,020,000			

Figure 3.1 – Sample sales report

The following screenshot is a sample `Products Database` table showing the product codes and unit costs of each product:

Products Database		Index_Num
Product	Product Code	Unit Cost N
Washing Machine	SK001	70,000
Cooker	SK002	55,000
Microwave	SK003	27,000
Hoover	PVC01	25,000
Standing Fan	PVC02	18,000
Desk Fan	PVC03	16,000
Desktop PC	BN001	65,000
Laptop	BN002	70,000
Ptinter	BN003	45,000

Figure 3.2 – Sample products database

In order to calculate `Cost of Sales` and `Profit` in the sales report, you will need to populate the `Unit Cost` column.

The unit cost values are in a different dataset, in this case, the `Products Database` table. We will need to use a `Lookup` function to get Excel to fetch the unit cost from the `Products Database` table into the sales report, for each product.

To ensure that your lookup selects the correct item, you must use a `key` field with unique values. Items in the `key` field must not occur more than once, and the field must be present in both tables. People could have the same name, so you would use employee IDs as the `key` field rather than employee names; similarly, product names could be duplicated, so you would use `Product Code` instead as the `key` field.

There are a number of lookup functions, each of them having particular scenarios to which they are best suited. We will have a look at some of the more popular ones.

In our datasets, the `Salesperson` field has duplicates as the names appear more than once in that field. In any case, `Salesperson` only appears in the sales report dataset. The `Product` field appears in both datasets but it also has duplicates, as products appear more than once. The field that appears in both datasets and has unique values in one of the datasets is the `Product Code` field.

We can use the `VLOOKUP` function to fetch the unit cost from the `Products Database` table into the sales report.

The VLOOKUP function

The arguments for VLOOKUP are shown in *Figure 3.3*:

Figure 3.3 – VLOOKUP arguments

Any argument enclosed in square brackets, [], is optional; therefore, if no value is entered for that argument, a default value is taken. Values must be entered for all other arguments; otherwise, the formula will result in an error.

For the VLOOKUP function, the optional argument is range_lookup. This requires you to select True if you are looking for an approximate match for your lookup value, or False if you are looking for an exact match. Excel allows you to substitute 1 for True and 0 for False. If no value is selected, then the argument defaults to False.

Since we want to fetch the unit cost, we will enter our formula in the Unit Cost field for each record.

Starting with the first record in row 5, we will type =, then V, then L, then O; as we spell out the name of the function, Excel lists suggested functions narrowing down to the function we want. As soon as the VLOOKUP function is highlighted, we do not need to complete the spelling; we simply press *Tab* or double-click on the highlighted function to select it from the list.

The first argument of the VLOOKUP function is lookup_value. This is the value in the key field of this row or record. In this case, the lookup value is BN001, which is in cell D5.

The following screenshot shows the selection of lookup_value in the Sales Report table:

	A	B	C	D	E	F	G	H	I	J
1										
2		**Sales Report**								
3										
4		Date	Product	Product Code	Salesperson	Units Sold	Unit Price	Sales	Unit Cost	Cost of Sales
5		01-11-18	Desktop PC	BN001	Mobola	30	78,000	2,340,000	=VLOOKUP(D5	
6		02-11-18	Desk Fan	PVC03	Iyabo	36	19,200	691,200	VLOOKUP(lookup_value, table_array,	
7		03-11-18	Printer	BN003	Dupe	27	54,000	1,458,000		
8		04-11-18	Microwave	SK003	Mobola	44	32,400	1,425,600		
9		06-11-18	Standing Fan	PVC02	Deji	26	21,600	561,600		

Figure 3.4 – VLOOKUP lookup value

The second argument is `table_array`. You select `table_array` from the source dataset that contains the value you want to fetch, in this case, the `Products Database` table.

In selecting your array, you must start with the `key` field, select all values in the `key` field, then continue to the right, and end with the field containing the value you wish to fetch, in this case, the `Unit Cost` field.

So, `table_array` must start from column C in the `Products Database` table, as this is where the `Product Code` field lies (note that this is the second column of the `Products Database` table), and end at column D. Please note that, since we intend to copy our VLOOKUP formula to the other cells in the `Unit Cost` field, we will need to make `table_array` absolute by pressing the *F4* key to place $ signs before the row and column parts of the reference. In our example, the `lookup` array is `$C$5:$D$13` on the `Products Database` worksheet.

Products Database		Index_Num
Product	**Product Code**	**Unit Cost N**
Washing Machine	SK001	70,000
Cooker	SK002	55,000
Microwave	SK003	27,000
Hoover	PVC01	25,000
Standing Fan	PVC02	18,000
Desk Fan	PVC03	16,000
Desktop PC	BN001	65,000
Laptop	BN002	70,000
Ptinter	BN003	45,000

Figure 3.5 – Lookup array

Excel will then locate the position of the `lookup` value in this first column, as shown in the following screenshot:

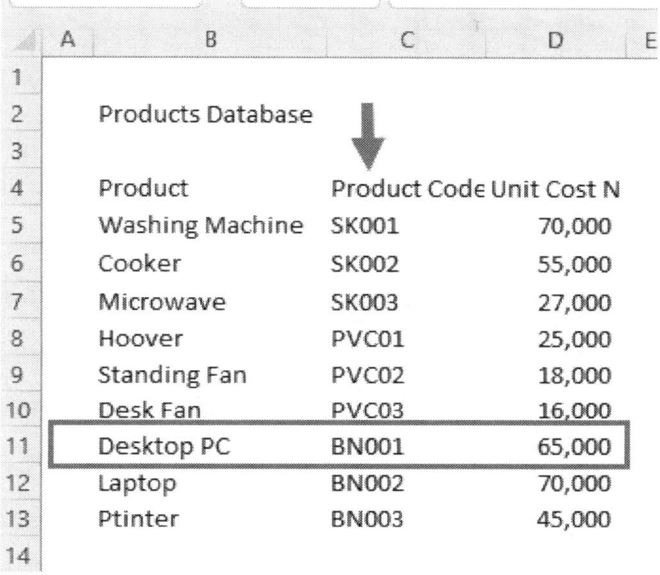

	A	B	C	D	E
1					
2		Products Database			
3					
4		Product	Product Code	Unit Cost N	
5		Washing Machine	SK001	70,000	
6		Cooker	SK002	55,000	
7		Microwave	SK003	27,000	
8		Hoover	PVC01	25,000	
9		Standing Fan	PVC02	18,000	
10		Desk Fan	PVC03	16,000	
11		Desktop PC	BN001	65,000	
12		Laptop	BN002	70,000	
13		Ptinter	BN003	45,000	
14					

Figure 3.6 – Position of the lookup value

From the preceding screenshot, we can see that product BN001 is in row 11 of the Products Database table, in the Product Code field.

The next argument is the column_index_num (column index number) value, which refers to the position of the source field in table_array, starting from the key field as column 1. The **source field** is the field from which you want to retrieve data. In our example, the source field is Unit Cost, which is column D, the second column of our lookup array. This gives us col_index_num of 2.

In this way, we have identified column D and row 11 for the source cell. Excel will then retrieve the data from cell D11 (65,000) and place it in our target cell in the Sales Report table:

	A	B	C	D	E
1					
2		Products Database			
3					
4		Product	Product Code	Unit Cost N	
5		Washing Machine	SK001	70,000	
6		Cooker	SK002	55,000	
7		Microwave	SK003	27,000	
8		Hoover	PVC01	25,000	
9		Standing Fan	PVC02	18,000	
10		Desk Fan	PVC03	16,000	
11		Desktop PC	BN001	65,000	
12		Laptop	BN002	70,000	
13		Ptinter	BN003	45,000	
14					

Figure 3.7 – Lookup value identified

Once you have completed your formula and successfully extracted the unit cost for the first record in our Sales Report table, copy the formula down the column for the other records in the Sales Report table.

You can now calculate the cost of sales and profit.

The INDEX and MATCH functions

The main restriction of the VLOOKUP formula is that in selecting your table array, you must start with the column containing the key field so that the source field will always be to the right. In other words, if the source dataset is set up with the source field to the left of the Key field, in our example, if Unit Cost came before Product Code in the Products Database table, we would not be able to use the VLOOKUP formula without first rearranging the dataset; this isn't always possible or feasible.

An alternative to VLOOKUP that can look up to the left as well as the right without having to rearrange the dataset is the INDEX and MATCH combination of functions.

The primary function, INDEX, has arguments to specify the row and column of the source cell.

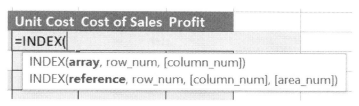

Figure 3.8 – INDEX function arguments

In general, datasets have few columns or fields and several rows of records, often running to thousands and sometimes tens of thousands or even more. So, while the column can most often be quickly ascertained, the challenge is usually to identify the relevant row.

This is where the MATCH function is introduced.

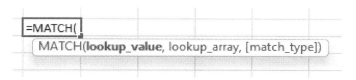

Figure 3.9 – MATCH function arguments

The MATCH function arguments are similar to the VLOOKUP arguments. They both have lookup_value, and lookup_array is the equivalent of the VLOOKUP table array. The MATCH function does not have column_index_num as the focus here is on identifying the row. As a result, the restriction on the first column of lookup_array does not apply to the MATCH function. Finally, match_type is the equivalent of VLOOKUP's range_lookup.

Let's now perform the same lookup exercise with the unit cost using INDEX and MATCH.

We start with the INDEX primary function. The first argument is array/reference. If you restrict the index array/reference to one column, you have effectively identified the column of the source cell. In our example, we have selected cells D5 to D13 as our reference, since Unit Cost is the key field where we can find lookup_value:

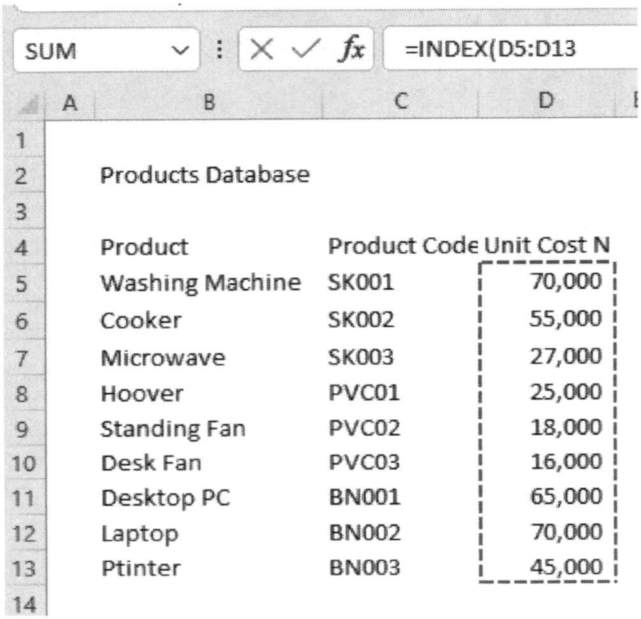

A	B	Product Code	Unit Cost N
1			
2	Products Database		
3			
4	Product	Product Code	Unit Cost N
5	Washing Machine	SK001	70,000
6	Cooker	SK002	55,000
7	Microwave	SK003	27,000
8	Hoover	PVC01	25,000
9	Standing Fan	PVC02	18,000
10	Desk Fan	PVC03	16,000
11	Desktop PC	BN001	65,000
12	Laptop	BN002	70,000
13	Ptinter	BN003	45,000
14			

Figure 3.10 – Single column index array

The next argument is row_num. In order to substitute it for the row argument, you will need to embed the MATCH function within the INDEX function, which is still active. To do this, just start typing the new function after the comma. As long as you have not yet entered the final parentheses for a function, Excel recognizes that the formula is still active, so there is no need to type = again. The first argument in the MATCH function is the lookup_value argument, which you look for in the lookup array. In this case, however, there is no restriction as to the location of the lookup array. We are using the same lookup value as in the VLOOKUP example, BN001, in cell D5 of the Sales Report worksheet.

Here, again, as shown in the following screenshot, you can restrict the lookup array to one column. In our example, we know that the match for our lookup value is under the Product Code field in column C of the Products Database worksheet. We, therefore, select cells C5 to C13 as our lookup array:

A	B	C	D
1			
2	Products Database		
3			
4	Product	Product Code	Unit Cost N
5	Washing Machine	SK001	70,000
6	Cooker	SK002	55,000
7	Microwave	SK003	27,000
8	Hoover	PVC01	25,000
9	Standing Fan	PVC02	18,000
10	Desk Fan	PVC03	16,000
11	Desktop PC	BN001	65,000
12	Laptop	BN002	70,000
13	Ptinter	BN003	45,000

Figure 3.11 – Single column MATCH lookup array

Note that the MATCH lookup array must start from the same worksheet row as the reference in the INDEX function and extend for the same number of rows. In our example, they both start from worksheet row 5 and end at worksheet row 13. You end the match formula with match_type, which is the same as range_lookup in the VLOOKUP function. You need to specify whether you want an approximate match, less than (1), greater than the lookup value (-1), or an exact match (0). An approximate match would be relevant, for example, where the lookup value falls within a range, such as exam scores, where a score between 60 and 75 will be considered Grade C.

The MATCH function returns an integer that corresponds to the position of the row within the lookup array in which the lookup value is found. This should not be mistaken for the worksheet row number.

In our example, the MATCH function will return the number 7 because the lookup value, BN001, is found in the seventh row of our lookup array, worksheet row 11.

As soon as you close the final bracket of the MATCH formula, Excel takes you back to the INDEX function.

The next argument is column_num. Since we have already determined the column number by restricting our reference to one column, we can ignore this argument. The final argument, area_num, is for more complex situations where we introduce a third dimension after row and column, such as multiple tables with the same field layouts. Again, we can ignore this argument as we will not be using it.

Having identified worksheet row 11 and column D, we now have the source cell, D11, which returns the value of 65000. You will note that the INDEX and MATCH combination overcomes the restriction in VLOOKUP, where the unique field must be the first column of the lookup array and you can only look up values to the right of this field.

Just to recap, in simple lookup situations, the INDEX formula is used to identify the column, and the MATCH function to identify the row, which together will give the location of the value you wish to fetch.

As a result, many users prefer to use INDEX and MATCH, even where VLOOKUP would work. Those who are intimidated by the function combination of INDEX and MATCH prefer to stick to VLOOKUP and would rather change the order of table columns to make it suitable for VLOOKUP. There is nothing wrong with that as long as the situation allows it.

The CHOOSE function

The CHOOSE function allows you to create a list of values or actions to perform and then select which value to use or action to perform, by choosing a number corresponding to the position of the values or actions in the list. The syntax for CHOOSE (as shown in the following screenshot) has two arguments: index_num, then the list of values or actions shown as value1, value2, and so on.

This screenshot shows the arguments of the CHOOSE function:

Figure 3.12 – The CHOOSE syntax

Let's consider an example where we wish to compare two methods of arriving at a growth driver for turnover, which will be applied to the next 5 forecast years. One method could be the average of the previous 5 years' actual results, and the second method could be to simply take the latest actual results available. We will use the dataset in *Figure 3.13* as follows:

	A	B	C	D	E	F	G	H	I	J	K	L	M	N
1														
2				Units	Y01A	Y02A	Y03A	Y04A	Y05A	Y06F	Y07F	Y08F	Y08F	Y10F
3														
4		Revenue			260,810	272,241	285,009	297,938	311,453					
5														
6														

Figure 3.13 – Dataset for the CHOOSE function

In our dataset, the latest actual results are for Y05A.

As stated, we are comparing two methods, so the first argument of the CHOOSE function, index_num, will either be 1 or 2. Here, 1 would mean we use the *method 1* average, and 2 would mean we use *method 2*, the latest available actual results.

We now need to find a way of switching between 1 and 2. A simple and effective way is to use **Data Validation…**.

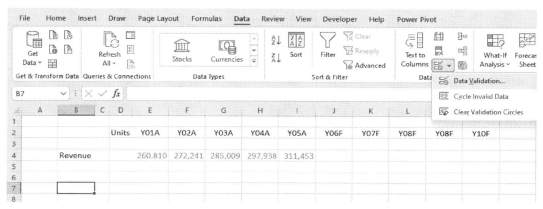

Figure 3.14 – Dataset for the CHOOSE function

Data Validation… can be found on the **Data** ribbon in the **Data tools** group. Once you select it, the following dialog box is launched:

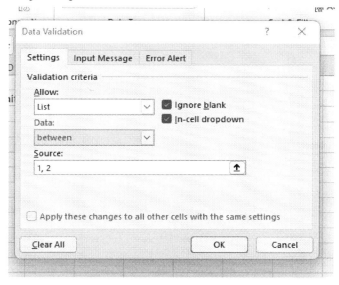

Figure 3.15 – Data validation dialog box

From the drop-down under **Allow**, select **List**, and under **Source**, type 1, 2. We are now ready for our CHOOSE function. Highlight cells J4 to N4. Since we are entering the same formula in all those cells, a quick way to do it is to highlight all the cells in that range, enter the formula once, then press *Ctrl + Enter* to conclude.

	A	B	C	D	E	F	G	H	I	J	K	L	M	N
SUM fx										=CHOOSE($B$7,AVERAGE($E$4:$I$4),$I$4)				
1														
2				Units	Y01A	Y02A	Y03A	Y04A	Y05A	Y06F	Y07F	Y08F	Y08F	Y10F
3														
4		Revenue			260,810	272,241	285,009	297,938	311,453	=CHOOSE($B$7,AVERAGE($E$4:$I$4),$I$4)				
5										CHOOSE(index_num, value1, [value2], [value3], [value4], ...)				
6														
7		1												
8														

Figure 3.16 – The CHOOSE function on turnover

The index_num cell is the one with the data validation, which we will switch between 1 and 2. You will then enter the formulas or references for the two options as value1 and value2. As can be seen from *Figure 3.16*, value1 is the average of the previous 5 years' results, and value2 is the value in cell I4.

Since we are effectively copying the formula to all other cells in the range highlighted, we need to make the references absolute. Now press *Ctrl + Enter*:

	A	B	C	D	E	F	G	H	I	J	K	L	M	N
J4 fx										=CHOOSE($B$7,AVERAGE($E$4:$I$4),$I$4)				
1														
2				Units	Y01A	Y02A	Y03A	Y04A	Y05A	Y06F	Y07F	Y08F	Y08F	Y10F
3														
4		Revenue			260,810	272,241	285,009	297,938	311,453	285,490	285,490	285,490	285,490	285,490
5														
6														
7		1												
8														

Figure 3.17 – Results of CHOOSE with method 1

Note the formula in the formula bar. The result with method 1 is 285,490.

	A	B	C	D	E	F	G	H	I	J	K	L	M	N
J4 fx										=CHOOSE($B$7,AVERAGE($E$4:$I$4),$I$4)				
1														
2				Units	Y01A	Y02A	Y03A	Y04A	Y05A	Y06F	Y07F	Y08F	Y08F	Y10F
3														
4		Revenue			260,810	272,241	285,009	297,938	311,453	311,453	311,453	311,453	311,453	311,453
5														
6														
7		2												
8														

Figure 3.18 – Results of CHOOSE with method 2

You will notice that the CHOOSE function in the formula bar does not change. We have only switched from 1 to 2 in cell B7. Method 2 results in 311,453.

You would then want to look at the bigger picture and see how the final value in your model is affected by your choice.

Utility type functions

Utility type functions can be used on their own. However, they come into their own when embedded in other, more complex functions. In such cases, they expand the scope and functionality of the enclosing function by providing access to more conditions or variables.

Some examples of utility type functions are IF, AND, OR, MAX, MIN, and MATCH. We will now look at a few of them here.

The IF function

This is one of the most widely used functions in Excel. It can be used on its own or as part of another formula. The IF function checks whether a condition is met, then returns one value if it is and another value if it isn't. The syntax contains three arguments:

- logical_test: The logical test is a statement that returns a value of true if the condition is met, or false if the condition is not met.

- value_if_true: This argument allows you to specify which value you wish to be returned if the condition is met and the result of the logical test is true.

- value_if_false: This argument allows you to specify which value you wish to be returned if the condition is not met and the result of the logical test is false.

Say you want to reward your salespersons with 2% of sales whenever the profit exceeds 300,000. You could write an IF formula to automate this. The logical test would be the statement, profit is greater than 300,000. In the following example, for the first record, this is K5>K2. The statement will either be true or false. If the result is true, the value to return is then Sales × Commission (2%). In our example, this is H5*H2. If the result is false, then the value returned will be 0. The following screenshot is an illustration of the IF formula:

M5		× ✓ fx	=IF(K5>$K$2,H5*$H$2,0									
	D	E	F	G	H	I	J	K	L	M	N	
1												
2				Bonus on Sales	2%		Hurdle	300,000				
3												
4			Sold	Unit Price	Sales	Unit Cost	Cost of Sales	Profit		IF	MAX	MIN
5			30	78,000	2,340,000	65,000	1,950,000	390,000		=IF(K5>$K$2,H5*$H$2,0		
6			36	19,200	691,200	16,000	576,000	115,200				
7			27	54,000	1,458,000	45,000	1,215,000	243,000				
8			44	32,400	1,425,600	27,000	1,188,000	237,600				
9			26	21,600	561,600	18,000	468,000	93,600				
10												

Figure 3.19 – An example of the IF function

This simple function is often used along with more complex functions.

The MAX and MIN functions

These functions are used to select either the maximum (MAX) or minimum (MIN) from a list of values. With a bit of imagination, you can put the MAX or MIN formulas to very efficient use.

For example, in your financial model, Cash Balance can turn out to be positive or negative. A positive balance would be posted to the Cash In Hand account on the asset side of the balance sheet, while a negative balance would be shown as Overdraft under current liabilities. If we simply related Cash In Hand or Overdraft to Cash Balance, then we could either have a negative balance displayed as Cash In Hand or a positive balance displayed as Overdraft.

A way around this is to use the MAX and MIN formulas, as shown in the following screenshot:

◢	A	B	C	D	E	F
1						
2						
3		**Cash Balance**	**Cash In Hand**	**Overdraft**		
4		1,450,422	=MAX(B4,0			
5		663,315	MAX(number1, **[number2]**, [number3], ...)			
6		(349,661)				
7		779,461				

Figure 3.20 – The MAX function

In the preceding screenshot, we are asking the MAX formula to display the greater value of Cash Balance and 0. A positive cash balance will always be greater than 0 and will, therefore, be displayed as Cash In Hand. However, whenever the cash balance is negative, since this will always be less than 0, Cash In Hand will display 0.

The following screenshot is an illustration of the MIN function:

◢	A	B	C	D	E	F	G
1							
2							
3		**Cash Balance**	**Cash In Hand**	**Overdraft**			
4		1,450,422	1,450,422	=MIN(B4,0			
5		663,315	663,315	MIN(number1, **[number2]**, [number3], ...)			
6		(349,661)	-				
7		779,461	779,461				
8		(393,443)	-				
9		717,832	717,832				
10		15,107	15,107				
11		(418,702)	-				

Figure 3.21 – The MIN function

In this case, we use the MIN formula to ensure that only negative cash balances will be displayed as Overdraft, since a negative cash balance will always be less than 0.

By copying the formulas, we can see how the cash balances have been neatly and accurately classified as Cash In Hand and Overdraft, as shown in the following screenshot, which shows the full result after applying the MAX and MIN formulas:

	A	B	C	D
1				
2				
3		Cash Balance	Cash In Hand	Overdraft
4		1,450,422	1,450,422	-
5		663,315	663,315	-
6		(349,661)	-	(349,661)
7		779,461	779,461	-
8		(393,443)	-	(393,443)
9		717,832	717,832	-
10		15,107	15,107	-
11		(418,702)	-	(418,702)
12		49,887	49,887	-
13		86,528	86,528	-
14		868,678	868,678	-
15		(319,840)	-	(319,840)
16		8,606	8,606	-
17		754,551	754,551	-
18		784,338	784,338	-
19		681,504	681,504	-
20				

Figure 3.22 – The MAX and MIN functions

This shows the final list after applying the MAX and MIN functions.

Pivot tables and charts

Pivot tables are one of the most powerful tools in Excel. A pivot table can summarize little or large amounts of data into a compact form that reveals trends and relationships that were not apparent from looking at the original data.

The pivot table allows you to introduce conditions based on the original data so that you can view the summarized data from different perspectives. It does all of this without you having to type any formulas. Most users are under the impression that pivot table reports are complex and difficult to prepare, but, in reality, the complexity is kept behind the scenes and taken care of by Excel. All you have to do is follow a few simple guidelines and you will be able to produce complex pivot tables with ease.

The first step is to ensure that your data is in the proper Excel table format, bearing in mind that you may have to work with data prepared by someone else.

Excel identification and navigation shortcuts depend on your table being in the proper format. Most actions require the specification of the target range. Excel can correctly identify the required range and isolate the field headers, but only if the data is in the proper table format, which can be seen in the following screenshot:

Proper Date Format

Field Headers

Blank Rows/Columns all round

Date	Product	Product Code	Salesperson	Units Sold	Unit Price	Sales
01/11/2018	Desktop PC	BN001	Mobola	30	78,000	2,340,000
02/11/2018	Desk Fan	PVC03	Iyabo	36	19,200	691,200
03/11/2018	Printer	BN003	Dupe	27	54,000	1,458,000
04/11/2018	Microwave	SK003	Mobola	44	32,400	1,425,600
06/11/2018	Standing Fan	PVC02	Deji	26	21,600	561,600
07/11/2018	Desktop PC	BN001	Deji	35	78,000	2,730,000
08/11/2018	Cooker	SK002	Lara	42	66,000	2,772,000
09/11/2018	Cooker	SK002	Tunde	48	66,000	3,168,000
10/11/2018	Desk Fan	PVC03	Mobola	43	19,200	825,600
11/11/2018	Printer	BN003	Dupe	31	54,000	1,674,000
13/11/2018	Standing Fan	PVC02	Mobola	25	21,600	540,000
14/11/2018	Desktop PC	BN001	Mobola	43	78,000	3,354,000
15/11/2018	Washing Machine	SK001	Dupe	50	84,000	4,200,000
16/11/2018	Laptop	BN002	Iyabo	36	84,000	3,024,000
17/11/2018	Standing Fan	PVC02	Lara	33	21,600	712,800
18/11/2018	Hoover	PVC01	Dupe	34	30,000	1,020,000

No Empty Cells

Figure 3.23 – Proper Excel dataset layout

In database terminology, each column of the table represents a field, and each row (apart from the first row) represents a record. The first row of the table should contain the field headers. There should be no empty cells in the table and no duplicate records.

Excel is very efficient at detecting data types and handling different forms of date formats, including 15/01/2019, 15-Jan-19, 15-01-2019, 01-15-2019, and 2019-01-15, among others. However, Excel is very sensitive, and any slight anomaly in the data may produce erratic results. For example, if you inadvertently type a *leading space* before the date, as shown on the left-hand side of the following screenshot, Excel treats it as a General data type.

The right-hand side of the following screenshot shows the same text without the leading space; Excel correctly recognizes it as a date and automatically assigns the Date format to the cell:

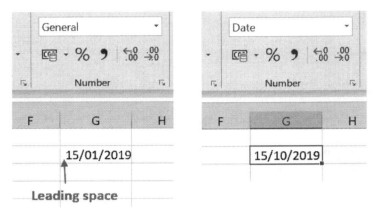

Figure 3.24 – Example of cell contents with a leading space

The reason for explaining this in detail is that pivot tables have a special relationship with dates and other data types. If a date field is included in your table, the pivot table will recognize it and allow you to group the dates into days, months, quarters, and years. However, if just one cell of the date field has an anomaly—as in the preceding example—the pivot table will not recognize it as a date and the group option will be unavailable. Once your data has been cleaned up and prepared, you are ready to create a pivot table. Ensure that the cursor is in any cell within the table, then click **Insert** and select **PivotTable** from the **Tables** group. The **Create PivotTable** dialog box is launched. Alternatively, you could use the keyboard shortcut "*Alt, N, V*", pressing the keys one after the other and not simultaneously. You will be required to select a range for the source data and then a location for the pivot table report. As long as it is a proper dataset, Excel will usually intelligently guess the correct range for the pivot table for the source data, but if it doesn't, you can manually select the required range.

By default, Excel will create the pivot table on a new worksheet. Again, you can override this, if you wish, and specify a location on either the same or another worksheet. If you choose to place the pivot table on the same sheet as the source data, be aware that you might have difficulty viewing or navigating the worksheet:

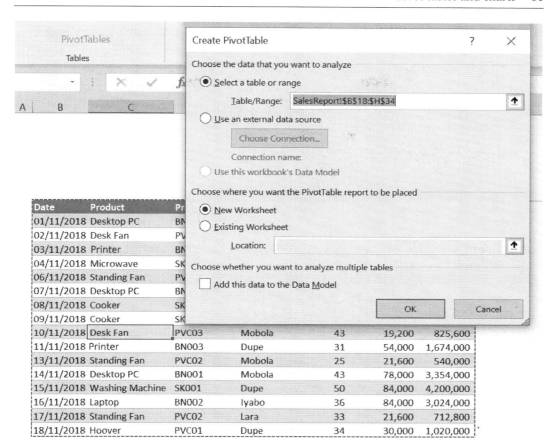

Figure 3.25 – Create PivotTable dialog box

When you press **OK**, a pivot table will be created. Initially, only the field list will be populated with the names of all of the fields in your table, which will be arranged vertically with checkboxes beside them. Below that, there are four boxes, titled **Filters**, **Columns**, **Rows**, and **Values**. You build the table by dragging the field names to the boxes as desired.

Before you start building your table, it would help if you try and envisage the layout you desire. The **Values** box is best suited for numerical fields, so you would drag the `Sales` field to this box, resulting in the updated table shown in the following screenshot, which shows how the **Values** field is displayed in the pivot table:

	A
1	
2	
3	**Sum of Sales**
4	30496800
5	
6	

Figure 3.26 – Pivot table displaying Sum of Sales

As you have not yet specified a condition or criteria, Excel simply totals the **Values** field and calls it `Sum of Sales`. You may then wish to display the *sales per salesperson* for each product. The following screenshot shows sales per salesperson:

	Row Labels	Sum of Sales
2		
3	**Row Labels** ▾	**Sum of Sales**
4	⊟ **Cooker**	**5940000**
5	Lara	2772000
6	Tunde	3168000
7	⊟ **Desk Fan**	**1516800**
8	Iyabo	691200
9	Mobola	825600
10	⊟ **Desktop PC**	**8424000**
11	Deji	2730000
12	Mobola	5694000
13	⊟ **Hoover**	**1020000**
14	Dupe	1020000
15	⊟ **Laptop**	**3024000**
16	Iyabo	3024000
17	⊟ **Microwave**	**1425600**
18	Mobola	1425600
19	⊟ **Printer**	**3132000**
20	Dupe	3132000
21	⊟ **Standing Fan**	**1814400**
22	Deji	561600
23	Lara	712800
24	Mobola	540000
25	⊟ **Washing Machine**	**4200000**
26	Dupe	4200000
27	**Grand Total**	**30496800**

Figure 3.27 – Pivot table showing sales per salesperson

For the previous screenshot, the field list would look like this:

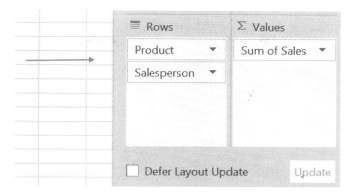

Figure 3.28 – Lower section of pivot table field list

Alternatively, you may wish to show the sales of products per salesperson, as shown in the following screenshot:

Row Labels	Sum of Sales
⊟ **Deji**	**3291600**
Desktop PC	2730000
Standing Fan	561600
⊟ **Dupe**	**8352000**
Hoover	1020000
Printer	3132000
Washing Machine	4200000
⊟ **Iyabo**	**3715200**
Desk Fan	691200
Laptop	3024000
⊟ **Lara**	**3484800**
Cooker	2772000
Standing Fan	712800
⊟ **Mobola**	**8485200**
Desk Fan	825600
Desktop PC	5694000
Microwave	1425600
Standing Fan	540000
⊟ **Tunde**	**3168000**
Cooker	3168000
Grand Total	**30496800**

Figure 3.29 – Pivot table showing product sales per salesperson

Notice that the positions of the `Product` and `Salesperson` fields are reversed in the **Rows** box, as shown in the following screenshot:

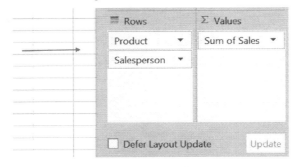

Figure 3.30 – Pivot table showing lower part of field list

An alternative layout could be achieved by displaying the products horizontally. This can be done by dragging the product field to the **Columns** box instead of the **Rows** box:

	A	B	C	D	E	F	G	H	I	J	K
3	Sum of Sales	Column Labels ▾									
4	Row Labels ▾	Cooker	Desk Fan	Desktop PC	Hoover	Laptop	Microwave	Printer	Standing Fan	Washing Machine	Grand Total
5	Deji			2730000					561600		3291600
6	Dupe				1020000			3132000		4200000	8352000
7	Iyabo		691200			3024000					3715200
8	Lara	2772000							712800		3484800
9	Mobola		825600	5694000			1425600		540000		8485200
10	Tunde	3168000									3168000
11	Grand Total	5940000	1516800	8424000	1020000	3024000	1425600	3132000	1814400	4200000	30496800
12											
13											

Figure 3.31 – Pivot table showing product sales in columns instead of rows

Doing that results in the following:

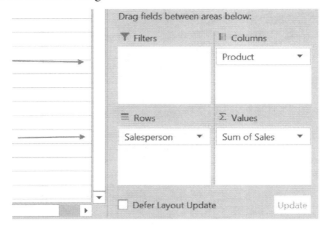

Figure 3.32 – Pivot table showing field list lower section

Another variation to the layout is to show sales by product, then show `Salesperson` as a filter:

	A	B
1	Salesperson	(All)
2		
3	**Row Labels**	**Sum of Sales**
4	Cooker	5,940,000
5	Desk Fan	1,516,800
6	Desktop PC	8,424,000
7	Hoover	1,020,000
8	Laptop	3,024,000
9	Microwave	1,425,600
10	Printer	3,132,000
11	Standing Fan	1,814,400
12	Washing Machine	4,200,000
13	**Grand Total**	**30,496,800**
14		

Figure 3.33 – Pivot table showing salesperson as a filter

This results in the following:

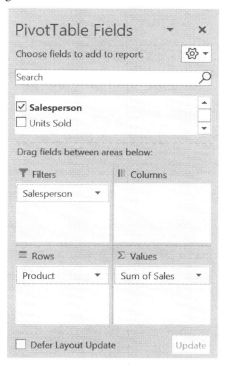

Figure 3.34 – Pivot table showing field list lower section

By clicking the drop-down arrow beside the `Salesperson (All)` filter, you can selectively display the results for any of the salespersons, any combination of them, or all of the salespersons.

Apart from showing the sales totals, you can also show sales as a percentage of the overall total or of average sales. In this way, you can show the contribution of a product or salesperson to the overall sales.

The following screenshot shows product sales in total and as percentages of gross sales. In order to achieve this, simply drag the **Sales** field to the **Values** box again so that it now appears twice. Right-click on the second **Sum of Sales** column to reveal a drop-down menu, then select **Show Values as…**, and then finally select **Grand Total** from the second menu that appears. An illustration of product sales in total and as percentages of gross sales is shown in the following screenshot:

	A	B	C	D	E	F	G	H
1								
2								
3	Row Labels ▾	Sum of Sales	Percentage		Row Labels ▾	Sum of Sales	Percentage	
4	Cooker	5940000	19.48%		Deji	3291600	10.79%	
5	Desk Fan	1516800	4.97%		Dupe	8352000	27.39%	
6	Desktop PC	8424000	27.62%		Iyabo	3715200	12.18%	
7	Hoover	1020000	3.34%		Lara	3484800	11.43%	
8	Laptop	3024000	9.92%		Mobola	8485200	27.82%	
9	Microwave	1425600	4.67%		Tunde	3168000	10.39%	
10	Printer	3132000	10.27%		Grand Total	30496800	100.00%	
11	Standing Fan	1814400	5.95%					
12	Washing Machine	4200000	13.77%					
13	Grand Total	30496800	100.00%					
14								

Figure 3.35 – Two pivot tables side by side from the same data source

The previous table shows sales by salespersons and as percentages of gross sales. This is actually a second pivot table that uses the same range but uses the table on cell E3 of the sheet housing the original pivot table. The **Show Values as…** menu has a wide range of options demonstrating the flexibility of pivot tables.

If, in trying out the various options, you mess up your table, you can simply discard it and create another one. Hopefully, this time, you would have learned from your mistakes and shifted up a notch in your experience of creating and working with pivot tables. Sometimes, people understand reports better when they are supported by diagrams and charts.

To create a pivot chart, select your pivot table, select **Analyze** from the pivot table tools context-sensitive menu, then select **Pivot Chart**. A wide range of chart types will be displayed. Select one and a pivot chart appears beside your pivot table:

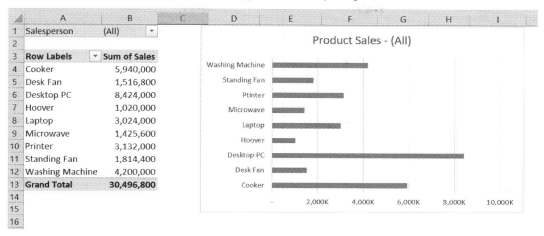

Figure 3.36 – Pivot table and pivot chart

The chart is dynamic so that if you filter your table to reflect, say, one salesperson, `Iyabo`, the chart automatically updates to reflect only Iyabo's results. This screenshot shows a pivot table and a pivot chart that have been filtered to show just Iyabo's sales:

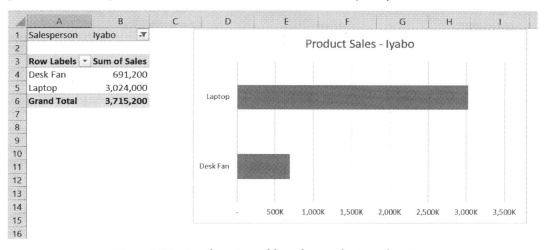

Figure 3.37 – Another pivot table and pivot chart combination

When you use pivot tables extensively, you will come to favor a particular style of layout. It then becomes a bit of a nuisance having to change the layout to your preferred layout each time you load pivot tables.

Excel 365 has now included a feature to address that.

Pitfalls to avoid

In constructing your formulas, it is easy to get carried away and, very soon, the formula becomes very complex and unfriendly. While it is desirable to keep formulas compact, they should be simple and easy for a third party to follow. If necessary, break up the formula into two or more parts so that it becomes easier to follow while retaining the original effect.

Alternatively, you can use *Alt + Enter* to force part of the formula to the next line. This will not affect the result of the formula, but it will make the formula easier to understand. Consider the following example:

```
=INDEX(C5:G10,MATCH(J20,C5:C10,0),MATCH(K19,C5:G5,0))
```

This complex formula can be broken down into three parts with the use of *Alt + Enter*, as follows:

```
=INDEX(C5:G10,
MATCH(J20,C5:C10,0),
MATCH(K19,C5:G5,0))
```

The formula remains within the same cell but is displayed on 3 lines. As we can see, this makes it easier to decipher.

Protect sheets

If you are going to share your model with others, it is important that you protect your formulas against inadvertent modifications that can render the model useless. To do this, first, highlight the cells without formulas that you want to modify, press *Ctrl + 1* to open the **Format Cells** dialog box, go to the **Protection** tab, check **Locked**, and click **OK**. This will unlock the cells that may be modified.

Now, go to the **Review** tab, then select **Protect Sheet**. The **Protect Sheet** dialog box appears. Enter a password to unprotect it if desired, then click **OK**. Now, the cells with formulas, which are protected, can only be viewed but not modified. You should enter a particular value only once. If you need to enter the same value in another location, simply refer to the original cell where the first entry was made. Any subsequent occurrences of the same value should also refer to the original entry rather than to any of the secondary cells containing the same value.

For example, an interest rate of 15% is first entered on **Sheet 1**, cell B5. If interest is required in **Sheet 2**, cell D16, rather than typing 15% again, you simply refer to **Sheet 1**, cell B5, by typing =, then entering Sheet 1, cell B5. If interest appears again on **Sheet 3**, cell J13, theoretically, you could refer to **Sheet 2**, cell D16. However, in order to preserve a simple audit trail, the reference should be to the original entry of that value, **Sheet 1**, cell B5. Try and use only one formula per row.

Use your knowledge of relative, absolute, and mixed cell referencing to construct your formulas so that you can enter them in one cell, then copy or fill the formulas across the other years. The fewer times you have to enter a formula, the lower the chances of making a mistake are.

New functions in Excel 365

With Excel 365, Microsoft has brought array formulas much more into mainstream use by introducing a number of revolutionary functions.

Throughout the book, we will explain these new functions, starting in this chapter with XLOOKUP.

XLOOKUP

This powerful new formula combines the features of VLOOKUP, HLOOKUP, INDEX, and MATCH, and does so in a much-simplified way while introducing a lot more options.

XLOOKUP has six arguments, three of which are compulsory with the other three optional. This does not make it more difficult or complex. Rather, as you will see, its application is quite simple.

The following screenshot shows the six XLOOKUP arguments:

	A	B	C	D	E	F	G	H	I	J	K	L
1												
2		Sales Report										
3												
4		Date	Product	Product Code	Salesperson	Units Sold	Unit Price	Sales	Unit Cost	Cost of Sales	Commission	
5		01/11/2018	Desktop PC	BN001	Mobola	30	78,000	2,340,000	=XLOOKUP(			
6		02/11/2018	Desk Fan	PVC03					XLOOKUP(**lookup_value**, lookup_array, return_array, [if_not_found], [match_mode], [search_mode])			
7		03/11/2018	Ptinter	BN003	Dupe	27	54,000	1,458,000				
8		04/11/2018	Microwave	SK003	Mobola	44	32,400	1,425,600				
9		06/11/2018	Standing Fan	PVC02	Deji	26	21,600	561,600				
10		07/11/2018	Desktop PC	BN001	Deji	35	78,000	2,730,000				
11		08/11/2018	Cooker	SK002	Lara	42	66,000	2,772,000				
12		09/11/2018	Cooker	SK002	Tunde	48	66,000	3,168,000				

Figure 3.38 – Example showing the full XLOOKUP syntax

Using the same example as in VLOOKUP as shown previously, the first argument, lookup_value, is the same: BN001 in cell D5.

We begin to see the differences with the second argument, lookup_array.

The following screenshot shows the lookup_array argument:

Products Database

Product	Product Code	Unit Cost N
Washing Machine	SK001	70000
Cooker	SK002	55000
Microwave	SK003	27000
Hoover	PVC01	25000
Standing Fan	PVC02	18000
Desk Fan	PVC03	16000
Desktop PC	BN001	65000
Laptop	BN002	70000
Ptinter	BN003	45000

Figure 3.39 – The XLOOKUP lookup array

We can see that `lookup_array` is simply the `key` field in the second dataset which, in this example, is `Product Code7`.

The next argument is new and asks for `return_array`.

The following screenshot shows `return_array` in XLOOKUP:

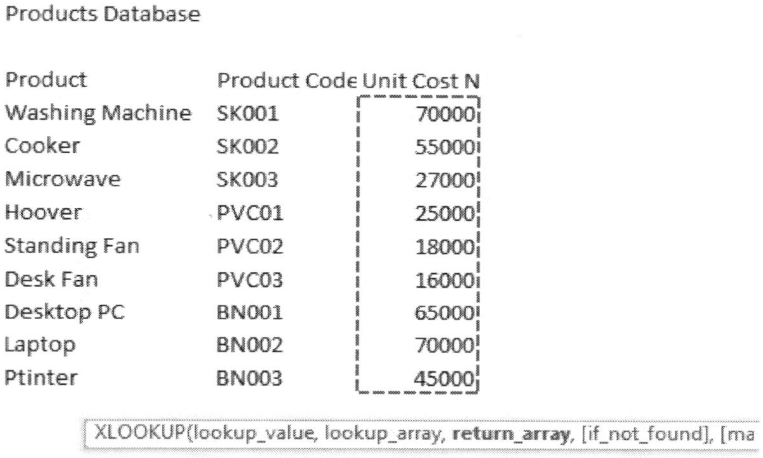

Products Database

Product	Product Code	Unit Cost N
Washing Machine	SK001	70000
Cooker	SK002	55000
Microwave	SK003	27000
Hoover	PVC01	25000
Standing Fan	PVC02	18000
Desk Fan	PVC03	16000
Desktop PC	BN001	65000
Laptop	BN002	70000
Ptinter	BN003	45000

XLOOKUP(lookup_value, lookup_array, **return_array**, [if_not_found], [ma

Figure 3.40 – The XLOOKUP return array

Again, we can see that `return_array` is simply the field with the value we want to return (or fetch), which, in this case, is `Unit Cost`, and that's it!

We can close the brackets; press *Enter* and the result 65,000 appears under `Unit Cost` in the first record of the `Sales Report` dataset.

You can now copy the formula down the other records but, don't forget that, since we are copying, we need to lock the references for the lookup array and return array by making them absolute using the *F4* key, as we do not want that range to move (see *Chapter 4, The Referencing Framework in Excel*).

This function is much simpler to implement and will become the go-to `lookup` function for most applications.

Let's now look at the other optional arguments:

- `if_not_found`: If the lookup value cannot be found in the lookup array, the function will display an error, #N/A. Once you have confirmed that the error is not due to a mistake in your formula, you may wish to display something other than #N/A in the cell.

  Previously, in order to do this, we had to include an `IFERROR` function, which made our formula much longer and more complex.

  With the `XLOOKUP` function, you simply respond to the fourth argument, `If_not_found`, by typing `Not Found` or `No Data`, or some other phrase of your choice. You just need to ensure that if you are returning text, you need to enclose it in quotation marks (`" "`).

- `match_mode`: This option allows you to look for the following:

  - `0` – Exact match

  - `-1` – Exact match or next smallest

  - `1` – Exact match or next largest

  - `2` – Wildcard character match

- `search_mode`: This option allows you to search for the following:

  - `1` – first to last

  - `-1` – last to first

  - `2` – binary search (sorted ascending order)

  - `-2` – binary search (sorted descending order)

FILTER

This is another formula introduced in Excel 365. If you have used the **Advanced Filter** option on the **Data** ribbon, you will be familiar with the results of a simple `FILTER` example. The difference is that, being a formula, `FILTER` is much more flexible and dynamic.

The `FILTER` function allows you to dynamically filter data based on any criteria you specify.

Consider the following dataset:

No.	LAST NAME	FIRST NAME	GROSS	PAYE	NET PAY	DEPT
1	Okilo	Natalie	450,000	13,500	436,500	1
2	Uba	Jeleel	390,000	11,700	378,300	1
3	Okeke	Dopsy	380,000	11,400	368,600	3
4	Bello	Peter	310,000	9,300	300,700	2
5	Saro-Wiwa	Stephanie	590,000	17,700	572,300	1
6	Gbadamosi	Lydia	420,000	12,600	407,400	3
7	Okorie	David	600,000	18,000	582,000	3
8	Ezekwesili	Joy	440,000	13,200	426,800	2
9	Ojukwu	Joseph	540,000	16,200	523,800	4
10	Anikulapo-Kuti	Henry	350,000	10,500	339,500	3
11	Awolowo	Adah	480,000	14,400	465,600	1
12	Asari-Dokubo	Olivia	400,000	12,000	388,000	4
13	Sekibo	Austin	400,000	12,000	388,000	2
14	Akiloye	Micheal	590,000	17,700	572,300	5
15	Olanrewaju	John	360,000	10,800	349,200	3
16	Attah	Ifeanyi	550,000	16,500	533,500	4
17	Akpabio	Ayobamidele	490,000	14,700	475,300	2
18	Akinjide	Dopsy	350,000	10,500	339,500	5
19	Kalu	Rex	460,000	13,800	446,200	2
20	Yar'Adua	Ada	310,000	9,300	300,700	3
21	Omehia	George	370,000	11,100	358,900	2
22	Ekwensi	Becca	470,000	14,100	455,900	4
23	Saro-Wiwa	Dickson	420,000	12,600	407,400	5
24	Jaja	Alex	480,000	14,400	465,600	1

Figure 3.41 – Staff salary details

We wish to filter the dataset to show only those staff with a gross (salary) greater than 500,000. However, we only want to show the LAST NAME, FIRST NAME, and GROSS fields.

Beside the main dataset, prepare a grid showing the criteria of the filter, gross income greater than 500,000 as well as the names of the columns we wish to display in our result.

In row K7, start to type the FILTER formula. The first argument is `array`, which refers to the range you want to show as your result.

No.	LAST NAME	FIRST NAME	GROSS	PAYE	NET PAY	DEPT
1	Okilo	Natalie	450,000	13,500	436,500	1
2	Uba	Jeleel	390,000	11,700	378,300	1
3	Okeke	Dopsy	380,000	11,400	368,600	3
4	Bello	Peter	310,000	9,300	300,700	2
5	Saro-Wiwa	Stephanie	590,000	17,700	572,300	1
6	Gbadamosi	Lydia	420,000	12,600	407,400	3
7	Okorie	David	600,000	18,000	582,000	3
8	Ezekwesili	Joy	440,000	13,200	426,800	2
9	Ojukwu	Joseph	540,000	16,200	523,800	4
10	Anikulapo-Kuti	Henry	350,000	10,500	339,500	3
11	Awolowo	Adah	480,000	14,400	465,600	1
12	Asari-Dokubo	Olivia	400,000	12,000	388,000	4
13	Sekibo	Austin	400,000	12,000	388,000	2
14	Akiloye	Micheal	590,000	17,700	572,300	5
15	Olanrewaju	John	360,000	10,800	349,200	3
16	Attah	Ifeanyi	550,000	16,500	533,500	4
17	Akpabio	Ayobamidele	490,000	14,700	475,300	2
18	Akinjide	Dopsy	350,000	10,500	339,500	5
19	Kalu	Rex	460,000	13,800	446,200	2
20	Yar'Adua	Ada	310,000	9,300	300,700	3
21	Omehia	George	370,000	11,100	358,900	2
22	Ekwensi	Becca	470,000	14,100	455,900	4
23	Saro-Wiwa	Dickson	420,000	12,600	407,400	5
24	Jaja	Alex	480,000	14,400	465,600	1

Criteria: Gross greater than 500,000

LAST NAME	FIRST NAME	GROSS
=FILTER(C4:E27		

FILTER(array, include, [if_empty])

Figure 3.42 – Filter array

Since we only want LAST NAME, FIRST NAME, and GROSS, our array will be the values in those fields for all the records. Our array will be C4:E27.

Press *the comma key* to highlight the second argument, `include`. This is where we specify the criteria on which to base our filter.

No.	LAST NAME	FIRST NAME	GROSS	PAYE	NET PAY	DEPT
1	Okilo	Natalie	450,000	13,500	436,500	1
2	Uba	Jeleel	390,000	11,700	378,300	1
3	Okeke	Dopsy	380,000	11,400	368,600	3
4	Bello	Peter	310,000	9,300	300,700	2
5	Saro-Wiwa	Stephanie	590,000	17,700	572,300	1
6	Gbadamosi	Lydia	420,000	12,600	407,400	3
7	Okorie	David	600,000	18,000	582,000	3
8	Ezekwesili	Joy	440,000	13,200	426,800	2
9	Ojukwu	Joseph	540,000	16,200	523,800	4
10	Anikulapo-Kuti	Henry	350,000	10,500	339,500	3
11	Awolowo	Adah	480,000	14,400	465,600	1
12	Asari-Dokubo	Olivia	400,000	12,000	388,000	4
13	Sekibo	Austin	400,000	12,000	388,000	2
14	Akiloye	Micheal	590,000	17,700	572,300	5
15	Olanrewaju	John	360,000	10,800	349,200	3
16	Attah	Ifeanyi	550,000	16,500	533,500	4
17	Akpabio	Ayobamidele	490,000	14,700	475,300	2
18	Akinjide	Dopsy	350,000	10,500	339,500	5
19	Kalu	Rex	460,000	13,800	446,200	2
20	Yar'Adua	Ada	310,000	9,300	300,700	3
21	Omehia	George	370,000	11,100	358,900	2
22	Ekwensi	Becca	470,000	14,100	455,900	4
23	Saro-Wiwa	Dickson	420,000	12,600	407,400	5
24	Jaja	Alex	480,000	14,400	465,600	1

Criteria — Gross greater than — 500,000

LAST NAME   FIRST NAME   GROSS
=FILTER(C4:E27,E4:E27>M4
FILTER(array, include, [if_empty])

Figure 3.43 – Filter criteria range

The argument will be built to display all records where GROSS is greater than 500,000. Highlight all records under the GROSS column, E4:E27, then type > (greater than), then point to cell M4, which contains the hurdle amount 500,000. This gives us E4:E27>M4.

The final argument, if_empty, is optional. It allows you to specify what you want Excel to return if there are no records that match your criteria. You can enter a comment such as not found or, since it is optional, you can just leave it blank, close brackets, and press *Enter*.

Criteria	Gross greater than	500,000
LAST NAME	**FIRST NAME**	**GROSS**
Saro-Wiwa	Stephanie	590000
Okorie	David	600000
Ojukwu	Joseph	540000
Akiloye	Micheal	590000
Attah	Ifeanyi	550000

Figure 3.44 – Staff with GROSS greater than 500,000

LAST NAME, FIRST NAME, and GROSS of all records whose GROSS is greater than 500,000 are displayed.

The action does not retain the number formatting and so the numbers are returned unformatted, as in *Figure 3.44*. Simply format the numbers using the Format Painter on the formatted number 500,000 or highlight the numbers and press *Ctrl + 1* to get to the **Format cells** dialog box.

Since FILTER is a function, it gives us the flexibility to alter any of the arguments and immediately display a whole new set of results. So, if we changed the criteria in cell M4 to 400,000 the formula will immediately update and display the following results:

No.	LAST NAME	FIRST NAME	GROSS	PAYE	NET PAY	DEPT			Criteria	Gross greater than	400,000
1	Okilo	Natalie	450,000	13,500	436,500	1					
2	Uba	Jeleel	390,000	11,700	378,300	1					
3	Okeke	Dopsy	380,000	11,400	368,600	3			LAST NAME	FIRST NAME	GROSS
4	Bello	Peter	310,000	9,300	300,700	2			Okilo	Natalie	450,000
5	Saro-Wiwa	Stephanie	590,000	17,700	572,300	1			Saro-Wiwa	Stephanie	590,000
6	Gbadamosi	Lydia	420,000	12,600	407,400	3			Gbadamosi	Lydia	420,000
7	Okorie	David	600,000	18,000	582,000	3			Okorie	David	600,000
8	Ezekwesili	Joy	440,000	13,200	426,800	2			Ezekwesili	Joy	440,000
9	Ojukwu	Joseph	540,000	16,200	523,800	4			Ojukwu	Joseph	540,000
10	Anikulapo-Kuti	Henry	350,000	10,500	339,500	3			Awolowo	Adah	480,000
11	Awolowo	Adah	480,000	14,400	465,600	1			Akiloye	Micheal	590,000
12	Asari-Dokubo	Olivia	400,000	12,000	388,000	4			Attah	Ifeanyi	550,000
13	Sekibo	Austin	400,000	12,000	388,000	2			Akpabio	Ayobamidele	490,000
14	Akiloye	Micheal	590,000	17,700	572,300	5			Kalu	Rex	460,000
15	Olanrewaju	John	360,000	10,800	349,200	3			Ekwensi	Becca	470,000
16	Attah	Ifeanyi	550,000	16,500	533,500	4			Saro-Wiwa	Dickson	420,000
17	Akpabio	Ayobamidele	490,000	14,700	475,300	2			Jaja	Alex	480,000
18	Akinjide	Dopsy	350,000	10,500	339,500	5					
19	Kalu	Rex	460,000	13,800	446,200	2					
20	Yar'Adua	Ada	310,000	9,300	300,700	3					
21	Omehia	George	370,000	11,100	358,900	2					
22	Ekwensi	Becca	470,000	14,100	455,900	4					
23	Saro-Wiwa	Dickson	420,000	12,600	407,400	5					
24	Jaja	Alex	480,000	14,400	465,600	1					

Figure 3.45 – Staff with GROSS greater than 400,000

If you decide that you only want to display the last and first name of those with GROSS greater than 400,000, simply change the array argument to C4:D27:

No.	LAST NAME	FIRST NAME	GROSS	PAYE	NET PAY	DEPT			Criteria	Gross greater than	400,000
1	Okilo	Natalie	450,000	13,500	436,500	1					
2	Uba	Jeleel	390,000	11,700	378,300	1					
3	Okeke	Dopsy	380,000	11,400	368,600	3			LAST NAME	FIRST NAME	GROSS
4	Bello	Peter	310,000	9,300	300,700	2			=FILTER(C4:D27,E4:E27>M4)		450,000
5	Saro-Wiwa	Stephanie	590,000	17,700	572,300	1			FILTER(array, include, [if_empty])		590,000
6	Gbadamosi	Lydia	420,000	12,600	407,400	3			Gbadamosi	Lydia	420,000
7	Okorie	David	600,000	18,000	582,000	3			Okorie	David	600,000
8	Ezekwesili	Joy	440,000	13,200	426,800	2			Ezekwesili	Joy	440,000
9	Ojukwu	Joseph	540,000	16,200	523,800	4			Ojukwu	Joseph	540,000

Figure 3.46 – Change array to show names only

When you press *Enter*, only the last and first names of staff with GROSS greater than 400,000 will be displayed.

No.	LAST NAME	FIRST NAME	GROSS	PAYE	NET PAY	DEPT		Criteria	Gross greater than	400,000
1	Okilo	Natalie	450,000	13,500	436,500	1				
2	Uba	Jeleel	390,000	11,700	378,300	1				
3	Okeke	Dopsy	380,000	11,400	368,600	3		LAST NAME	FIRST NAME	GROSS
4	Bello	Peter	310,000	9,300	300,700	2		=FILTER(C4:D27,E4:E27>M4)		
5	Saro-Wiwa	Stephanie	590,000	17,700	572,300	1		S FILTER(array, include, [if_empty])		
6	Gbadamosi	Lydia	420,000	12,600	407,400	3		Gbadamosi	Lydia	
7	Okorie	David	600,000	18,000	582,000	3		Okorie	David	
8	Ezekwesili	Joy	440,000	13,200	426,800	2		Ezekwesili	Joy	
9	Ojukwu	Joseph	540,000	16,200	523,800	4		Ojukwu	Joseph	
10	Anikulapo-Kuti	Henry	350,000	10,500	339,500	3		Awolowo	Adah	
11	Awolowo	Adah	480,000	14,400	465,600	1		Akiloye	Micheal	
12	Asari-Dokubo	Olivia	400,000	12,000	388,000	4		Attah	Ifeanyi	
13	Sekibo	Austin	400,000	12,000	388,000	2		Akpabio	Ayobamidele	
14	Akiloye	Micheal	590,000	17,700	572,300	5		Kalu	Rex	
15	Olanrewaju	John	360,000	10,800	349,200	3		Ekwensi	Becca	
16	Attah	Ifeanyi	550,000	16,500	533,500	4		Saro-Wiwa	Dickson	
17	Akpabio	Ayobamidele	490,000	14,700	475,300	2		Jaja	Alex	
18	Akinjide	Dopsy	350,000	10,500	339,500	5				
19	Kalu	Rex	460,000	13,800	446,200	2				
20	Yar'Adua	Ada	310,000	9,300	300,700	3				
21	Omehia	George	370,000	11,100	358,900	2				
22	Ekwensi	Becca	470,000	14,100	455,900	4				
23	Saro-Wiwa	Dickson	420,000	12,600	407,400	5				
24	Jaja	Alex	480,000	14,400	465,600	1				

Figure 3.47 – Display last and first names only

Note that the same records are displayed, as those are the ones that meet the criteria, only, in this case, the GROSS column of our results is not populated.

You should note that the FILTER function is an array function. We enter the formula in cell O4 only, but it returns values that fill multiple cells. Previously array formulas were considered advanced and complex and you needed to enter them with *Ctrl* + *Shift* + *Enter*, because simply pressing *Enter* would result in an error. However, this batch of new functions introduced in Excel 365 can handle arrays without having to press *Ctrl* + *Shift* + *Enter*.

With these new functions, as you can see, the formula is entered in one cell even though the results spread over several cells. So, you cannot alter the formula or any of the cells in the array directly except that cell in which you entered the formula.

Also, if a cell within the range of the results array is previously populated, a #SPILL error is shown and the results will not be displayed.

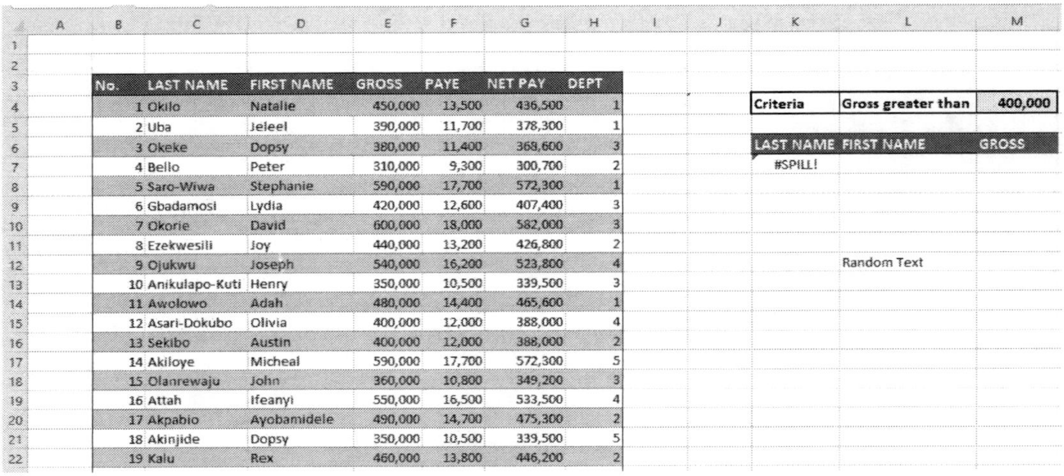

Figure 3.48 – #SPILL error

You only need to delete the obstructing data before the results can be displayed.

SORT

As the name suggests, this function allows you to sort a list or table according to the field of your choice and in the sort order, ascending or descending, that you choose.

Using the same staff salary dataset, we will sort by LAST NAME:

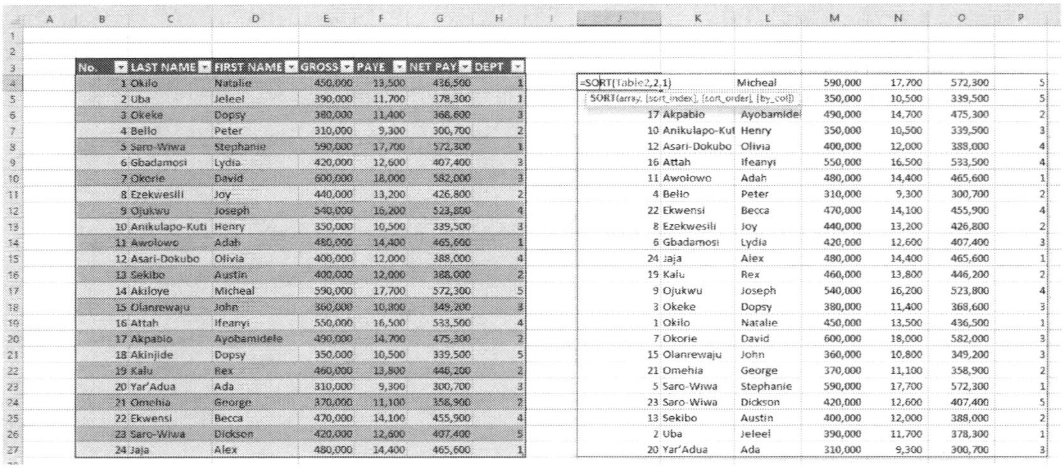

Figure 3.49 – Sort by last name

The SORT function has four arguments, three of which are optional. The first argument, array, is mandatory and asks for the range to be included in the search results. In our example, we have selected the full table.

The next argument is sort_index, which asks for the number of the column you wish to sort by, with the first column of the array you selected, No., being index number 1. We want to sort by LAST NAME, which is the second column in our array, so sort_index is 2.

The third argument is sort_order, which could be *ascending* (A to Z, or smallest to largest), represented by 1, or *descending* (Z to A, or largest to smallest), represented by –1. We have selected 1, ascending order. Now, press *Enter*, and the list sorted alphabetically according to the last name is displayed, as shown in *Figure 3.49*.

The final argument is by_col, which we will ignore as our data is arranged in rows, which is the default.

We will now select LAST NAME, FIRST NAME, and GROSS as the array, and sort according to GROSS in descending order.

	A	B	C	D	E	F	G	H	I	J	K	L	M
1													
2													
3		No.	LAST NAME	FIRST NAME	GROSS	PAYE	NET PAY	DEPT		=SORT(Table2[[#All],[LAST NAME]:[GROSS]],3,-1)			
4		1	Okilo	Natalie	450,000	13,500	436,500	1		C SORT(array, [sort_index], [sort_order], [by_col])			
5		2	Uba	Jeleel	390,000	11,700	378,300	1		Saro-Wiwa	Stephanie	590,000	
6		3	Okeke	Dopsy	380,000	11,400	368,600	3		Akiloye	Micheal	590,000	
7		4	Bello	Peter	310,000	9,300	300,700	2		Attah	Ifeanyi	550,000	
8		5	Saro-Wiwa	Stephanie	590,000	17,700	572,300	1		Ojukwu	Joseph	540,000	
9		6	Gbadamosi	Lydia	420,000	12,600	407,400	3		Akpabio	Ayobamidele	490,000	
10		7	Okorie	David	600,000	18,000	582,000	3		Awolowo	Adah	480,000	
11		8	Ezekwesili	Joy	440,000	13,200	426,800	2		Jaja	Alex	480,000	
12		9	Ojukwu	Joseph	540,000	16,200	523,800	4		Ekwensi	Becca	470,000	
13		10	Anikulapo-Kuti	Henry	350,000	10,500	339,500	3		Kalu	Rex	460,000	
14		11	Awolowo	Adah	480,000	14,400	465,600	1		Okilo	Natalie	450,000	
15		12	Asari-Dokubo	Olivia	400,000	12,000	388,000	4		Ezekwesili	Joy	440,000	
16		13	Sekibo	Austin	400,000	12,000	388,000	2		Gbadamosi	Lydia	420,000	
17		14	Akiloye	Micheal	590,000	17,700	572,300	5		Saro-Wiwa	Dickson	420,000	
18		15	Olanrewaju	John	360,000	10,800	349,200	3		Asari-Dokubo	Olivia	400,000	
19		16	Attah	Ifeanyi	550,000	16,500	533,500	4		Sekibo	Austin	400,000	
20		17	Akpabio	Ayobamidele	490,000	14,700	475,300	2		Uba	Jeleel	390,000	
21		18	Akinjide	Dopsy	350,000	10,500	339,500	5		Okeke	Dopsy	380,000	
22		19	Kalu	Rex	460,000	13,800	446,200	2		Omehia	George	370,000	
23		20	Yar'Adua	Ada	310,000	9,300	300,700	3		Olanrewaju	John	360,000	
24		21	Omehia	George	370,000	11,100	358,900	2		Anikulapo-Kuti	Henry	350,000	
25		22	Ekwensi	Becca	470,000	14,100	455,900	4		Akinjide	Dopsy	350,000	
26		23	Saro-Wiwa	Dickson	420,000	12,600	407,400	5		Bello	Peter	310,000	
27		24	Jaja	Alex	480,000	14,400	465,600	1		Yar'Adua	Ada	310,000	

Figure 3.50 – Sort by GROSS in descending order

You will notice in *Figure 3.50* that only the LAST NAME to GROSS fields are selected as the array, sort_index is 3 as the GROSS field is in the third column of our selected array, and sort_order is -1, which is descending order.

SORT BY

This is an extension of the SORT function. When the sort criteria are not part of the array you wish to return from your formula, or when you need to sort with multiple criteria, you use SORT BY.

Let's set an array of LAST NAME and FIRST NAME, and sort by GROSS in descending order:

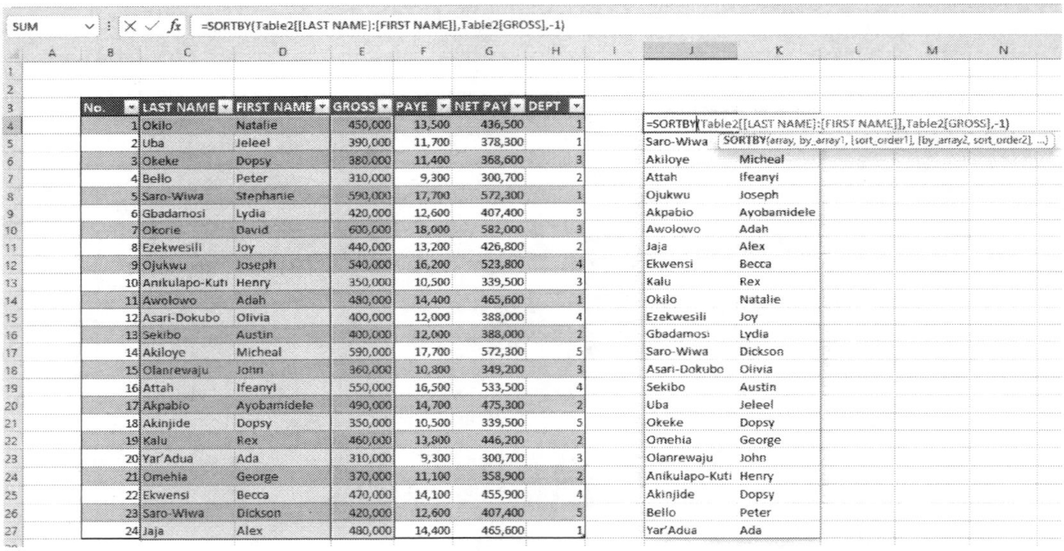

Figure 3.51 – Sort by GROSS displaying last and first name

The SORTBY function starts with the same argument as for the SORT array. You just select LAST NAME and FIRST NAME.

The second argument is `by_array1`, which stands for the first sort criteria. For this, you select the GROSS field.

The next argument is `sort_order1`, which is the sort order you desire for `criteria1`. Type in –1 for descending order. Since we only have one criterion, we can close brackets and press *Enter* to get the result displayed in *Figure 3.51*.

Finally, we will sort by DEPT then by GROSS. For the array, select all fields from LAST NAME to DEPT. For `by_array1`, select DEPT; for `sort_order1`, select 1 for ascending. The next argument is `by_array2`, select GROSS, and finally, for `sort_order2`, type –1 for descending order.

No.	LAST NAME	FIRST NAME	GROSS	PAYE	NET PAY	DEPT							
1	Okilo	Natalie	450,000	13,300	436,500	1		=SORTBY(Table2[[LAST NAME]:[DEPT]],Table2[DEPT],1,Table2[GROSS],-1)					
2	Uba	Jeleel	390,000	11,700	378,300	1		SORTBY(array, by_array1, [sort_order1], [by_array2, sort_order2], [by_array3, sort_order3], ...)					
3	Okeke	Dopsy	380,000	11,400	368,600	3		Jaja	Alex	480,000	14,400	465,600	1
4	Bello	Peter	310,000	9,300	300,700	2		Okilo	Natalie	450,000	13,500	436,500	1
5	Saro-Wiwa	Stephanie	590,000	17,700	572,300	1		Uba	Jeleel	390,000	11,700	378,300	1
6	Gbadamosi	Lydia	420,000	12,600	407,400	3		Akpabio	Ayobamidele	490,000	14,700	475,300	2
7	Okorie	David	600,000	18,000	582,000	3		Kalu	Rex	460,000	13,800	446,200	2
8	Ezekwesili	Joy	440,000	13,200	426,800	2		Ezekwesili	Joy	440,000	13,200	426,800	2
9	Ojukwu	Joseph	540,000	16,200	523,800	4		Sekibo	Austin	400,000	12,000	388,000	2
10	Anikulapo-Kuti	Henry	350,000	10,500	339,500	3		Omehia	George	370,000	11,100	358,900	2
11	Awolowo	Adah	480,000	14,400	465,600	1		Bello	Peter	310,000	9,300	300,700	2
12	Asari-Dokubo	Olivia	400,000	12,000	388,000	4		Okorie	David	600,000	18,000	582,000	3
13	Sekibo	Austin	400,000	12,000	388,000	2		Gbadamosi	Lydia	420,000	12,600	407,400	3
14	Akiloye	Micheal	590,000	17,700	572,300	5		Okeke	Dopsy	380,000	11,400	368,600	3
15	Olanrewaju	John	360,000	10,800	349,200	3		Olanrewaju	John	360,000	10,800	349,200	3
16	Attah	Ifeanyi	550,000	16,500	533,500	4		Anikulapo-Kuti	Henry	350,000	10,500	339,500	3
17	Akpabio	Ayobamidele	490,000	14,700	475,300	2		Yar'Adua	Ada	310,000	9,300	300,700	3
18	Akinjide	Dopsy	350,000	10,500	339,500	5		Attah	Ifeanyi	550,000	16,500	533,500	4
19	Kalu	Rex	460,000	13,800	446,200	2		Ojukwu	Joseph	540,000	16,200	523,800	4
20	Yar'Adua	Ada	310,000	9,300	300,700	3		Ekwensi	Becca	470,000	14,100	455,900	4
21	Omehia	George	370,000	11,100	358,900	2		Asari-Dokubo	Olivia	400,000	12,000	388,000	4
22	Ekwensi	Becca	470,000	14,100	455,900	4		Akiloye	Micheal	590,000	17,700	572,300	5
23	Saro-Wiwa	Dickson	420,000	12,600	407,400	5		Saro-Wiwa	Dickson	420,000	12,600	407,400	5
24	Jaja	Alex	480,000	14,400	465,600	1		Akinjide	Dopsy	350,000	10,500	339,500	5

Figure 3.52 – Sort by DEPT then by GROSS

When you press *Enter*, the result in *Figure 3.52* is what you get.

UNIQUE

In a list or range of cells, you might have some or all values repeated more than once. The UNIQUE function extracts unique values from a list or range, ignoring all repetitions.

For example, in the dataset in *Figure 3.53*, the SALESMAN, REGION, and PRODUCT fields all have several occurrences of the individual salesmen, regions, and products respectively.

	A	B	C	D	E	F	G	H
1								
2		**UNIQUE FUNCTION**						
3								
4		DATE	SALESMAN	REGION	PRODUCT	UNITS	UNIT PRICE	SALES
5		01/03/2018	DAVID	North	Gas Cooker	2398	45,000	107,910,000
6		02/03/2018	DAVID	North	Washing Mch.	2251	47,000	105,797,000
7		03/03/2018	MICHAEL	East	Washing Mch.	1926	47,000	90,522,000
8		04/03/2018	JOHN	West	Washing Mch.	1505	47,000	70,735,000
9		05/03/2018	ROBERT	West	MW Oven	2512	22,000	55,264,000
10		06/03/2018	WILLIAM	North	Washing Mch.	1700	47,000	79,900,000
11		07/03/2018	WILLIAM	South	Gas Cooker	1231	45,000	55,395,000
12		08/03/2018	WILLIAM	West	Washing Mch.	1849	47,000	86,903,000
13		09/03/2018	MICHAEL	North	MW Oven	2693	22,000	59,246,000
14		10/03/2018	WILLIAM	West	Gas Cooker	1995	45,000	89,775,000
15		11/03/2018	ROBERT	South	Fridge	2286	75,000	171,450,000
16		12/03/2018	JAMES	South	Fridge	2483	75,000	186,225,000
17		13/03/2018	ROBERT	East	MW Oven	1776	22,000	39,072,000
18		14/03/2018	MICHAEL	West	Gas Cooker	1813	45,000	81,585,000
19		15/03/2018	JOHN	North	Fridge	1771	75,000	132,825,000
20		16/03/2018	ROBERT	East	MW Oven	586	22,000	12,892,000
21		17/03/2018	JAMES	West	Fridge	2879	75,000	215,925,000
22		18/03/2018	WILLIAM	North	Washing Mch.	1909	47,000	89,723,000
23		19/03/2018	JOHN	East	Washing Mch.	1001	47,000	47,047,000
24		20/03/2018	ROBERT	West	Gas Cooker	2629	45,000	118,305,000
25		21/03/2018	ROBERT	East	Fridge	1946	75,000	145,950,000

Figure 3.53 – Sales report by salesman, by region, and by product

Since this report is formatted as an Excel table, we will be able to take advantage of some features specific to Excel tables to expedite our work. To convert to an Excel table, first, highlight the entire dataset, then press *Ctrl + T*.

In cell J5, enter the UNIQUE function. You will notice that there are three arguments, two of which are optional.

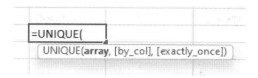

Figure 3.54 – Arguments of the UNIQUE function

To extract a unique list of salesmen, place the cursor arrow at the top border of the header of the Salesman field, cell C4, until the cursor turns to a thick black arrow, then click. The entire column of salesmen is selected, as shown in *Figure 3.55*:

	A	B	C	D	E	F	G	H	I	J	K	L
1												
2		UNIQUE FUNCTION										
3												
4		DATE	SALESMAN	REGION	PRODUCT	UNITS	UNIT PRICE	SALES				
5		01/03/2018	DAVID	North	Gas Cooker	2398	45,000	107,910,000		=UNIQUE(Table1[SALESMAN]		
6		02/03/2018	DAVID	North	Washing Mch.	2251	47,000	105,797,000		UNIQUE(**array**, [by_col], [exactly_once])		
7		03/03/2018	MICHAEL	East	Washing Mch.	1926	47,000	90,522,000				
8		04/03/2018	JOHN	West	Washing Mch.	1505	47,000	70,735,000				
9		05/03/2018	ROBERT	West	MW Oven	2512	22,000	55,264,000				
10		06/03/2018	WILLIAM	North	Washing Mch.	1700	47,000	79,900,000				
11		07/03/2018	WILLIAM	South	Gas Cooker	1231	45,000	55,395,000				
12		08/03/2018	WILLIAM	West	Washing Mch.	1849	47,000	86,903,000				
13		09/03/2018	MICHAEL	North	MW Oven	2693	22,000	59,246,000				
14		10/03/2018	WILLIAM	West	Gas Cooker	1995	45,000	89,775,000				
15		11/03/2018	ROBERT	South	Fridge	2286	75,000	171,450,000				
16		12/03/2018	JAMES	South	Fridge	2483	75,000	186,225,000				
17		13/03/2018	ROBERT	East	MW Oven	1776	22,000	39,072,000				
18		14/03/2018	MICHAEL	West	Gas Cooker	1813	45,000	81,585,000				
19		15/03/2018	JOHN	North	Fridge	1771	75,000	132,825,000				
20		16/03/2018	ROBERT	East	MW Oven	586	22,000	12,892,000				
21		17/03/2018	JAMES	West	Fridge	2879	75,000	215,925,000				
22		18/03/2018	WILLIAM	North	Washing Mch.	1909	47,000	89,723,000				
23		19/03/2018	JOHN	East	Washing Mch.	1001	47,000	47,047,000				
24		20/03/2018	ROBERT	West	Gas Cooker	2629	45,000	118,305,000				
25		21/03/2018	ROBERT	East	Fridge	1946	75,000	145,950,000				
26		22/03/2018	DAVID	West	Washing Mch.	1042	47,000	48,974,000				

Figure 3.55 – Salesmen selected as the array

Since the remaining arguments are optional, we can ignore them, and just press *Enter* to get the unique list:

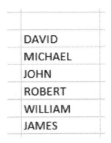

| DAVID |
| MICHAEL |
| JOHN |
| ROBERT |
| WILLIAM |
| JAMES |

Figure 3.56 – Unique list of salesmen

The sales report has 47 records, but only six unique salesmen. The rest are repetitions.

If we want a unique list of regions, we just need to edit the formula and replace the SALESMAN field with the REGION field. Select cell J4, which contains the UNIQUE formula, press the *F2* function key on your keyboard to get into *Edit* mode, press the left arrow key on the keyboard to get back into the formula syntax, and then click on the first argument, array.

	DATE	SALESMAN	REGION	PRODUCT	UNITS	UNIT PRICE	SALES					
5	01/03/2018	DAVID	North	Gas Cooker	2398	45,000	107,910,000		=UNIQUE(Table1[REGION])			
6	02/03/2018	DAVID	North	Washing Mch.	2251	47,000	105,797,000		N UNIQUE(array, [by_col], [exactly_once])			
7	03/03/2018	MICHAEL	East	Washing Mch.	1926	47,000	90,522,000		JOHN			
8	04/03/2018	JOHN	West	Washing Mch.	1505	47,000	70,735,000		ROBERT			
9	05/03/2018	ROBERT	West	MW Oven	2512	22,000	55,264,000		WILLIAM			
10	06/03/2018	WILLIAM	North	Washing Mch.	1700	47,000	79,900,000		JAMES			
11	07/03/2018	WILLIAM	South	Gas Cooker	1231	45,000	55,395,000					
12	08/03/2018	WILLIAM	West	Washing Mch	1849	47,000	86,903,000					
13	09/03/2018	MICHAEL	North	MW Oven	2693	22,000	59,246,000					
14	10/03/2018	WILLIAM	West	Gas Cooker	1995	45,000	89,775,000					
15	11/03/2018	ROBERT	South	Fridge	2286	75,000	171,450,000					
16	12/03/2018	JAMES	South	Fridge	2483	75,000	186,225,000					
17	13/03/2018	ROBERT	East	MW Oven	1776	22,000	39,072,000					
18	14/03/2018	MICHAEL	West	Gas Cooker	1813	45,000	81,585,000					
19	15/03/2018	JOHN	North	Fridge	1771	75,000	132,825,000					
20	16/03/2018	ROBERT	East	MW Oven	586	22,000	12,892,000					
21	17/03/2018	JAMES	West	Fridge	2879	75,000	215,925,000					
22	18/03/2018	WILLIAM	North	Washing Mch.	1909	47,000	89,723,000					

Figure 3.57 – Formula to extract the unique list of regions

The `array` argument becomes bold and the original range selected, SALESMAN, will be highlighted. You just need to select the REGION field in the same way you selected the SALESMAN field earlier. Then, press *Enter*.

North

East

West

South

Figure 3.58 – Unique list of regions

To select a unique list of salesmen and regions, in cell K4, repeat the previous steps for selecting the salesmen as the array, but this time, once you have selected the SALESMAN column, before you release the cursor, drag it to the REGION field then release, so that both the SALESMAN and REGION fields are selected:

	A	B	C	D	E	F	G	H	I	J	K	L	M
1													
2		UNIQUE FUNCTION											
3													
4		DATE	SALESMAN	REGION	PRODUCT	UNITS	UNIT PRIC	SALES					
5		01/03/2018	DAVID	North	Gas Cooker	2398	45,000	107,910,000		North	=UNIQUE(Table1[[SALESMAN]:[REGION]])		
6		02/03/2018	DAVID	North	Washing Mch.	2251	47,000	105,797,000		East	N UNIQUE(array, [by_col], [exactly_once])		
7		03/03/2018	MICHAEL	East	Washing Mch.	1926	47,000	90,522,000		West	JOHN	West	
8		04/03/2018	JOHN	West	Washing Mch.	1505	47,000	70,735,000		South	ROBERT	West	
9		05/03/2018	ROBERT	West	MW Oven	2512	22,000	55,264,000			WILLIAM	North	
10		06/03/2018	WILLIAM	North	Washing Mch.	1700	47,000	79,900,000			WILLIAM	South	
11		07/03/2018	WILLIAM	South	Gas Cooker	1231	45,000	55,395,000			WILLIAM	West	
12		08/03/2018	WILLIAM	West	Washing Mch.	1849	47,000	86,903,000			MICHAEL	North	
13		09/03/2018	MICHAEL	North	MW Oven	2693	22,000	59,246,000			ROBERT	South	
14		10/03/2018	WILLIAM	West	Gas Cooker	1995	45,000	89,775,000			JAMES	South	
15		11/03/2018	ROBERT	South	Fridge	2286	75,000	171,450,000			ROBERT	East	
16		12/03/2018	JAMES	South	Fridge	2483	75,000	186,225,000			MICHAEL	West	
17		13/03/2018	ROBERT	East	MW Oven	1776	22,000	39,072,000			JOHN	North	
18		14/03/2018	MICHAEL	West	Gas Cooker	1813	45,000	81,585,000			JAMES	West	
19		15/03/2018	JOHN	North	Fridge	1771	75,000	132,825,000			JOHN	East	
20		16/03/2018	ROBERT	East	MW Oven	586	22,000	12,892,000			DAVID	West	
21		17/03/2018	JAMES	West	Fridge	2879	75,000	215,925,000			MICHAEL	South	
22		18/03/2018	WILLIAM	North	Washing Mch.	1909	47,000	89,723,000			DAVID	East	
23		19/03/2018	JOHN	East	Washing Mch.	1001	47,000	47,047,000			JAMES	East	
24		20/03/2018	ROBERT	West	Gas Cooker	2629	45,000	118,305,000			ROBERT	North	
25		21/03/2018	ROBERT	East	Fridge	1946	75,000	145,950,000			JAMES	North	
26		22/03/2018	DAVID	West	Washing Mch.	1042	47,000	48,974,000					

Figure 3.59 – Unique list of salesmen and regions

The next argument, `by_col`, is not applicable, since our data is arranged in rows and not columns. Since this argument is optional, we can just type a *comma* (,) to move on to the final argument, `exactly_once`. This argument is asking which of those unique salesman and region combinations occur only once. There are two options: 1 or `True` – `Return items that appear exactly once`, and 0 or `False` – `Return every distinct item`. Type 1:

North	DAVID	North	`=UNIQUE(Table1[[SALESMAN]:[REGION]],,1`
			Only return rows or columns that appear exactly once in the ar `UNIQUE(array, [by_col], [exactly_once])` (...) TRUE - Return items that appear exactly once
West	JOHN	West	(...) FALSE - Return every distinct item
South	ROBERT	West	
	WILLIAM	North	
	WILLIAM	South	

Figure 3.60 – The exactly_once argument

Press *Enter*, and you get the following:

	A	B	C	D	E	F	G	H	I	J	K	L	M	N	O
1															
2		UNIQUE FUNCTION													
3															
4		DATE	SALESMAN	REGION	PRODUCT	UNITS	UNIT PRIC	SALES							
5		01/03/2018	DAVID	North	Gas Cooker	2398	45.000	107,910,000		North	DAVID	North		MICHAEL	East
6		02/03/2018	DAVID	North	Washing Mch.	2251	47.000	105,797,000		East	MICHAEL	East		JAMES	South
7		03/03/2018	MICHAEL	East	Washing Mch.	1926	47.000	90,522,000		West	JOHN	West		JAMES	West
8		04/03/2018	JOHN	West	Washing Mch.	1505	47.000	70,735,000		South	ROBERT	West		JOHN	East
9		05/03/2018	ROBERT	West	MW Oven	2512	22.000	55,264,000			WILLIAM	North		ROBERT	North
10		06/03/2018	WILLIAM	North	Washing Mch.	1700	47.000	79,900,000			WILLIAM	South		JAMES	North
11		07/03/2018	WILLIAM	South	Gas Cooker	1231	45.000	55,395,000			WILLIAM	West			
12		08/03/2018	WILLIAM	West	Washing Mch.	1849	47.000	86,903,000			MICHAEL	North			
13		09/03/2018	MICHAEL	North	MW Oven	2693	22.000	59,246,000			ROBERT	South			
14		10/03/2018	WILLIAM	West	Gas Cooker	1995	45.000	89,775,000			JAMES	South			
15		11/03/2018	ROBERT	South	Fridge	2286	75.000	171,450,000			ROBERT	East			
16		12/03/2018	JAMES	South	Fridge	2483	75.000	186,225,000			MICHAEL	West			
17		13/03/2018	ROBERT	East	MW Oven	1776	22.000	39,072,000			JOHN	North			
18		14/03/2018	MICHAEL	West	Gas Cooker	1813	45.000	81,585,000			JAMES	West			
19		15/03/2018	JOHN	North	Fridge	1771	75.000	132,825,000			JOHN	East			
20		16/03/2018	ROBERT	East	MW Oven	586	22.000	12,892,000			DAVID	West			
21		17/03/2018	JAMES	West	Fridge	2879	75.000	215,925,000			MICHAEL	South			
22		18/03/2018	WILLIAM	North	Washing Mch.	1909	47.000	89,723,000			DAVID	East			
23		19/03/2018	JOHN	East	Washing Mch.	1001	47.000	47,047,000			JAMES	East			
24		20/03/2018	ROBERT	West	Gas Cooker	2629	45.000	118,305,000			ROBERT	North			
25		21/03/2018	ROBERT	East	Fridge	1946	75.000	145,950,000			JAMES	North			

Figure 3.61 – Unique list of salesmen and regions that appear just once

Since our dataset is formatted as an Excel table, if we add a new record to the bottom of the table, any formula that refers to the table will be automatically updated with the new record.

Suppose we add the following record to the bottom of our table: 16/04/2018; MICHAEL; North East; MW Oven; 1000; 22,000; 22,000,000; as shown in *Figure 3.62*:

47	12/04/2018	JAMES	East	MW Oven	1194	22,000	26,268,000
48	13/04/2018	ROBERT	South	Washing Mch.	2137	47,000	100,439,000
49	14/04/2018	WILLIAM	North	Washing Mch.	770	47,000	36,190,000
50	15/04/2018	JAMES	North	Fridge	771	75,000	57,825,000
51	16/04/2018	MICHAEL	North East	MW Oven	1000	22,000	22,000,000	←

Figure 3.62 – New record added to the bottom of the table

As soon as you press *Enter*, all formulas related to this table will be updated accordingly!

	North	DAVID	North		MICHAEL	East
	East	MICHAEL	East		JAMES	South
	West	JOHN	West		JAMES	West
	South	ROBERT	West		JOHN	East
→	North East	WILLIAM	North		ROBERT	North
		WILLIAM	South		JAMES	North
		WILLIAM	West		MICHAEL	North East ←
		MICHAEL	North			
		ROBERT	South			
		JAMES	South			
		ROBERT	East			
		MICHAEL	West			
		JOHN	North			
		JAMES	West			
		JOHN	East			
		DAVID	West			
		MICHAEL	South			
		DAVID	East			
		JAMES	East			
		ROBERT	North			
		JAMES	North			
		MICHAEL	North East ←			

Figure 3.63 – Formulas updated with new data

The arrows in *Figure 3.63* show where the new data has been added to each of the formula output arrays.

You could take this a step further and produce a sorted, filtered list. Go to the formula in cell K5, which extracts a unique list of SALESMAN and REGION, and press the *F2* function key to go into *Edit* mode.

Immediately after the = sign, type SORT, then press *Tab*. This inserts and activates the SORT function.

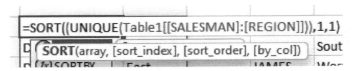

Figure 3.64 – Sort unique list syntax

The SORT array is the UNIQUE formula, so you need to put brackets at the beginning and end of the UNIQUE formula, (these are the inside brackets in *Figure 3.64*). Now, press the comma key; then, for sort_index, type 1, followed by a comma, then 1 for sort_order to sort in ascending order, or from A to Z.

North	DAVID	North	MICHAEL	East
East	DAVID	West	JAMES	South
West	DAVID	East	JAMES	West
South	JAMES	South	JOHN	East
North East	JAMES	West	ROBERT	North
	JAMES	East	JAMES	North
	JAMES	North	MICHAEL	North East
	JOHN	West		
	JOHN	North		
	JOHN	East		
	MICHAEL	East		
	MICHAEL	North		
	MICHAEL	West		
	MICHAEL	South		
	MICHAEL	North East		
	ROBERT	West		
	ROBERT	South		
	ROBERT	East		
	ROBERT	North		
	WILLIAM	North		
	WILLIAM	South		
	WILLIAM	West		

Figure 3.65 – Sorted unique list of salesmen and regions

The unique list of salesmen and regions is now sorted alphabetically, in ascending order, in the SALESMAN column.

Summary

In this chapter, we learned about the power of formulas and functions and how we can use them to speed up our modeling and make it more interesting. We worked through examples of some of the more common functions, such as the VLOOKUP, MATCH, and CHOOSE functions. We were also introduced to some of the new functions introduced in Excel 365: XLOOKUP, FILTER, UNIQUE, and SORT. We will see another new function, SEQUENCE, in a practical example in *Chapter 7, Asset and Debt Schedules.*

In the next chapter, we will look at one of the features that forms the backbone of Excel, the referencing framework. Understanding this framework and knowing how to apply its principles will help to speed up your work and improve your productivity.

4

Referencing Framework in Excel

In the course of your modeling, you will have to deal with a lot of repetitive and time-consuming calculations. Apart from taking up a lot of your time, it can make the practice of modeling boring and unattractive. Fortunately, Excel has a number of tools and features that can speed up your actions and make modeling a much more pleasing exercise. The referencing framework in Excel is one such feature.

At the end of the chapter, you will understand what the referencing framework is all about. You will have learned the different types of referencing and how and when to use them to improve your productivity.

This chapter specifically covers the following topics:

- An introduction to the framework
- Relative referencing
- Absolute referencing
- Mixed referencing

An introduction to the framework

A worksheet in Microsoft Excel is divided into over 1 million rows and over 16,000 columns. The rows are labeled 1, 2, 3, and so on to 1,048,576, and the columns are labeled A, B, C, and so on to XFD. The rows and columns intersect to form over 16 billion cells in one worksheet. However, since a cell is identified by the column and row that intersect to form it, each cell has a unique identification that is conventionally written as the intersecting column and row. Thus, at the intersection of column UV and row 59, we have the cell UV59. There is no other cell UV59 on that worksheet in that workbook on that computer. This feature forms the basis for the referencing framework in Excel. It means that you can use the contents of any cell simply by including its cell reference in a formula.

The following screenshot gives the simplest example of this. By typing =D4 in cell F5, the contents of cell D4, **Happy day**, have been duplicated in cell F5:

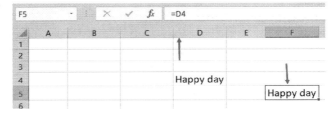

Figure 4.1 – The cell reference in the formula

You can enter a formula in Excel by typing the values for each part of the formula directly into the cell, as shown in the following screenshot:

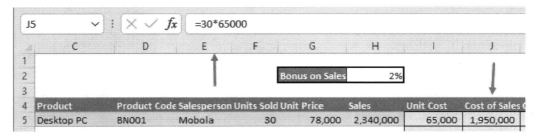

Figure 4.2 – A hardcoded formula

The cost of sales is *units sold x unit cost*, which in this case is *30 x 65000*. The formula bar shows that we entered =30*65000 to get **1,950.000**.

The two major shortcomings of this method, which is referred to as hardcoding, are the following:

- It is not clear where the figures have come from. Several months down the line when you come to review your model, you don't want to have to think the whole process through again in order to determine the source of the input.

- If the cells containing the values you have entered need to be modified in order to accommodate new and/or more accurate information, wherever those variables occur or have been used in formulas in your model, you would need to go and update them one by one accordingly.

Let's now look at the different types of referencing in Excel and how they affect your formulas.

Relative referencing

Relative referencing is the default type of referencing in Excel. A reference is relative because when it is included as part of a formula that is copied to another location, the column and row of the reference will change by the same amount, relative to the position of the cell to which the formula is being copied.

Rather than type in values directly into cells, you should type the value in another cell and then enter the cell references of the cells containing the values, as shown in the following screenshot:

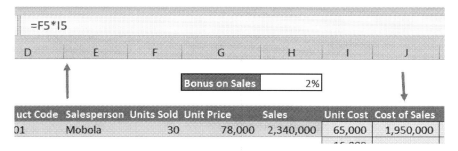

Figure 4.3 – The formula with the cell references

Entering the cell references rather than the values in the cells being referred to does not change the result of the formula. The only thing that changes is that you are now seeing cell references rather than values in the cells with formulas. However, when you decide to copy the formula to another location, the rules governing cell referencing come into play. Instead of hardcoding, Excel allows you to make use of the contents of a cell by simply referring to that cell.

The formula bar shows that we entered =F5*I5. This way, it is clear where the input is coming from. The formula is saying to multiply the value in cell F5 with the value in cell I5. Currently, this means *30 x 65.000* to give **1,950,000**.

This way, the formula is not linked to the contents of the cell but rather to the cell and, more specifically, the cell references. This means that if we modify the contents of one or more of the cells referred to, it is the new value that Excel will use, and the result will be adjusted accordingly.

So, if we change the units sold by Mobola from 30 to 50, the cost of sales becomes *50 x 65,000 = 3,250.000*:

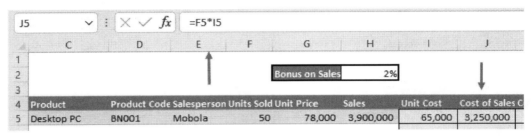

Figure 4.4 – The updated cost of sales

You should note that the **Sales** amount, which is *units sold x unit price*, is also updated to **3,900,000**, as that formula also refers to cell F5, the units sold by Mobola. So, all cells that have formulas that refer directly or indirectly to the modified cell will be automatically updated accordingly.

Another advantage of referencing is that, by default, Excel registers the position of the cell references, relative to the active cell. So, in the preceding example, F5 is registered in the same row but four cells to the left and I5, in one cell to the left of the active cell, J5.

The relevance of this is that if you copy that formula to another location, Excel remembers the positions of the original cell references relative to the original location of the formula and then adjusts the references accordingly in order to maintain those positions relative to the new active cell. So, if the formula is copied one cell down (which is one row down), the row part of the references is adjusted by one row down, Thus, F5*I5 automatically becomes F6*I6, as illustrated in *Figure 4.5*:

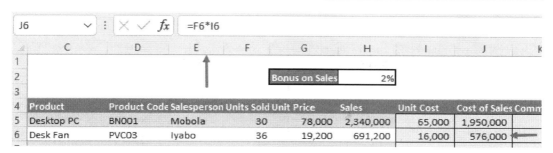

Figure 4.5 – The cost of the sales formula copied down by one cell

This way, since the formula is the same, *units sold x unit cost*, we can simply copy our formula down the list and still obtain the correct answers.

> **Important Note**
>
> This would not work in the earlier example where we entered the values directly into the active cell. In that case, if we copied down, we would get the same value, 1,950,000, all the way down the list.

The following screenshot shows the result of copying the formula down the column:

Date	Product	Product Code	Salesperson	Units Sold	Unit Price	Sales	Unit Cost	Cost of Sales	Commission
01/11/2018	Desktop PC	BN001	Mobola	30	78,000	2,340,000	65,000	1,950,000	
02/11/2018	Desk Fan	PVC03	Iyabo	36	19,200	691,200	16,000	576,000	
03/11/2018	Ptinter	BN003	Dupe	27	54,000	1,458,000	45,000	1,215,000	
04/11/2018	Microwave	SK003	Mobola	44	32,400	1,425,600	27,000	1,188,000	
06/11/2018	Standing Fan	PVC02	Deji	26	21,600	561,600	18,000	468,000	
07/11/2018	Desktop PC	BN001	Deji	35	78,000	2,730,000	65,000	2,275,000	
08/11/2018	Cooker	SK002	Lara	42	66,000	2,772,000	55,000	2,310,000	
09/11/2018	Cooker	SK002	Tunde	48	66,000	3,168,000	55,000	2,640,000	
10/11/2018	Desk Fan	PVC03	Mobola	43	19,200	825,600	16,000	688,000	
11/11/2018	Ptinter	BN003	Dupe	31	54,000	1,674,000	45,000	1,395,000	
13/11/2018	Standing Fan	PVC02	Mobola	25	21,600	540,000	18,000	450,000	
14/11/2018	Desktop PC	BN001	Mobola	43	78,000	3,354,000	65,000	2,795,000	
15/11/2018	Washing Machin	SK001	Dupe	50	84,000	4,200,000	70,000	3,500,000	
16/11/2018	Laptop	BN002	Iyabo	36	84,000	3,024,000	70,000	2,520,000	
17/11/2018	Standing Fan	PVC02	Lara	33	21,600	712,800	18,000	594,000	
18/11/2018	Hoover	PVC01	Dupe	34	30,000	1,020,000	25,000	850,000	

Figure 4.6 – The cost of the sales formula copied down to other cells in that column/field

This type of referencing is referred to as relative referencing.

Absolute referencing

Sometimes, you will have a formula containing a reference that you want to remain the same when you copy the formula to another location. For example, if we wanted to calculate the commission on sales for each salesperson, this would be *sales x commission*.

As we move down the list of salespersons, the row number changes so that the reference to the sales made by the salesperson moves from H5 to H6 to H7 and eventually to H20, the last record in our list. This is what we want so that the salesperson is matched with the correct sales.

However, we are using the same commission percentage that is in cell H2, and when we copy down the list, we want the cell reference to remain as H2. In other words, we need to lock this cell reference or make it absolute. We do this by putting a $ sign before the column and row parts of the reference, so H2 becomes $H$2. From the following screenshot, we can see that the formula has been entered in cell K5 as =H5*$H$2:

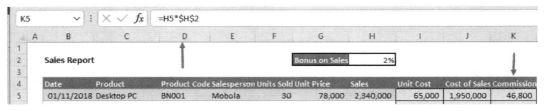

Figure 4.7 – The absolute reference to the commission

Instead of typing in the $ signs, Excel allows you to press the *F4* key to put $ signs before the column and row references. This means that when we copy this formula down the list from one row to the next, the reference to sales will change accordingly, but the reference to the commission will be locked on cell H2.

The following screenshot shows the result of copying the formula, with the locked cell, down the column:

| K5 | | | ✕ ✓ f_x | =H5*$H$2 | | | | | | |

◢	A	B	C	D	E	F	G	H	I	J	K
1											
2		Sales Report						Bonus on Sales	2%		
3											
4		Date	Product	Product Code	Salesperson	Units Sold	Unit Price	Sales	Unit Cost	Cost of Sales	Commission
5		01/11/2018	Desktop PC	BN001	Mobola	30	78,000	2,340,000	65,000	1,950,000	46,800
6		02/11/2018	Desk Fan	PVC03	Iyabo	36	19,200	691,200	16,000	576,000	13,824
7		03/11/2018	Ptinter	BN003	Dupe	27	54,000	1,458,000	45,000	1,215,000	29,160
8		04/11/2018	Microwave	SK003	Mobola	44	32,400	1,425,600	27,000	1,188,000	28,512
9		06/11/2018	Standing Fan	PVC02	Deji	26	21,600	561,600	18,000	468,000	11,232
10		07/11/2018	Desktop PC	BN001	Deji	35	78,000	2,730,000	65,000	2,275,000	54,600
11		08/11/2018	Cooker	SK002	Lara	42	66,000	2,772,000	55,000	2,310,000	55,440
12		09/11/2018	Cooker	SK002	Tunde	48	66,000	3,168,000	55,000	2,640,000	63,360
13		10/11/2018	Desk Fan	PVC03	Mobola	43	19,200	825,600	16,000	688,000	16,512
14		11/11/2018	Ptinter	BN003	Dupe	31	54,000	1,674,000	45,000	1,395,000	33,480
15		13/11/2018	Standing Fan	PVC02	Mobola	25	21,600	540,000	18,000	450,000	10,800
16		14/11/2018	Desktop PC	BN001	Mobola	43	78,000	3,354,000	65,000	2,795,000	67,080
17		15/11/2018	Washing Machin	SK001	Dupe	50	84,000	4,200,000	70,000	3,500,000	84,000
18		16/11/2018	Laptop	BN002	Iyabo	36	84,000	3,024,000	70,000	2,520,000	60,480
19		17/11/2018	Standing Fan	PVC02	Lara	33	21,600	712,800	18,000	594,000	14,256
20		18/11/2018	Hoover	PVC01	Dupe	34	30,000	1,020,000	25,000	850,000	20,400

Figure 4.8 – The formula with the absolute reference copied down

This type of referencing is an example of absolute referencing.

Mixed referencing

As mentioned earlier, a cell reference is made up of the row and column that intercept to form that cell. Thus, if a cell is in column G, row 59, its cell reference is G59, G being the column part and 59 the row part of the cell reference. No two cells can have the same cell reference on the same worksheet.

Mixed referencing occurs when you need to lock either the column part only, leaving the row part of the reference relative, or lock the row part only, leaving the column part of the reference relative. This is demonstrated in the following example.

You should take note of the following two things:

- Firstly, the referencing framework is only relevant when you want to copy a formula to another location.

- Secondly, its main function is to make it possible for you to enter a formula once and then copy it over a range that contains cells with formulas that have cell references in a similar position to the active cells.

While this framework allows you to save copious amounts of valuable time, it is not mandatory, and if you find that you are struggling to understand this framework, you can ignore it and repeat the formula manually down the list.

Our example, using the same sales report, seeks to compare sales obtained by using markups of 15%, 20%, and 25%. Sales are calculated as *cost of sales x (1+markup)*. The sales markup is illustrated in the following screenshot:

Figure 4.9 – A dataset for mixed referencing

You would use mixed referencing in a situation where you need to copy the same formula down (rows) and across (columns) and lock the row and allow just the column reference to vary, and vice versa.

In our example, you will create the formula once in cell I5 and then copy it down rows 6 to 20 and across columns J and K. The following screenshot shows the formula we will use for mixed referencing:

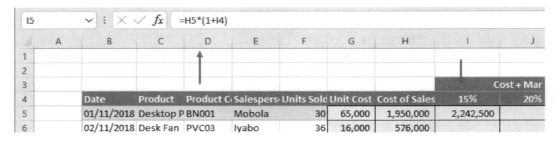

Figure 4.10 – The core formula for 15% markup on the cost of sales

As shown in the previous screenshot, the core formula is **=H5*(1+I4)**. Note that there are two cell references in the formula, H5 and I4, which you will consider separately. Cell H5 is the cost of sales. The column part is H, which we will look at when we consider copying to the right, across columns. The row part is 5, which we will look at when we consider copying down the rows.

When copying the formula down the rows, you want the cost of sales to change from one record to the next one down. In other words, the row part of the reference, 5, should not be locked; it should remain relative – that is, with no $ sign in front of it.

When copying the formula across the columns, the cost of sales remains the same, as you move along the same row from one markup percentage to the next. In other words, the column part of the reference should be locked on column H with a $ sign in front of it so that from one markup percentage to the next, it is still referring to cell H5. Thus, our first reference should look like this – $H5.

Cell I4 is the markup margin, 15%. The column part is I, which we will look at when we consider copying to the right, across columns. The row part is 4, which we will look at when we consider copying down the rows.

When copying the formula down the rows, you want the markup margin, 15%, to remain the same from one record to the next one down. In other words, the row part of the reference, 4, should be locked; it should have a $ sign in front of it so that it always refers to cell I4 when we copy down from one row to the next.

When copying the formula across the columns, the markup should move from 15% to 20%, and so on. In other words, the column part of the reference, I, should not be locked; it should remain relative with no $ sign in front of it. Thus, our second reference should look like this – I$5. The complete formula should thus be $H5*(1+I$4). The following screenshot shows the complete formula with mixed referencing:

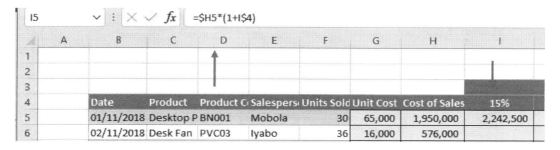

Figure 4.11 – The mixed referencing formula

Again, you do not need to type in the $ signs. The *F4* key on your keyboard is a toggle key that cycles through four options:

1. Using the H5 cell reference as an example, pressing the *F4* key once will put $ before both the column and row parts to give $H$5.

2. A second press of the *F4* key will put the $ sign in front of the row part only to give H$5.

3. A third press of the *F4* key will put the $ sign in front of the column part only to give $H5.

4. Finally, a fourth press of the *F4* key will return the reference to a relative reference, H5, with no $ signs.

Now, copy the formula across and down. The following screenshot confirms that the furthest cell to which the formula was copied points to the correct cells:

	Product C	Salespers	Units Sold	Unit Cost	Cost of Sales	15%	20%	25%
							Cost + MarkUp %	
5	BN001	Mobola	30	65,000	1,950,000	2,242,500	2,340,000	2,437,500
6	PVC03	Iyabo	36	16,000	576,000	662,400	691,200	720,000
7	BN003	Dupe	27	45,000	1,215,000	1,397,250	1,458,000	1,518,750
8	SK003	Mobola	44	27,000	1,188,000	1,366,200	1,425,600	1,485,000
9	PVC02	Deji	26	18,000	468,000	538,200	561,600	585,000
10	BN001	Deji	35	65,000	2,275,000	2,616,250	2,730,000	2,843,750
11	SK002	Lara	42	55,000	2,310,000	2,656,500	2,772,000	2,887,500
12	SK002	Tunde	48	55,000	2,640,000	3,036,000	3,168,000	3,300,000
13	PVC03	Mobola	43	16,000	688,000	791,200	825,600	860,000
14	BN003	Dupe	31	45,000	1,395,000	1,604,250	1,674,000	1,743,750
15	PVC02	Mobola	25	18,000	450,000	517,500	540,000	562,500
16	BN001	Mobola	43	65,000	2,795,000	3,214,250	3,354,000	3,493,750
17	SK001	Dupe	50	70,000	3,500,000	4,025,000	4,200,000	4,375,000
18	BN002	Iyabo	36	70,000	2,520,000	2,898,000	3,024,000	3,150,000
19	PVC02	Lara	33	18,000	594,000	683,100	712,800	742,500
20	PVC01	Dupe	34	25,000	850,000	977,500	1,020,000	=$H20*(1+K$4)

SUM   fx   =$H20*(1+K$4)

Figure 4.12 – Check on the furthermost cell to confirm that the formula is correct

It is always prudent to check that the copied formula gives the correct answer. You do this by checking the cell at the bottom right of the range to which you have copied – in this case, cell K20, which correctly refers to the cells H20 and K$4.

Summary

In this chapter, we have learned about the referencing framework in Excel.

We have learned about the three types of referencing, **relative**, **absolute**, and **mixed** referencing, and when to use each of them.

We have understood that these concepts can save us a lot of time in our Excel work, but it is only relevant when we need to copy a cell or range of cells that contain one or more cell references to another location.

We have learned about the *F4* shortcut key and how it toggles between the different forms of referencing.

In the next chapter, we will cover the need to understand the purpose of the assignment and how to build assumptions that are necessary to project our actual results for the next 3 to 5 years.

5

An Introduction to Power Query

Power Query is one of the most innovative and game-changing features introduced to Microsoft Excel. In this chapter, we will offer an introduction to Power Query, including its advantages and a step-by-step illustration of how to use it.

A financial analyst or financial modeler receives data from a wide range of sources. Most of the time, you don't have control over this, so you might end up having to work with data in different formats such as `.txt`, `.csv`, `.xls`, and `.pdf`. Also, the data would have been prepared by people of vastly varying Excel competence and discipline.

As a result of this, the data usually comes with a lot of formatting and layout inconsistencies that have to be addressed before it is ready for your model. Traditionally, correcting these errors used to be one of the most tedious aspects of modeling, until the advent of Power Query.

By the end of this chapter, you will be able to get and transform data using Power Query and break through some of the barriers to transforming data that existed before Power Query.

In this chapter, we will cover the following topics:

- Highlighting common formatting mistakes
- What is Power Query?
- Different ways to use Power Query
- Advantages of Power Query
- Illustrative example

Highlighting common formatting mistakes

Excel is a wonderful tool for financial analysts. However, in order to make use of many of its great features, certain protocols have to be observed.

The following are some of the common types of formatting anomalies that introduce complications in using Excel data analysis tools:

- **Numbers formatted as text**: When you enter data into an Excel cell, by default, the text is aligned to the left of the cell, and numbers and dates are aligned to the right of the cell. In this way, Excel can recognize numbers as such and easily apply number-related actions to the data.

  Unfortunately, imported data and even data prepared in Excel by a novice often comes with numbers formatted as text. This immediately limits how you can manipulate the data in Excel, as many of the time-saving features will not work or will give erratic results.

- **Partially summarized dataset**: Excel analytical tools are designed to work with clean datasets with one column per field and one row per record. So, when fields are combined, (for example, grouping actual results separately from expected results, and sales displayed separately according to the region, as in *Figure 5.1*), the analytical tools are unable to function properly until the data is cleaned up or *unpivoted*.

Jan-21					
			ACTUAL		
SALESMAN	PRODUCT	North West	South East	Mid Central	North W
Sade	Washing Mch.	24,987	54,926	18,212	26,4
	MW Oven	32,401	51,334	15,286	25,9
	Fridge		51,126	22,502	
	Gas Cooker	28,290	61,865	22,309	29,9
Sade Total		**85,678**	**219,251**	**78,309**	**82,3**
Habiba	Washing Mch.	24,884	57,230	21,310	20,8
	MW Oven	20,619	54,220	19,560	28,7
	Fridge	27,878	62,502		30,8
	Gas Cooker	21,565	55,316	16,479	24,7
Habiba Total		**94,946**	**229,268**	**57,349**	**105,2**

Figure 5.1 – Partially summarized dataset

- **Subtotals within a dataset**: Subtotals are very common and often help to clarify some datasets by breaking up the monotony of a mass of figures, as can be seen in *Figure 5.1*, where sales are subtotaled according to the salesman.

  Unfortunately, this gives a very limited amount of structured information. Data analysis tools such as pivot tables are so much more flexible and can give a much wider range of presentation and display options. However, they need the dataset to be in proper Excel format without any of the anomalies listed here.

  Once the pivot table is set up, you can display the information according to salesman, product, or region, alternating between them with just a few mouse clicks.

- **Leading spaces**: This refers to a space at the beginning of a word or sentence in addition to normal spaces that separate words.

  Since Excel considers space to be a separate character, leading spaces introduce anomalies in dealing with datasets. For example, a leading space before a number forces Excel to treat that number as text.

  This formatting error is made more difficult to trace since a space is mostly invisible and not so easy to detect.

  As a result of this, the analyst or modeler must typically spend a vast amount of time cleaning up data, often with the use of formulas that can sometimes get quite complex, before they can start working properly on the data.

In 2013, Microsoft announced the release of Power Query, and the entire landscape of data preparation and analysis changed. Tasks that hitherto required complex formulas could now be completed with just a few keystrokes.

We have looked at a selection of mistakes and anomalies that have sometimes made data preparation and analysis a tedious chore in identifying and constructing complex formulas to correct them. Let's now look at Power Query and how it can simplify the whole process.

What is Power Query?

Power Query is an **extract-transform-load** (**ETL**) tool. It has greatly extended the sources from which data can be imported into Excel. Power Query has an impressive array of transform tools that crucially can be accessed and applied without the use of formulas. Finally, with the option to create a connection only, it reduces the file size tremendously over previous methods.

The first step in using Power Query is to import data (**Get Data**) into Excel. In Excel 365, you do this by selecting the desired source from the **Get Data** button in the **Get & Transform Data** group under the **Data** ribbon.

> **Note**
> From 2010 to 2013, you could access Power Query as a separate ribbon in Excel. However, from 2016 on, Power Query is now found in the **Data** ribbon as the **Get & Transform** group.

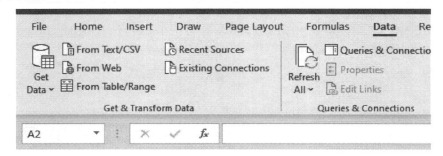

Figure 5.2 – The Get Data button in the Get & Transform Data group

Here, you are given the option of extracting data from a wide range of sources including the following:

- From other workbooks

- From a file or folder on your device
- From text/CSV files
- From a table/range
- From PDF files
- From the web
- From databases (SQL, Access, and others)

There are also options to extract data from several other sources.

The data is loaded into the **Power Query Editor** window. This window bears some similarities to the Excel spreadsheet window, as can be seen in *Figure 5.3*:

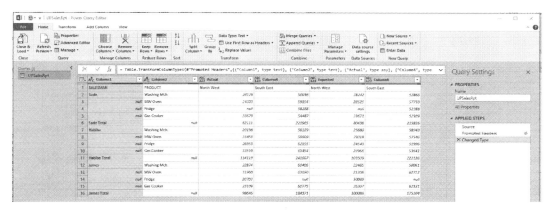

Figure 5.3 – Power Query Editor window

You should note that when the editor window is open, you cannot access the parent Excel file or indeed, any other Excel file. The editor window has the **File**, **Home**, **Transform**, **Add Column**, and **View** ribbons. However, the similarities pretty much end there. The ribbons are populated with buttons to transform and prepare data for eventual upload back to Excel.

The **Transform** and **Add Column** ribbons contain several similar commands. The difference is that under the **Transform** ribbon, the transformations are applied to the selected column(s); however, with the **Add Column** ribbon, the selected column remains unchanged and a new column is created with the transformed data. To the left of the main window, there is a list of the queries you have created. On the right, you have **PROPERTIES** including **Name** (of the query), and **APPLIED STEPS**.

In Power Query, there is no undo feature. Rather, every action is recorded under **APPLIED STEPS** and you have the option of going to any of the previous steps to modify or even cancel that step. You need to be aware, however, that every step is dependent on the step before it so that, if you modify or delete a feature that is essential to a later step, that step will be flagged as an error. You will then need to delete the error and modify that step or leave it out altogether.

You can now proceed to transform the data using the various tools in the ribbons. Usually, the aim is to clean up and transform the data into a proper dataset or simply to add the data to the data model.

The next step would be to close and load the data with the **Close & Load to** option. The tab allows you to select from a number of destinations, as shown in *Figure 5.4*. You can load to the current worksheet or a new worksheet. You can also load as **Table**, **PivotTable Report**, **PivotChart**, or just create a connection.

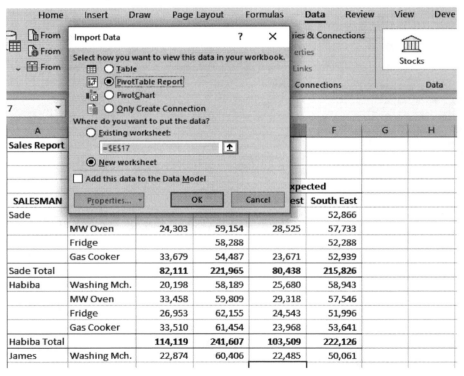

Figure 5.4 – Import data dialog box

The data will then be loaded to Excel in the manner you have selected as a table, pivot table, and so on.

One of the limitations of Excel for heavy users is that a worksheet has a maximum of 1,048,576 rows. However, with Power Query, you have the advantage of loading a data model where there is no limit to the number of rows you can work with.

Different ways to use Power Query

Power Query is extremely versatile and user-friendly. The following are just a few of the many different ways to use Power Query:

- **Create a connection/Merge queries**:

  The simplest way to use Power Query is to get a table into the Power Query window, then immediately create a connection from the **Import data** dialog box, as seen in *Figure 5.4*. Repeat this for one or more other tables.

  You can then merge two or more queries with the same headers using the **Data** ribbon to go to **Get Data | Combine Queries | Merge** (see *Figure 5.5*):

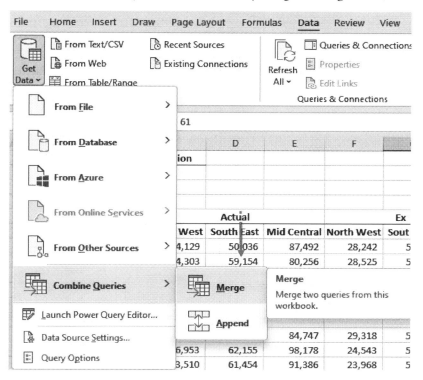

Figure 5.5 – Merge queries from the Data ribbon, Combine Queries, and Merge

- **Append queries**: This option allows you to append a table to the bottom of another.

  For example, if you have monthly sales reports, you can upload January and February sales separately into Power Query, and then create a connection for each.

  You can then append February sales to January sales using the **Data** ribbon to go to **Get Data** | **Combine Queries** | **Append** (see *Figure 5.5*).

  As the monthly reports arrive, you can repeat the process, this time appending to the newly-combined table of January and February sales, and so on.

- **Transform data**: The descriptions in the merge and append queries assume that the data arrives without any of the formatting anomalies mentioned earlier in this chapter, in the *Highlighting common formatting mistakes* section.

  However, this is not normally the case, and you will find that you have to transform the data once it is loaded into the Power Query Editor.

The following are some of the actions taken to clean and transform datasets in Power Query:

- **Fill**: This action fills cell contents into adjacent empty cells, usually when a heading has been entered only once to represent several rows of records instead of repeating the heading for each record as is required in a proper Excel dataset. You would use the **Fill** | **Down** option to fill the relevant blank cells with the heading.

  In *Figure 5.6*, **Sade** is entered once to represent her sales of **Washing Mch**, **MW oven**, **Fridge**, and **Gas Cooker**, and the same is done for other salespersons:

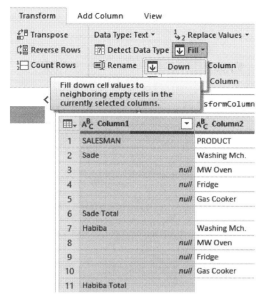

Figure 5.6 – Fill button and empty cells

Select **Column1**, then on the **Transform** ribbon, select **Fill**, and then **Down**. The blank cells are now filled with the appropriate salesperson's name, as shown in *Figure 5.7*:

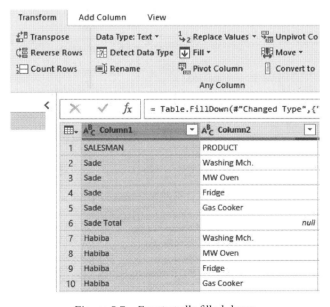

Figure 5.7 – Empty cells filled down

- **Format**: This button on the **Transform** ribbon displays a drop-down list of options to transform text data, as shown in *Figure 5.8*:

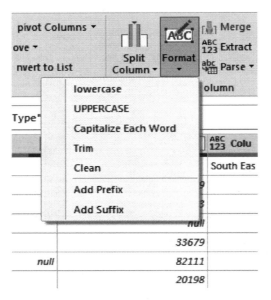

Figure 5.8 – Format button on the Transform ribbon

There are three options for modifying the capitalization of text. This is very important because Power Query, unlike Excel, is case-sensitive:

- The **Trim** option removes superfluous spaces, especially leading spaces.

- The **Clean** option removes non-printable characters from the selected column/s.

- The **Add Prefix/Add Suffix** option will add text that you specify to the beginning or end respectively of the selected column/s.

- **Unpivot**: Imported data often comes with some datasets pivoted or partially pivoted; for example, in *Figure 5.9*, where there are separate columns for **Actual**, **Expected**, **North West**, and **South East** in separate columns.

When the data comes like this, it does not allow pivot tables or formulas to work the way they were designed to work by Excel.

In an attempt to work with this bad layout, you previously had to construct extremely complex formulas just to create a proper dataset in a format friendly to pivot tables and formulas. Power Query has greatly simplified this cleanup process to fix such bad layouts with just a few clicks of the mouse.

	A	B	C	D	E	F
1	Sales Report By Salesman and Region					
2						
3						
4			Actual		Expected	
5	SALESMAN	PRODUCT	North West	South East	North West	South East
6	Sade	Washing Mch.	24,129	50,036	28,242	52,866
7		MW Oven	24,303	59,154	28,525	57,733
8		Fridge		58,288		52,288
9		Gas Cooker	33,679	54,487	23,671	52,939
10	Sade Total		82,111	221,965	80,438	215,826
11	Habiba	Washing Mch.	20,198	58,189	25,680	58,943
12		MW Oven	33,458	59,809	29,318	57,546
13		Fridge	26,953	62,155	24,543	51,996
14		Gas Cooker	33,510	61,454	23,968	53,641
15	Habiba Total		114,119	241,607	103,509	222,126
16	James	Washing Mch.	22,874	60,406	22,485	50,061
17		MW Oven	31,960	63,190	21,208	62,722
18		Fridge	20,703		30,089	
19		Gas Cooker	23,109	60,775	26,307	62,321
20	James Total		98,646	184,371	100,089	175,104
21						

Figure 5.9 – Pivoted/partially pivoted data

Power Query allows you to unpivot the data so that there is one column each for **Actual/Expected**, **Salesman**, **Region**, **Product**, and **Sales** amounts, as seen in *Figure 5.10*:

	A$_C^B$ Scenario	A$_C^B$ Salesman	A$_C^B$ Region	A$_C^B$ Product	$ Sales
1	Actual	Sade	North West	Washing Mch.	24,129.00
2	Actual	Sade	North West	MW Oven	24,303.00
3	Actual	Sade	North West	Gas Cooker	33,679.00
4	Actual	Habiba	North West	Washing Mch.	20,198.00
5	Actual	Habiba	North West	MW Oven	33,458.00
6	Actual	Habiba	North West	Fridge	26,953.00
7	Actual	Habiba	North West	Gas Cooker	33,510.00
8	Actual	James	North West	Washing Mch.	22,874.00
9	Actual	James	North West	MW Oven	31,960.00
10	Actual	James	North West	Fridge	20,703.00
11	Actual	James	North West	Gas Cooker	23,109.00
12	Actual	Sade	South East	Washing Mch.	50,036.00
13	Actual	Sade	South East	MW Oven	59,154.00
14	Actual	Sade	South East	Fridge	58,288.00
15	Actual	Sade	South East	Gas Cooker	54,487.00
16	Actual	Habiba	South East	Washing Mch.	58,189.00
17	Actual	Habiba	South East	MW Oven	59,809.00
18	Actual	Habiba	South East	Fridge	62,155.00
19	Actual	Habiba	South East	Gas Cooker	61,454.00
20	Actual	James	South East	Washing Mch.	60,406.00
21	Actual	James	South East	MW Oven	63,190.00
22	Actual	James	South East	Gas Cooker	60,775.00
23	Expected	Sade	North West	Washing Mch.	28,242.00

profiling based on top 1000 rows

Figure 5.10 – Dataset unpivoted

There is a host of other transform tools, some of which we will come across in the examples in the following sections of this chapter.

Advantages of Power Query

Although many of the actions taken in it could be done using traditional Excel formulas, Power Query has several advantages that make it irresistible:

- **Import data from multiple sources**: With Power Query, you can now import data in a wide range of different formats such as `.txt`, `.csv`, `.xls`, and PDF. You can even extract data from databases and the web.

- **Simplicity**: Especially for users who find formulas a daunting prospect, Power Query provides a simpler and much more pleasant way of getting things done.

    With a few clicks of the mouse, you are able to achieve what complex formulas can do and much more.

- **Large datasets**: Power Query can comfortably work with datasets of tens, and even hundreds, of millions of rows.

- **Speed**: Working out what formulas to use to clean data, constructing the formulas, and then applying them can be time-consuming. The same result can be achieved in Power Query with just a few clicks of the mouse.

- **File size**: Especially with the option of creating a connection only, files created using Power Query are several times smaller than comparable Excel files created using formulas.

- **Applied steps**: This great feature creates a record of all the steps you take, from importing the data into Power Query to loading the transformed data into Excel.

As a result, if you update the data in the original dataset, by just pressing the **Refresh** or **Refresh All** button, the data is run through all the applied steps and the output is updated almost immediately. This is done without having to reopen the Power Query editor.

Let's have a look at some examples in the following section.

Illustrative example

Some of the many errors found in source data include partial summarization of the data and grouping of some field headers. In this example, we are going to clean and transform data using various tools, including **Unpivot**.

You are given a dataset of sales per salesperson in two regions. The dataset includes a number of anomalies, including subtotals and headers in more than one row, as shown in *Figure 5.11*. You are asked to prepare a pivot table from the data.

(Sample data is available for download to give a more hands-on experience.)

	A	B	C	D	E	F
1	Sales Report By Salesman and Region					
2						
3						
4			Actual		Expected	
5	SALESMAN	PRODUCT	North West	South East	North West	South East
6	Sade	Washing Mch.	24,129	50,036	28,242	52,866
7		MW Oven	24,303	59,154	28,525	57,733
8		Fridge		58,288		52,288
9		Gas Cooker	33,679	54,487	23,671	52,939
10	Sade Total		82,111	221,965	80,438	215,826
11	Habiba	Washing Mch.	20,198	58,189	25,680	58,943
12		MW Oven	33,458	59,809	29,318	57,546
13		Fridge	26,953	62,155	24,543	51,996
14		Gas Cooker	33,510	61,454	23,968	53,641
15	Habiba Total		114,119	241,607	103,509	222,126
16	James	Washing Mch.	22,874	60,406	22,485	50,061
17		MW Oven	31,960	63,190	21,208	62,722
18		Fridge	20,703		30,089	
19		Gas Cooker	23,109	60,775	26,307	62,321
20	James Total		98,646	184,371	100,089	175,104
21						

Figure 5.11 – Sales by salesperson, by product, and by region

Use the following steps to load the table into Power Query, transform the data, and finally load it back into Excel as clean data ready for further analysis:

1. The first step is to convert the data into a table.

    Since the data has multiple header rows (see *Figure 5.12*), you will have to uncheck the option that says **My table has headers**:

Actual		Expected	
North West	South East	North West	South East
24,129	50,036	28,242	52,866

Figure 5.12 – Multiple header rows

2.   Select the dataset, then press *Ctrl + T*. The **Create Table** dialog box is launched (see *Figure 5.13*):

Figure 5.13 – Create Table dialog box

The dataset is converted into a table with dummy headers as the first row, such as **Column1**, **Column2**, up to **Column6**. The data is now ready to be sent to Power Query.

3.   Give your table a name, highlight it, and select **Range/Table** from the **Get & Transform** group. The **Power Query Editor** window is launched (see *Figure 5.14*):

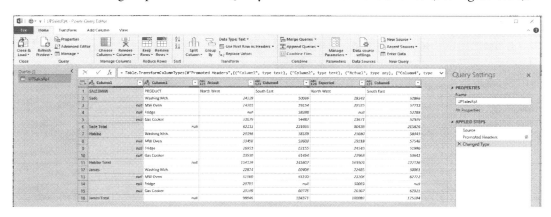

Figure 5.14 – Full Power Query Editor window

4. Select **Column1**, then from the **Transform** ribbon, select **Fill | Down**:

Figure 5.15 – Fill/fill down

This fills in the gaps in the **SALESMAN** column.

As noted earlier, our headers are in two rows; however, in Power Query, we can only merge columns and not rows. We, therefore, have to first transpose the dataset so that rows become columns and vice versa before dealing with the multiple row headers.

5. From the **Transform** ribbon, select **Transpose**. The transposed data appears, as shown in *Figure 5.16*. Rows and columns have now been swapped:

Figure 5.16 – Transposed dataset

6. Once again, fill down **Column1** to fill the blank cells with the appropriate value.

7. Next, you should identify the anchor columns, which are those columns that will not be unpivoted. In this case, columns 1 and 2. Now, merge these columns:

Figure 5.17 – Columns 1 and 2 merged to form a merged column

With the headers now grouped together in one column, we can transpose back and promote the first row as headers:

Figure 5.18 – Transposed back and first row promoted as headers

You might have noticed that we still have subtotals for salesmen that will need to be removed.

8. You can do this by clicking the drop-down filter arrow beside the **SALESMAN** header, then text filters.

9. Now, select **Filter Rows** to include only those records that do not end with **Total**:

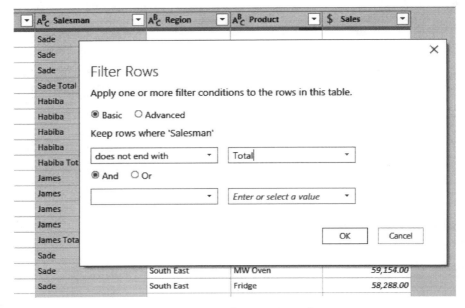

Figure 5.19 – Filter rows/records

The rows with the subtotals will be filtered out, as shown in the following figure:

	:SALESMAN	:PRODUCT	Actual:North West	Actual:South East	Expected:North West	Expected:South East
1	Sade	Washing Mch.	24129	50036	28242	52866
2	Sade	MW Oven	24303	59154	28525	57733
3	Sade	Fridge	null	58288	null	52288
4	Sade	Gas Cooker	33679	54487	23671	52939
5	Habiba	Washing Mch.	20198	58189	25680	58943
6	Habiba	MW Oven	33458	59809	29318	57546
7	Habiba	Fridge	26953	62155	24543	51996
8	Habiba	Gas Cooker	33510	61454	23968	53641
9	James	Washing Mch.	22874	60406	22485	50061
10	James	MW Oven	31960	63190	21208	62722
11	James	Fridge	20703	null	30089	null
12	James	Gas Cooker	23109	60775	26307	62321

Figure 5.20 – Subtotals removed

This filter is different from the filter in Excel, which only filters the list in place without deleting anything. In this case, the filtered records are removed.

We are now set to unpivot the data.

10. In general, you unpivot value columns and not text columns. In this case, select the four value columns and select **Unpivot Selected Columns**.

You could also select the text columns, which in this case are the first two columns, then select **Unpivot Other Columns**.

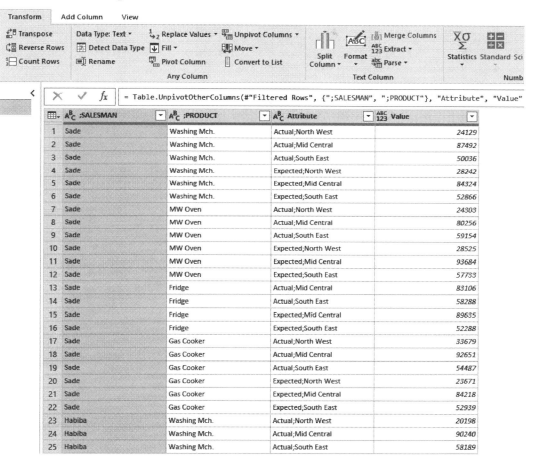

Figure 5.21 – Unpivoted data

What is left to do now is to split the attributes column and tidy up the headings.

We split the column using the delimiter, which is what you used to merge columns in the first place.

	A^B_C SALESMAN	A^B_C PRODUCT	A^B_C SCENARIO	A^B_C REGION	1²₃ VALUE
1	Sade	Washing Mch.	Actual	North West	24129
2	Sade	Washing Mch.	Actual	Mid Central	87492
3	Sade	Washing Mch.	Actual	South East	50036
4	Sade	Washing Mch.	Expected	North West	28242
5	Sade	Washing Mch.	Expected	Mid Central	84324
6	Sade	Washing Mch.	Expected	South East	52866
7	Sade	MW Oven	Actual	North West	24303
8	Sade	MW Oven	Actual	Mid Central	80256
9	Sade	MW Oven	Actual	South East	59154
10	Sade	MW Oven	Expected	North West	28525
11	Sade	MW Oven	Expected	Mid Central	93684
12	Sade	MW Oven	Expected	South East	57733
13	Sade	Fridge	Actual	Mid Central	83106
14	Sade	Fridge	Actual	South East	58288
15	Sade	Fridge	Expected	Mid Central	89635
16	Sade	Fridge	Expected	South East	52288
17	Sade	Gas Cooker	Actual	North West	33679
18	Sade	Gas Cooker	Actual	Mid Central	92651
19	Sade	Gas Cooker	Actual	South East	54487
20	Sade	Gas Cooker	Expected	North West	23671
21	Sade	Gas Cooker	Expected	Mid Central	84218
22	Sade	Gas Cooker	Expected	South East	52939
23	Habiba	Washing Mch.	Actual	North West	20198
24	Habiba	Washing Mch.	Actual	Mid Central	90240
25	Habiba	Washing Mch.	Actual	South East	58189
26	Habiba	Washing Mch.	Expected	North West	25680
27	Habiba	Washing Mch.	Expected	Mid Central	96561
28	Habiba	Washing Mch.	Expected	South East	58943

Figure 5.22 – Split attribute columns

11. Finally, you can select **Close & Load/Close & Load To** from the **Home** ribbon. Then, select the pivot table on a new worksheet.

    You are taken back to Excel and a pivot table is created on a new worksheet.

12. Arrange the pivot table to display the salespeople and products in rows, **SCENARIO** and **REGION** in columns, and sales amounts under the values, as shown in *Figure 5.23*:

	A	B	C	D	E	F	G
1	Sum of VALUE		SCENARIO ▼	REGION ▼			
2			⊟ Actual		⊟ Expected		Grand Total
3	SALESMAN ▼	PRODUCT ▼	North West	South East	North West	South East	
4	⊟ Habiba	Fridge	26,953	62,155	24,543	51,996	165,647
5		Gas Cooker	33,510	61,454	23,968	53,641	172,573
6		MW Oven	33,458	59,809	29,318	57,546	180,131
7		Washing Mch.	20,198	58,189	25,680	58,943	163,010
8	Habiba Total		114,119	241,607	103,509	222,126	681,361
9	⊟ James	Fridge	20,703		30,089		50,792
10		Gas Cooker	23,109	60,775	26,307	62,321	172,512
11		MW Oven	31,960	63,190	21,208	62,722	179,080
12		Washing Mch.	22,874	60,406	22,485	50,061	155,826
13	James Total		98,646	184,371	100,089	175,104	558,210
14	⊟ Sade	Fridge		58,288		52,288	110,576
15		Gas Cooker	33,679	54,487	23,671	52,939	164,776
16		MW Oven	24,303	59,154	28,525	57,733	169,715
17		Washing Mch.	24,129	50,036	28,242	52,866	155,273
18	Sade Total		82,111	221,965	80,438	215,826	600,340
19	Grand Total		294,876	647,943	284,036	613,056	1,839,911

Figure 5.23 – Loaded to pivot table on a new worksheet

The real beauty of Power Query is in the next step, which brings in fresh data.

You are told that sales data for Mid Central is now available and they would like you to update the query to include this.

Actual	Expected
Mid Central	Mid Central
87,492	84,324
80,256	93,684
83,106	89,635
92,651	84,218
343,505	351,861
90,240	96,561
84,747	84,772
98,178	89,073
91,386	80,610
364,551	351,016
84,050	88,247
91,025	97,826
81,560	95,997
94,775	97,663
351,410	379,733

Figure 5.24 – Additional data

The additional data, in the outlined box in *Figure 5.24*, includes actual and expected results for the **Mid Central** region.

	SALESMAN	PRODUCT	Actual			Expected		
			North West	South East	Mid Central	North West	South East	Mid Central
7	Sade	Washing Mch.	24,129	50,036	87,492	28,242	52,866	84,324
8		MW Oven	24,303	59,154	80,256	28,525	57,733	93,684
9		Fridge		58,288	83,106		52,288	89,635
10		Gas Cooker	33,679	54,487	92,651	23,671	52,939	84,218
11	Sade Total		82,111	221,965	343,505	80,438	215,826	351,861
12	Habiba	Washing Mch.	20,198	58,189	90,240	25,680	58,943	96,561
13		MW Oven	33,458	59,809	84,747	29,318	57,546	84,772
14		Fridge	26,953	62,155	98,178	24,543	51,996	89,073
15		Gas Cooker	33,510	61,454	91,386	23,968	53,641	80,610
16	Habiba Total		114,119	241,607	364,551	103,509	222,126	351,016
17	James	Washing Mch.	22,874	60,406	84,050	22,485	50,061	88,247
18		MW Oven	31,960	63,190	91,025	21,208	62,722	97,826
19		Fridge	20,703		81,560	30,089		95,997
20		Gas Cooker	23,109	60,775	94,775	26,307	62,321	97,663
21	James Total		98,646	184,371	351,410	100,089	175,104	379,733

Figure 5.25 – Original table updated with new region

13. Once the original dataset has been updated, you simply need to click **Refresh All** on the **Data** ribbon in the **Queries & Connections** group, and the transformed pivot table is updated automatically within seconds:

	A	B	C	D	E	F	G	H	I
1	Sum of VALUE		SCENARIO	REGION					
2			Actual			Expected			Grand Total
3	SALESMAN	PRODUCT	North West	South East	Mid Central	North West	South East	Mid Central	
4	Habiba	Fridge	26,953	62,155	98,178	24,543	51,996	89,073	352,898
5		Gas Cooker	33,510	61,454	91,386	23,968	53,641	80,610	344,569
6		MW Oven	33,458	59,809	84,747	29,318	57,546	84,772	349,650
7		Washing Mch.	20,198	58,189	90,240	25,680	58,943	96,561	349,811
8	Habiba Total		114,119	241,607	364,551	103,509	222,126	351,016	1,396,928
9	James	Fridge	20,703		81,560	30,089		95,997	228,349
10		Gas Cooker	23,109	60,775	94,775	26,307	62,321	97,663	364,950
11		MW Oven	31,960	63,190	91,025	21,208	62,722	97,826	367,931
12		Washing Mch.	22,874	60,406	84,050	22,485	50,061	88,247	328,123
13	James Total		98,646	184,371	351,410	100,089	175,104	379,733	1,289,353
14	Sade	Fridge		58,288	83,106		52,288	89,635	283,317
15		Gas Cooker	33,679	54,487	92,651	23,671	52,939	84,218	341,645
16		MW Oven	24,303	59,154	80,256	28,525	57,733	93,684	343,655
17		Washing Mch.	24,129	50,036	87,492	28,242	52,866	84,324	327,089
18	Sade Total		82,111	221,965	343,505	80,438	215,826	351,861	1,295,706
19	Grand Total		294,876	647,943	1,059,466	284,036	613,056	1,082,610	3,981,987

Figure 5.26 – Updated pivot table

This is possible because the updated original table is taken through the steps recorded in the **APPLIED STEPS** section of the Power Query editor:

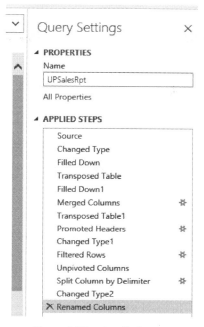

Figure 5.27 – Applied steps

A second example involves getting data from a folder. The SalesreportA folder contains three files with sales reports for January, February, and March in files named Jan-21b, Feb-21b, and Mar-21b:

Figure 5.28 – Files in the folder

Each of the files has a sales report for the respective month showing salesman, product, and regions, and they are all in the same format, as shown in *Figure 5.29*:

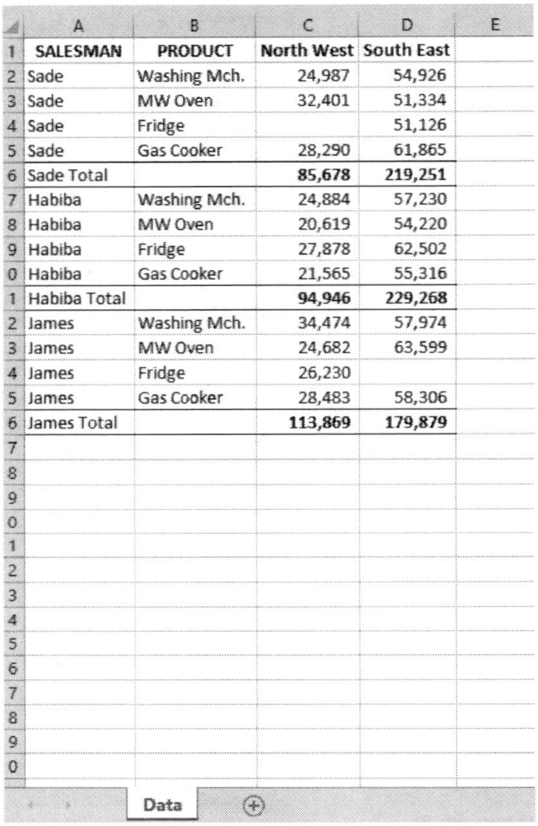

	A	B	C	D	E
1	**SALESMAN**	**PRODUCT**	**North West**	**South East**	
2	Sade	Washing Mch.	24,987	54,926	
3	Sade	MW Oven	32,401	51,334	
4	Sade	Fridge		51,126	
5	Sade	Gas Cooker	28,290	61,865	
6	Sade Total		**85,678**	**219,251**	
7	Habiba	Washing Mch.	24,884	57,230	
8	Habiba	MW Oven	20,619	54,220	
9	Habiba	Fridge	27,878	62,502	
0	Habiba	Gas Cooker	21,565	55,316	
1	Habiba Total		**94,946**	**229,268**	
2	James	Washing Mch.	34,474	57,974	
3	James	MW Oven	24,682	63,599	
4	James	Fridge	26,230		
5	James	Gas Cooker	28,483	58,306	
6	James Total		**113,869**	**179,879**	
7					
8					
9					
0					
1					
2					
3					
4					
5					
6					
7					
8					
9					
0					

Data ⊕

Figure 5.29 – Format of file contents

You are required to clean the data, then append the files for January followed by February and then March so that it forms one continuous report, then load the report to a pivot table on a new worksheet. Finally, you will copy the file with April's data into the same folder as the other 3 months, and when you refresh, Power Query will automatically append the new data in a cleaned format to the pivot table:

1. The first step is to open a new workbook and then get the data into Power Query. On the **Data** ribbon, select **Get Data | From File | From Folder**:

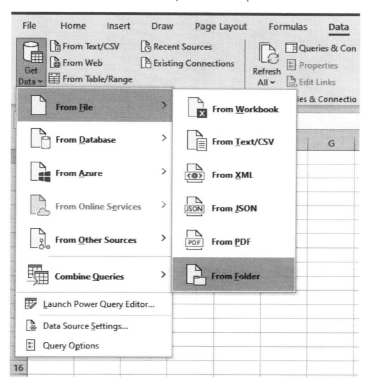

Figure 5.30 – Get data from file and folder

2. A **File Explorer** window opens up giving you access to files and folders on your hard drive. Navigate to the correct location and select the SalesreportA folder:

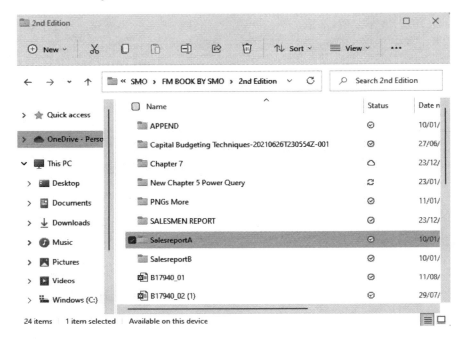

Figure 5.31 – File Explorer window

When you select the folder, a dialog box opens up showing details and attributes of all the files in the folder selected:

Content	Name	Extension	Date accessed	Date modified	Date created	Attributes	Folder Path
Binary	Feb-21b.xlsx	.xlsx	29/11/2021 13:19:29	16/11/2021 00:21:33	16/11/2021 00:21:31	Record	C:\Users\shmue\OneDrive\Document
Binary	Jan-21b.xlsx	.xlsx	29/11/2021 13:32:06	16/11/2021 00:21:58	16/11/2021 00:20:27	Record	C:\Users\shmue\OneDrive\Document
Binary	Mar-21b.xlsx	.xlsx	29/11/2021 13:24:37	16/11/2021 00:23:05	16/11/2021 00:23:03	Record	C:\Users\shmue\OneDrive\Document

Figure 5.32 – Attributes of files in the selected folder

Options are shown at the bottom of the dialog box:

Figure 5.33 – Options at bottom of Get From Folder dialog box

3. If our data was in the format we need, we would simply select **Combine** and **Load or Combine** and then **Load To…** and Power Query would continue with the process of appending the files.

    However, our data is already partially pivoted with sales summarized by region and subtotals by salesman. This prevents pivot tables and formulas from functioning the way they were designed. So, we will, first of all, transform the data before loading it to Excel. Select **Transform Data**.

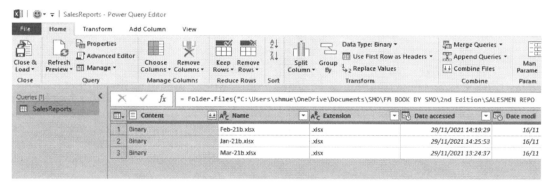

Figure 5.34 – Transform data

Currently, our folder contains only those Excel files we wish to append.

However, we will be adding content to this folder, so we need to ensure that it is only the desired file types that will be loaded into our query whenever we refresh our data.

4.   To do this, we will filter the **Extension** column for only files beginning with `.xlsx`:

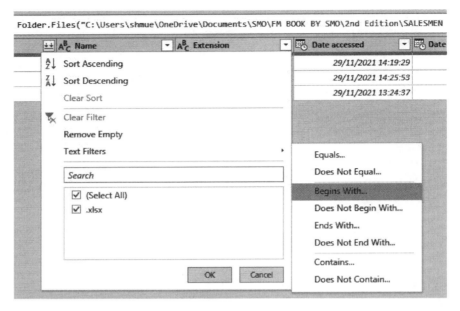

Figure 5.35 – Filter the Extension column

5.   Click on the **Filter** button beside the **Extension** column header, then under **Text Filters**, select **Begins With...** as shown in *Figure 5.36*.

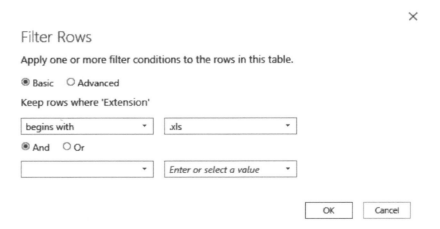

Figure 5.36 – Filter for extensions that begin with .xls

In the **Filter Rows** dialog box, in the box next to **begins with**, type `.xls`. This will ensure that files with the following extensions are captured: `.xls`, `.xlsx`, `.xlsb`, and `.xlsm`. Then, click **OK**.

6. You will notice that in *Step 3* in *Figure 5.33*, an additional column was created when we selected **Transform Data**. The column header is **Content** and there is a double-headed arrow pointing downward beside it:

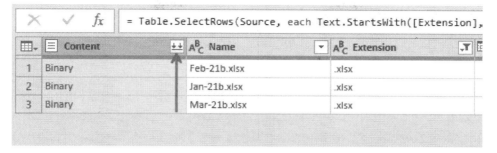

Figure 5.37 – Content column

Each of the **Binary** cells actually contains the table found in each of the files.

7. Click on the downward pointing arrows. This launches the **Combine Files** dialogue box:

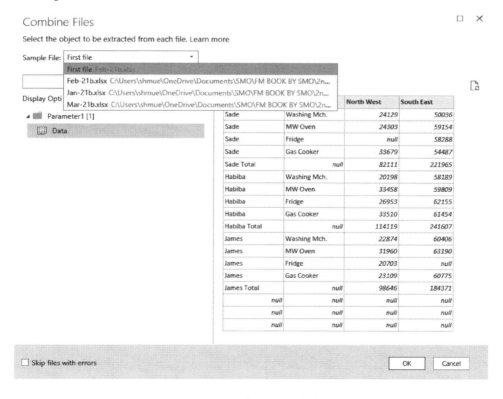

Figure 5.38 – Combine Files dialog box

8. In the **Combine Files** dialog box under **Sample File**, a drop-down list appears starting with **First file** and then the names of the files in the selected folder. You need to select the file you want Power Query to use as the sample on which to effect the transformations you require, if any. The other files will automatically be transformed in the same way. Since all three files have the same format, you can simply select the default, **First file**, which refers to the file that comes first in the list of files in the directory.

9. **Display Options** lists the names of the worksheet tabs found in the sample file, and when you select **Data** (which is the only tab in our sample), it will display the contents of the worksheet on the right. Click **OK**.

10. The **Power Query Editor** window opens with the sample file uploaded and with the other files appended below it:

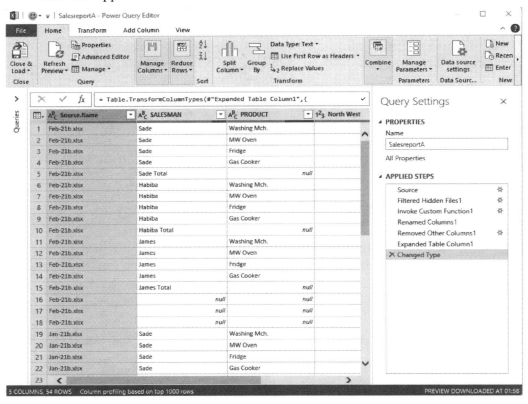

Figure 5.39 – Power Query Editor

A new column is created with the title **Source.Name**, and it contains the filename and extension for each record. The filename includes the month and year, so we will want to extract the date from it.

APPLIED STEPS over to the right of *Figure 5.39* lists the actions that have been taken so far to get the data to how it is displayed in the editor window in the figure.

11. Select the **Source.Name** column, then in the **Transform** ribbon, in the **Text Column** group, select **Extract**:

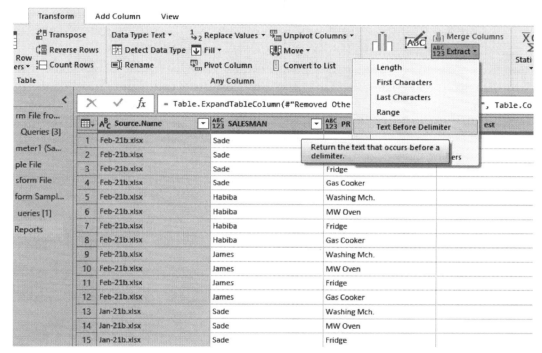

Figure 5.40 – Extract text before delimiter

12. From the drop-down list, select **Text Before Delimiter**.

The **Text Before Delimiter** dialog box opens up:

Text Before Delimiter

Enter the delimiter that marks the end of what you would like to extract.

Delimiter

b.

▷ Advanced options

OK   Cancel

Figure 5.41 – Text Before Delimiter dialog box

13. An example of the filename is `Feb-21b.xslx` and it is standard for all the filenames. As you can see, the month and year come immediately before `b.xslx`. We need to choose a delimiter from those characters that come after the date. In doing this, we should be mindful that this, along with the other steps, will be applied to all other files that will be added to the parent folder.

   With this in mind, we can select `b.` as our delimiter, thus instructing Power Query to extract everything before `b.`.

14. The date, month, and year alone are extracted from the filename. You should note that the **Add Column** ribbon contains most of the commands found on the **Transform** ribbon. The difference is that where the commands on the **Transform** ribbon replace the original contents, the same commands under the **Add Column** ribbon will create a new column and place the transformed data in it leaving the original data intact.

   As seen in *Figure 5.41*, the **Source.Name** column now contains only the date. Now, select the columns you wish to unpivot, the **North West** and **South East** columns:

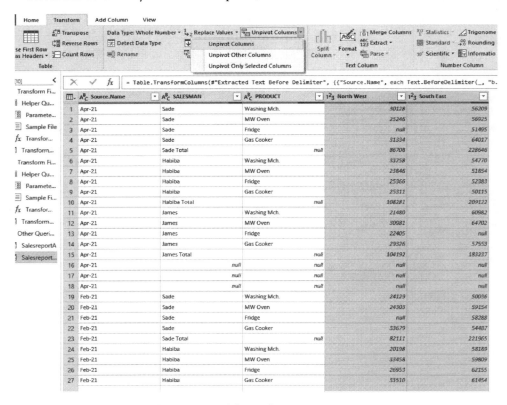

Figure 5.42 – Select columns to unpivot

15. On the **Transform** ribbon, go to **Unpivot Columns** and then select **Unpivot Columns**.

16. The columns will be unpivoted. Now, select the **SALESMAN** column and filter to show only data by selecting the **Does Not End With…** option:

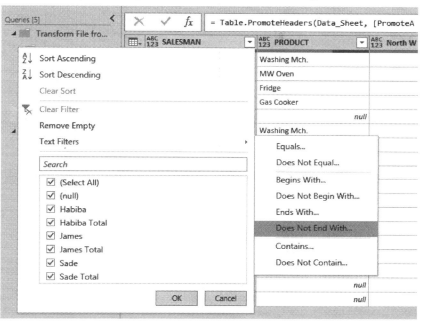

Figure 5.43 – Filter for rows not ending with…

17. Then, in the **Filter Rows** dialog box, select **Total** in the box beside **does not end with**. This will remove the total rows as well as empty rows that are currently displayed as Null:

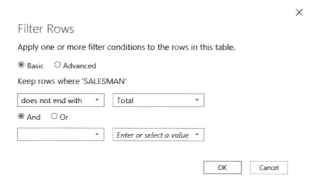

Figure 5.44 – Keep rows not ending in Total

18. Now, rename the **Source.Name** column to `Date` and correct **Data Type** to **Date**. Also, rename the **Attributes** column to `Region` and give the query an appropriate name, `CombinedSales`.

19. Finally, close and load to **PivotTable Report**:

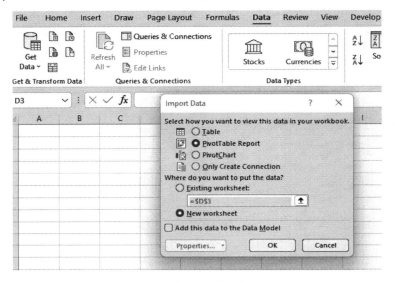

Figure 5.45 – Close and load to options

20. The Power Query window closes, and a pivot table opens on a new worksheet. Arrange the pivot table to show product sales per salesman per month with the regions in columns:

	A	B	C	D	E	F
2	Months	SALESMAN	PRODUCT	North West	South East	Grand Total
3	⊟Jan	⊟Habiba	Fridge	27878	62502	90380
4			Gas Cooker	21565	55316	76881
5			MW Oven	20619	54220	74839
6			Washing Mch.	24884	57230	82114
7		Habiba Total		94946	229268	324214
8		⊟James	Fridge	26230		26230
9			Gas Cooker	28483	58306	86789
10			MW Oven	24682	63599	88281
11			Washing Mch.	34474	57974	92448
12		James Total		113869	179879	293748
13		⊟Sade	Fridge		51126	51126
14			Gas Cooker	28290	61865	90155
15			MW Oven	32401	51334	83735
16			Washing Mch.	24987	54926	79913
17		Sade Total		85678	219251	304929
18	⊟Feb	⊟Habiba	Fridge	26953	62155	89108
19			Gas Cooker	33510	61454	94964
20			MW Oven	33458	59809	93267
21			Washing Mch.	20198	58189	78387
22		Habiba Total		114119	241607	355726

Figure 5.46 – Pivot table report

21. We now want to include data for the following month, April:

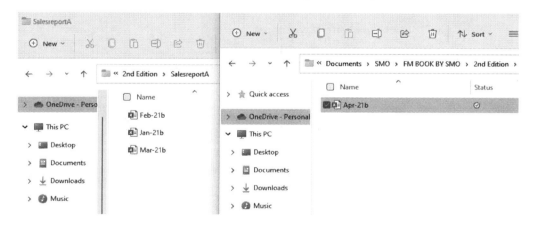

Figure 5.47 – Copy April data to the SalesreportA folder

22. All we need to do is copy the file containing the April data and paste it into the folder with the first 3 months' data:

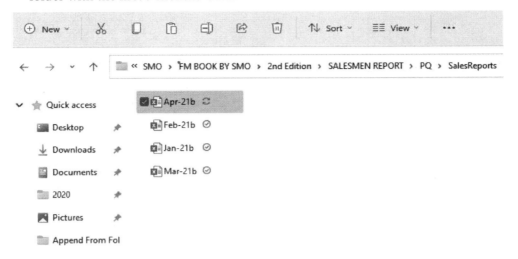

Figure 5.48 – New file posted to target folder containing the other files

23. Then, on the **Data** ribbon, select **Refresh All | Refresh**. The pivot table is automatically updated with the April data:

	SALESMAN	REGION	PRODUCT	Jan	Feb	Mar	Apr	Grand Total
4								
5	Habiba	North West	Fridge	27,878	26,953	20,800	25,366	100,997
6			Gas Cooker	21,565	33,510	30,029	25,311	110,415
7			MW Oven	20,619	33,458	26,662	23,846	104,585
8			Washing Mch.	24,884	20,198	32,002	33,758	110,842
9		North West Total		94,946	114,119	109,493	108,281	426,839
10		South East	Fridge	62,502	62,155	57,331	52,383	234,371
11			Gas Cooker	55,316	61,454	64,960	50,115	231,845
12			MW Oven	54,220	59,809	50,576	51,854	216,459
13			Washing Mch.	57,230	58,189	56,411	54,770	226,600
14		South East Total		229,268	241,607	229,278	209,122	909,275
15	Habiba Total			324,214	355,726	338,771	317,403	1,336,114
16	James	North West	Fridge	26,230	20,703	33,964	22,405	103,302
17			Gas Cooker	28,483	23,109	28,063	29,326	108,981
18			MW Oven	24,682	31,960	22,482	30,981	110,105
19			Washing Mch.	34,474	22,874	20,733	21,480	99,561
20		North West Total		113,869	98,646	105,242	104,192	421,949
21		South East	Gas Cooker	58,306	60,775	58,988	57,553	235,622
22			MW Oven	63,599	63,190	60,564	64,702	252,055
23			Washing Mch.	57,974	60,406	64,172	60,982	243,534

Figure 5.49 – Updated pivot table

The April data has been cleaned and is now incorporated into the main pivot table.

Summary

In this chapter, we have highlighted some of the mistakes and anomalies found in data that make data preparation using traditional formulas a tedious chore. We have learned how Power Query makes this exercise so much easier and removes the emphasis from complex formulas that many shy away from to simple keystrokes.

We have covered just some of the uses of Power Query. There is still a lot more you can do with it, such as extracting data from the web, extracting data from PDF files, and a host of other transform tools that we have not touched.

Finally, Power Query has its own language called **M**, which can be used to write formulas and further expand its capabilities.

In the next chapter, we will look at actions to take to ensure that you understand your project assignment, as well as how to build your assumptions.

Part 3 –
Building an Integrated
3-Statement Financial Model
with Valuation by DCF

A financial model is integrated when the various sections are linked together in such a way that any alteration will ripple right through the model and update all relevant values. This part will take you systematically through the stages to follow in building your model.

This part includes the following chapters:

- *Chapter 6, Understanding Project and Building Assumptions*
- *Chapter 7, Asset and Debt Schedules*
- *Chapter 8, Preparing a Cash Flow Statement*
- *Chapter 9, Ratio Analysis*
- *Chapter 10, Valuation*
- *Chapter 11, Model Testing for Reasonableness and Accuracy*

6
Understanding Project and Building Assumptions

In financial modeling, there is no one-size-fits-all. Financial models can vary widely in size, purpose, and complexity. A valuation model is vastly different from a loan repayment model. A model that's created to expand a business will be different from one that's created to dispose of a business. A model that's created to give someone a rough idea of the value of a business will be far less complex than one that's created in support of a private placement or an initial public offering of the shares of the business. It is imperative that you understand the scope and purpose of the model you have been asked to prepare. No matter how impressive your model is, it is of no use if it doesn't meet the requirements of the user.

In this chapter, you will learn how to analyze projects and learn what the purpose of a project is. You will also learn how to create assumptions about the reasons for historic growth and expected future growth with the use of growth drivers.

In this chapter, we will cover the following topics:

- Understanding the nature and purpose of a project and discussions with management
- Building assumptions
- Selecting profit and loss growth drivers
- Selecting balance sheet growth drivers

Understanding the nature and purpose of a project and discussions with management

In order to determine the nature and purpose of a project, you will need to address a number of questions, which are as follows:

- What is the project seeking to do?
- Are you seeking to value something, project something, or both?
- What is the focus or scope of the project?
- Are you looking at the business as a whole, a section of the business, or a particular asset, plant, or equipment?
- Who is the target audience?
- Is it for internal or personal use, or for presentation to a wider audience?
- Is it for a select, knowledgeable audience or the general public?
- Is there any specialist or technical part of the project that will require you to engage an expert in that field?

The answers to each one of these questions will have an impact on how you approach your model, what type of model you build, and how detailed it is.

Conducting interviews

A significant amount of your modeling time should be allocated to discussions with the client's management.

People are generally apprehensive when they're called into discussions with professionals, so you will need to allay their fears and create a non-threatening environment for your discussions. You need to make them understand that they are the experts and that you need their help to understand the business.

These interviews will help you understand why the decision was taken to prepare a financial model. They should cover the history of the company, including key policy decisions that have been taken and their impact on the company's results.

You will need to make an assessment of key management personnel and the extent to which you can place reliance on their assertions. You will need to document your discussions as thoroughly as possible but prepare the client for follow-up interviews should the need arise.

Building assumptions

A financial model can be defined as a collection of mathematical assumptions for the purpose of projecting the results, financial position, and cash flow of a business into the future, often with the aim of arriving at value for the business.

Building reliable assumptions is critical to the success and viability of your model.

The following is a quick checklist. Your assumptions should be as follows:

- Based on actual historical figures
- Realistic
- Clearly explained
- Easily verifiable
- Properly documented
- Visually distinguishable in your model (usually with a different font) from calculated cells

Let's dive deeper into the history and foundation of building assumptions.

Historical data

The foundation for building assumptions that we will use to forecast the company's results for the next 5 years is the company's historical financials. You will therefore need to obtain 3 or 5 years of the company's financial statements for this purpose. Ideally, you would want a soft copy of the accounts in Excel format. Unfortunately, what is usually available is a hard copy or a PDF file. Even when it is in Excel or CSV format, the layout will more than likely require modifications in order to bring it in line with your preferred layout.

You should therefore be prepared to find a way to get the accounts into Excel, in a layout that's suitable for your model. This used to mean that you often had to type out the accounts again; however, with the advent of Power Query, you can now import data from a wide range of sources, including PDF files and the web. An introduction to Power Query can be seen in *Chapter 5, An Introduction to Power Query*.

You would need to extract the balance sheets and profit and loss accounts for every year. The historical financials are extremely important since, apart from forming the basis of our assumptions and projections, they will also play a very important role when troubleshooting is required. Since we will be using the same concepts and formulas for our projected years, it helps to use a set of complete and balanced accounts as the starting point.

General assumptions

The overall assumptions of your model are that the business will be profitable and cash flow will ultimately be positive.

You also assume that the business is a growing concern (that it will be able to meet its liabilities, as they fall due, for the foreseeable future) and that information you have obtained or been given, about competitors and projected costs and revenue, is accurate.

Profit and loss and balance sheet assumptions

When you're building your financial statement assumptions, you start by identifying growth drivers. In this context, growth drivers are those indices or indicators that best capture the growth in individual items over the past 3 or 5 years.

In carrying out this exercise, you need to consider the cost-effectiveness of your decisions, particularly when dealing with items that aren't material. Sometimes, a simple best-judgment projection will be sufficient.

Selecting profit and loss account growth drivers

Turnover is the most prominent item in a profit and loss account. It, therefore, makes sense to concentrate on identifying a driver for turnover and then relating some of the less significant line expenses to projected turnover.

Appropriate drivers could be **year-on-year growth** or **inflation**, or **compound annual growth rate** (**CAGR**). Let's take a look at these two drivers in more detail now.

Year-on-year growth

This is simply the growth from one year to the next. It is usually expressed as a percentage. Year-on-year growth in turnover from *year1* to *year2* can be calculated as follows:

$$Growth\ rate = \frac{Turnover(year2) - Turnover(year1)}{Turnover(year1)}$$

This can be simplified as follows:

$$Growth\ rate = \frac{Turnover(year2)}{Turnover(year1)} - 1$$

This will give the historical growth driver in turnover for *year2*.

The growth driver for *year3* will be as follows:

$$Growth\ rate = \frac{Turnover(year3)}{Turnover(year3)} - 1$$

In this way, you will calculate growth drivers for each of the historical years (except for year 1 as there is no previous year to consider).

Compound annual growth rate

To understand CAGR, you must understand the concept of compounding.

If you invest N100m (one hundred million Naira) at 10% per annum, you would expect to collect N10m in interest at the end of the year (10% of N100m). At the end of the second year, you would collect another N10m in interest, and so on.

If, however, at the end of the first year you decided not to withdraw the interest of N10m, but rather to compound it, you would have *N100m + N10m = N110m* to invest at 10% at the beginning of the second year. So, at the end of the second year, you would receive N11m in interest (10% of N110m). You would therefore have *N110m + N11m = N121m* to invest at 10% at the beginning of the third year, and so on.

Note that compounding over multiple years gives a higher overall return than if you withdrew the interest at the end of each year. You could also say that your N100m today is worth N110m at the end of 1 year and N121m at the end of 2 years, and so on. Money today is worth more tomorrow; N100m today is worth more than N100m tomorrow. Year-on-year growth is seldom constant over multiple periods; it varies from year to year.

In practice, you might have a scenario like the one displayed in the following screenshot:

	=(D4-C4)/C4				
B	C	D	E	F	G
	Yr1	Yr2	Yr3	Yr4	Yr5
Revenue	150	280	320	350	450
Year on Year Growth		87%	14%	9%	29%

Figure 6.1 – Year-on-year growth calculation

CAGR is an index that's used to convert diverse growth rates over multiple periods into a single growth rate over all the periods.

The CAGR of an item takes the value of that item in the first year and the value in the final year and, assuming compounding, calculates a growth rate for the period.

The formula for CAGR is as follows:

$$Value\ in\ year\ 1\ =\ V1;$$
$$Value\ in\ year\ 2\ is\ V2 = V1 + (V1 \times r);$$
$$where\ r\ is\ the\ CAGR$$

We can simplify this by isolating *V1* on the right-hand side of the equation, as follows:

$$V2 = V1 \times (1 + r)$$

Thus, the value in year 3 is as follows:

$$V3 = V2 \times (1 + r)$$

By substituting for the value of *V2* in the preceding equation, we get the following:

$$V3 = V1 \times (1 + r) \times (1 + r) = V1 \times (1 + r)^2$$

Now, *V4* is as follows:

$$V4 = V3 \times (1 + r)$$

Substituting for $V3$, we get the following:

$$V4 = V1 \times (1+r) \times (1+r) \times (1+r) = V1 \times (1+r)^3$$

This leads to the following general formula:

$$V_n = V1 \times (1+r)^{n-1}$$

Where n is the year.

We take the following steps to rearrange and make r the subject of the formula:

$$V1 \times (1+r)^{n-1} = V_n$$

Move $V1$ to the right-hand side of the equation so that it becomes $V_n/V1$:

$$(1+r)^{n-1} = \frac{V_n}{V1}$$

We move the power sign to the other side so that it becomes $1/(n-1)$:

$$1+r = \left[\frac{V_n}{V1}\right]^{\frac{1}{n-1}}$$

This gives us the following formula for CAGR:

$$r = \left[\frac{V_n}{V1}\right]^{\frac{1}{n-1}} - 1$$

When this is written out in full, it's as follows:

$$\left[\frac{Value\ in\ year\ n}{Value\ in\ year\ 1}\right]^{\frac{1}{n-1}} - 1$$

Here, n is the number of years.

The CAGR in revenue in our example will be as follows:

$$\left[\frac{Revenue\ in\ first\ year}{Revenue\ in\ final\ year}\right]^{\frac{1}{4}} - 1$$

The power or exponent is represented by ^ in Excel. Therefore, 2^2 becomes 2^2 in Excel.

The following is a screenshot of the CAGR formula:

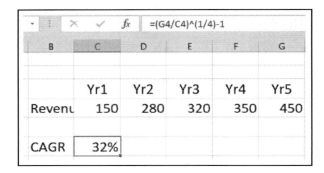

Figure 6.2 – CAGR formula

This gives us a CAGR of 32%, as shown in the following screenshot:

Figure 6.3 – CAGR calculated

Note that you can use the same formula to calculate the CAGR of other items, such as the cost of sales.

In general, we apply our growth drivers to the following values:

- **Turnover—price and volume**: For a simple model, you can base your projections on turnover. However, in order to make your model more flexible, you may wish to increase the detail or granularity of it. In such cases, you would break down the turnover into its component parts and base your projections on price and volume.

- **Purchases—cost and volume**: Similarly, for purchases and other direct expenses, if necessary, you can make your model more granular and base your projections on cost and volume.

- **Overheads**: Most overheads can be projected based on the historical percentage of turnover. Then, the average percentage of turnover—over the historical 5 years—will be applied to the estimated turnover for each of the next 5 estimated years.

Often, items considered immaterial are simply retained at their last recorded amount or a straight average of the historical amounts.

Selecting balance sheet growth drivers

Balance sheet growth drivers are not as straightforward as profit and loss drivers. While a profit and loss item is the sum of occurrences of that item within the period under review, a balance sheet item is made up of an opening balance, plus or minus movements in that item during the period, in order to arrive at a balance at a specific point in time, that is, the period end.

A wise man once said that *revenue is vanity, profit is sanity, but cash is reality*. We identify appropriate drivers for the balance sheet by considering cash flow.

Balance sheet items that drive cash flow are the elements of working capital—inventory, debtors, and creditors. An increase or decrease in these items has a direct effect on cash flow.

The following diagram shows this process:

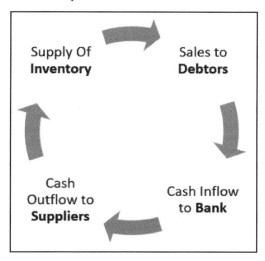

Figure 6.4 – Elements of working capital

The working capital cycle consists of how quickly you turn over your stock, how quickly your debtors pay, and how quickly you pay your creditors.

In general, the faster the cycle turns, the quicker its components are converted into cash. Balance sheet growth drivers are calculated using the concept of *days of....* The following diagram shows the different labels for each process:

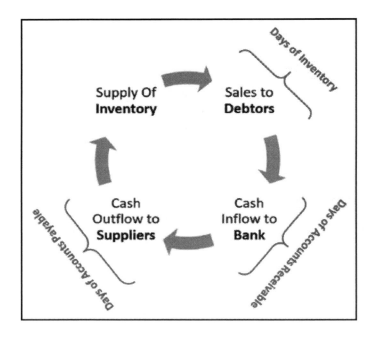

Figure 6.5 – Days of indicators as relate to working capital

This forms the basis for balance sheet growth drivers.

Days of inventory

The management of a company will need to ensure that they have enough stock to satisfy customers and avoid supply delays. On the other hand, they shouldn't keep too much stock, as this ties down cash that could otherwise be utilized productively.

Over time, management will learn the optimum level of stock to hold, as well as when to reorder stock, so as to strike an appropriate balance between satisfying customers and not overstocking. Once proper stock control has been achieved, the amount of time it takes before the stock is sold (days of inventory) should be fairly constant and can be used as a basis for estimating future inventory.

The days of inventory, or inventory days, are calculated as follows:

$$\frac{average\ inventory}{daily\ cost\ of\ goods\ sold\ (COGS)} = \frac{opening\ inventory + closing\ inventory}{2} \div \frac{annual\ COGS}{365}$$

Here, *opening inventory* is the inventory at the beginning of the year, *closing inventory* is the inventory at the end of the year, and *COGS* is the cost of the goods that were sold.

Debtor days

A similar assumption holds for debtors. Once management has established an efficient debt collection process, the number of days it takes, on average, for trade debtors to pay becomes fairly constant over time and can be used to estimate future debtors.

The formula for debtor days is as follows:

$$\frac{average\ debtors}{daily\ sales}$$

If we expand the formula for average debtors' daily sales, we get the following:

$$\frac{opening\ debtors + closing\ debtors}{2} \div \frac{annual\ sales}{365}$$

Here, *opening debtors* is the count of debtors at the beginning of the year, and *closing debtors* is the count of debtors at the end of the year.

Creditor days

Finally, once management has been able to negotiate favorable credit terms with its suppliers and an efficient payment process has been put in place, the amount of time it takes to pay suppliers becomes fairly constant.

The formula for creditor days is as follows:

$$\frac{average\ creditors}{daily\ COGS}$$

If we expand the formula for average debtors' daily sales, we get the following:

$$\frac{opening\ creditors + closing\ creditors}{2} \div \frac{annual\ COGS}{365}$$

Here, *opening creditors* is the count of creditors at the beginning of the year and *closing creditors* is the count of creditors at the end of the year.

Once we have established our historical growth drivers, we turn to our notes from discussions with management and our own assessments in order to create assumptions about the projected behavior of the selected items and balances over the next 5 years.

For profit and loss items, we will be looking out for phrases such as ...*x should increase by historic CAGR over the next 5 years, should increase by 0.5% more (or less) than historic CAGR, should show a gradual increase from y% to z% over the next 5 years*, or *will stay the same for the next 2 years, then increase gradually to y% in the fifth year.*

Continuing with our example, say the sales manager projects that turnover will increase by 2% less than the historical CAGR over the next 5 years; we would proceed as follows.

Using your knowledge of the referencing framework in Excel, you would highlight all the cells for the projected years to be populated with the growth driver, CAGR – 2% (cells H4 to L4), construct your formula for CAGR using the appropriate absolute and relative referencing, and subtract 2%:

```
CAGR = ($G$4/$C$4)^(1/4)-1-2%
```

Then, press *Ctrl + Enter*. This will give you the projected growth drivers for the next 5 years, as shown in the following diagram:

	f_x =($G$4/$C$4)^(1/4)-1-2%									
B	C	D	E	F	G	H	I	J	K	L
	Yr1A	Yr2A	Yr3A	Yr4A	Yr5A	Yr6E	Yr7E	Yr8E	Yr9E	Yr10E
Revenue	150	280	320	350	450					
Growth						30%	30%	30%	30%	30%

Figure 6.6 – Projected growth drivers

Next, we apply the growth to the turnover of the last year with actual results, `Yr5A` (the **A** stands for **actual**), to get the turnover for the first year of estimated figures, `Yr6E` (the **E** stands for **estimate**), using the following formula:

```
=G4*(1+H5)
```

We will repeat this for Yr7E and each subsequent projected year. In practice, you would highlight cells H4 to L4, type the formula once, and then press *Ctrl + Enter* to populate all the highlighted cells at once, as follows:

	B	C	D	E	F	G	H	I	J	K	L
		Yr1A	Yr2A	Yr3A	Yr4A	Yr5A	Yr6E	Yr7E	Yr8E	Yr9E	Yr10E
	Revenue	150	280	320	350	450	583	756	980	1270	1646
	Growth						30%	30%	30%	30%	30%

fx =G4*(1+H5)

Figure 6.7 – Absolute revenue from growth driver and historical amount

Apply the same procedure to other major profit and loss items. For less significant profit and loss items, such as sales and distribution, you first calculate the percentage turnover for each of the historical years. The following screenshot shows overheads as a percentage of turnover:

SUM   *fx* =E8/E4%

	A	B	C	D	E	F	G	H	I	J	K	L	M	N
1														
2														
3					Yr1A	Yr2A	Yr3A	Yr4A	Yr5A	Yr6E	Yr7E	Yr8E	Yr9E	Yr10E
4		Revenue			150	280	320	350	450	583	756	980	1270	1646
5		Growth		CAGR - 2%						30%	30%	30%	30%	30%
6														
7														
8		Sales & distribution			15	25	30	30	35					
9				% of sales	=E8/E4%									
10														

Figure 6.8 – Overhead as percentage of turnover

You would then project this driver forward as the average of the 5 historical years.

Note that the quickest way to populate a range of cells with the same formula is to do the following:

1. Select the range of cells.
2. Construct the formula using relative, absolute, and mixed referencing as appropriate (see *Chapter 4, The Referencing Framework in Excel*, for more information).
3. Hold down *Ctrl*, and then press *Enter* (*Ctrl + Enter*).

All the cells in the range will now be filled with the same formula as if you had copied the formula to each of them.

If you forget *Step 1* and fail to select the range of cells before constructing the formula, all is not lost:

1. Construct the formula using relative, absolute, and mixed referencing as appropriate (see *Chapter 4, The Referencing Framework in Excel*, for more information).

2. Select the range of cells to be populated with the same formula, starting with and including the cell in which you have typed the formula.

3. Now, press *Ctrl + D* if the range of cells is downward or *Ctrl + R* if the range of cells is to the right.

The following screenshot shows how to calculate the growth drivers to be used over the 5 forecasted years:

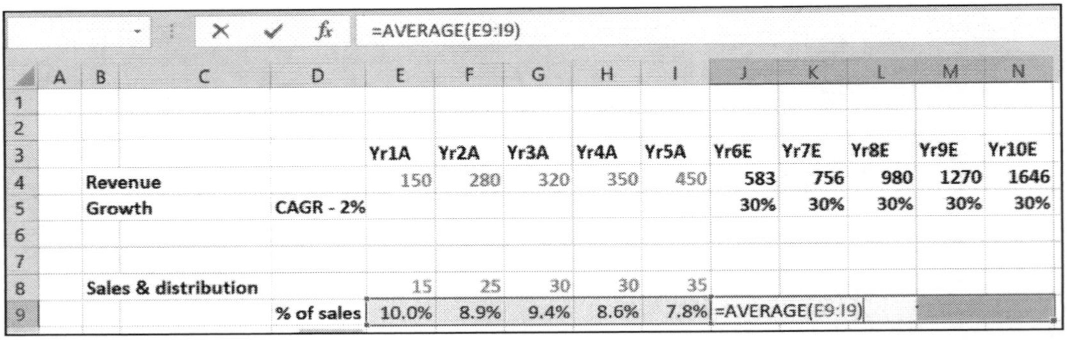

	A	B	C	D	E	F	G	H	I	J	K	L	M	N
1														
2														
3					Yr1A	Yr2A	Yr3A	Yr4A	Yr5A	Yr6E	Yr7E	Yr8E	Yr9E	Yr10E
4		Revenue			150	280	320	350	450	583	756	980	1270	1646
5		Growth		CAGR - 2%						30%	30%	30%	30%	30%
6														
7														
8		Sales & distribution			15	25	30	30	35					
9				% of sales	10.0%	8.9%	9.4%	8.6%	7.8%	=AVERAGE(E9:I9)				

fx =AVERAGE(E9:I9)

Figure 6.9 – Projected driver for sales and distribution using the average of historical years

Finally, you would apply the projected drivers to each of the estimated years, `Yr6E` to `Yr10E`.

The following screenshot shows grossing up the expense by applying the growth driver to last year's value:

	A	B	C	D	E	F	G	H	I	J	K	L	M	N
					J9		fx	=J4*J9						
1														
2														
3					Yr1A	Yr2A	Yr3A	Yr4A	Yr5A	Yr6E	Yr7E	Yr8E	Yr9E	Yr10E
4		Revenue			150	280	320	350	450	583	756	980	1270	1646
5		Growth		CAGR - 2%						30%	30%	30%	30%	30%
6														
7														
8		Sales & distribution			15	25	30	30	35	=J4*J9				
9				% of sales	10.0%	8.9%	9.4%	8.6%	7.8%	8.9%	8.9%	8.9%	8.9%	8.9%
10														

Figure 6.10 – Sales and distribution grossed up from driver and actual

By doing this, you will arrive at the projected sales and distribution costs for Yr6E to Yr10E.

The following screenshot shows filling the other forecast years with the same formula:

	A	B	C	D	E	F	G	H	I	J	K	L	M	N
					J8		fx	=J4*J9						
1														
2														
3					Yr1A	Yr2A	Yr3A	Yr4A	Yr5A	Yr6E	Yr7E	Yr8E	Yr9E	Yr10E
4		Revenue			150	280	320	350	450	583	756	980	1270	1646
5		Growth		CAGR - 2%						30%	30%	30%	30%	30%
6														
7														
8		Sales & distribution			15	25	30	30	35	52	68	87	113	147
9				% of sales	10.0%	8.9%	9.4%	8.6%	7.8%	8.9%	8.9%	8.9%	8.9%	8.9%

Figure 6.11 – Projected years populated

In this way, you would build up your profit and loss account for the projected/estimated years, Yr6E to Yr10E. At this stage, your profit and loss account would be complete, except for depreciation and interest.

For balance sheet items, we will need to revisit our formulas for *days of…*:

$$Days\ of\ inventory\ =\ \frac{average\ inventory}{daily\ COGS}$$

Rearranging the formula, we get the following:

$$average\ inventory\ =\ days\ of\ inventory\ \times\ daily\ COGS$$

Let's expand the average inventory and daily cost of goods sold:

$$\frac{opening\ inventory + closing\ inventory}{2} = days\ of\ inventory\ \times\ \frac{annual\ COGS}{365}$$

Then, by rearranging the formula again, we get the following:

$$closing\ inventory = 2 \times days\ of\ inventory \times \frac{annual\ COGS}{365} - opening\ inventory$$

The following list describes the separate components of the days of measurements:

- **Days of inventory**: We have mentioned that days of inventory is expected to be stable over the years. You could therefore take the average of historical days of inventory over the past 5 years and use this as the projected driver for inventory over the next 5 years. If there have been any occurrences that indicate that activity may be affected in such a way as to have a significant effect on COGS, you could apply a best-judgment adjustment to the average days of inventory calculated. For example, a big competitor entering the market could result in a temporary slowdown in sales, thereby leading to a reduction in COGS and thus an increase in days of inventory.

- **Opening inventory**: The opening inventory of 1 year is the closing inventory for the previous year. So, the opening inventory for Yr6E is the closing inventory from Yr5A.

- **Annual COGS**: This will have been calculated earlier in the projection and be built up of your profit and loss account for Yr6E to Yr10E. Since all the items on the right of the equation are known, we can calculate the closing inventory for Yr6E and then repeat the procedure for Yr7E to Yr10E. The following screenshot shows the computation of inventory for the projected years:

SUM	▾	:	✕	✓	*fx*	=AVERAGE(E28:F28)/(F23/365)					

	A	B	C	D	E	F	G	H	I
1					Yr1A	Yr2A	Yr3A	Yr4A	Yr5A
14	**Balance Sheet Assumptions**								
15		**Key Ratios (Days of...)**							
16			Inventories (Daily cost of sales)			=AVERAGE(E28:F28)/(F23/365)			
17			Trade and other receivables (Daily sales)						
18			Trade and other payables (Daily cost of sales)						
19									
20	**PROFIT & LOSS**								
21									
22		Revenue			260,810	272,241	245,009	297,938	311,453
23		Cost of sales			177,782	181,657	186,876	193,989	200,786
24		GROSS PROFIT			83,028	90,584	58,133	103,949	110,667
25									
26	**BALANCE SHEET**								
27									
28	Inventories				15,545	18,007	21,731	14,530	21,860
29	Trade and other receivables				20,864	31,568	35,901	33,812	39,063
30	Cash and cash equivalents				7,459	17,252	9,265	65,106	67,707
31	**Total current assets**				43,868	66,827	66,897	113,447	128,630

Figure 6.12 – Days of inventory

- **Debtor days**: In the same way, debtor days can be represented as follows:

$$closing\ debtors = 2 \times days\ of\ debtors \times \frac{annual\ turnover}{365} - opening\ debtors$$

The average of the historical debtor days will be taken as projected debtor days for Yr6E to Yr10E.

The following screenshot shows the computation of debtors for the projected years:

SUM		▾	⋮	✕	✓	*fx*	=AVERAGE(E28:F28)/(F22/365)				

◢	A	B	C	D	E	F	G	H	I
1					Yr1A	Yr2A	Yr3A	Yr4A	Yr5A
14	**Balance Sheet Assumptions**								
15		**Key Ratios (Days of…)**							
16			Inventories (Daily cost of sales)			34	39	34	33
17			Trade and other receivables (Daily sales)		=AVERAGE(E28:F28)/(F22/365)				
18			Trade and other payables (Daily cost of sales)						
19									
20	**PROFIT & LOSS**								
21									
22		Revenue			260,810	272,241	245,009	297,938	311,453
23		Cost of sales			177,782	181,657	186,876	193,989	200,786
24		GROSS PROFIT			83,028	90,584	58,133	103,949	110,667
25									
26	**BALANCE SHEET**								
27									
28	Inventories				15,545	18,007	21,731	14,530	21,860
29	Trade and other receivables				20,864	31,568	35,901	33,812	39,063
30	Cash and cash equivalents				7,459	17,252	9,265	65,106	67,707
31	Total current assets				43,868	66,827	66,897	113,447	128,630

Figure 6.13 – Days of accounts receivable

- **Creditor days**: Finally, we have the following equation:

$$closing\ creditors = 2 \times days\ of\ creditors \times \frac{annual\ COGS}{365} - opening\ creditors$$

The average of the historical creditor days will be used to estimate creditor days for `Yr6E` to `Yr10E`.

The following screenshot shows the computation of creditors for the projected years:

	SUM	▾ : × ✓ fx	=AVERAGE(E33:F33)/(F23/365)					
A B	C	D	E	F	G	H	I
				Yr1A	Yr2A	Yr3A	Yr4A	Yr5A
14	Balance Sheet Assumptions							
15	Key Ratios (Days of...)							
16	Inventories (Daily cost of sales)				34	39	34	33
17	Trade and other receivables (Daily sales)				22	30	22	21
18	Trade and other payables (Daily cost of sales)			=AVERAGE(E33:F33)/(F23/365)				
19								
20	PROFIT & LOSS							
21								
22	Revenue			260,810	272,241	245,009	297,938	311,453
23	Cost of sales			177,782	181,657	186,876	193,989	200,786
24	GROSS PROFIT			83,028	90,584	58,133	103,949	110,667
25								
26	BALANCE SHEET							
27								
28	Inventories			15,545	18,007	21,731	14,530	21,860
29	Trade and other receivables			20,864	31,568	35,901	33,812	39,063
30	Cash and cash equivalents			7,459	17,252	9,265	65,106	67,707
31	Total current assets			43,868	66,827	66,897	113,447	128,630
32	Current liabilities							
33	Trade and other payables			12,530	16,054	15,831	14,072	15,938

Figure 6.14 – Days of accounts payable

Once we have populated the balance sheet with these items, we will have complete projected balance sheets, except for long-term assets, loans, and, of course, cash. These accounts will require separate individual treatment and are dealt with in the following chapters.

Summary

In this chapter, we have seen that without a thorough knowledge of the nature and purpose of a project, you could end up with a model that doesn't meet the specifications of your client. We have learned about the nature of and reason for assumptions, as well as the importance of discussions with management in projecting your assumptions into the future. In making our assumptions, we have realized the importance of historical financials, balance sheets, profit and loss accounts, and cash flow statements. We have also learned about historical financials, which are an essential starting point in resolving anomalies that may arise in our model.

In the next chapter, *Chapter 7, Asset and Debt Schedules*, we will learn how to project long-term assets and borrowings. We will be introduced to different approaches: a complex but more accurate method and a simple, more subjective approach. We will also learn how to update the balance sheet and profit and loss with output from our asset and debt schedules.

7
Asset and Debt Schedules

The projected balance sheets and profit and loss accounts are now complete, except for the effects of **Capital Expenditure (CapEx)**—purchase, disposal, and depreciation of long-term assets and long-term debt; fresh issues; repayments; and interest charges.

The fixed asset, depreciation, interest, and debt schedules are very important to our model as they tend to be very significant amounts in financial statements. They are long-term balances and are not covered by growth drivers.

You will learn how long-term assets and long-term debts are treated in financial statements, along with how we arrive at the different amounts to be included in the balance sheet and profit and loss account and how the values change from year to year.

This chapter covers the following topics:

- Understanding the BASE and corkscrew concepts
- Asset schedule
- Approaches to modeling assets
- Asset and depreciation schedule
- Debt schedule
- Creating a simple loan amortization schedule

Understanding the BASE and corkscrew concepts

These are common standards to follow in modeling our balance sheet items. **BASE** stands for **Beginning add Additions less Subtractions equals End**. The **corkscrew** concept refers to the way in which the BASE setup is connected from one period to the next. In the following screenshot, we will see that the closing balance from one year is carried forward as the opening balance of the next year:

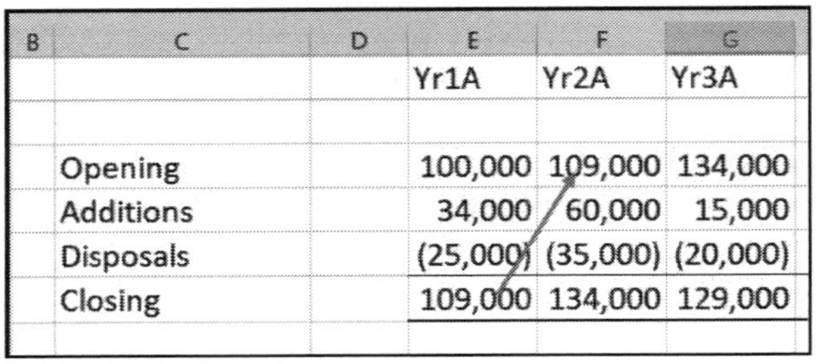

B	C	D	E	F	G
			Yr1A	Yr2A	Yr3A
	Opening		100,000	109,000	134,000
	Additions		34,000	60,000	15,000
	Disposals		(25,000)	(35,000)	(20,000)
	Closing		109,000	134,000	129,000

Figure 7.1 – BASE formation

We notice that the movement starts from the opening balance, goes down the rows of the first year to the closing balance, then goes back up to the opening balance of the second year, then down the rows of the second year, and so on:

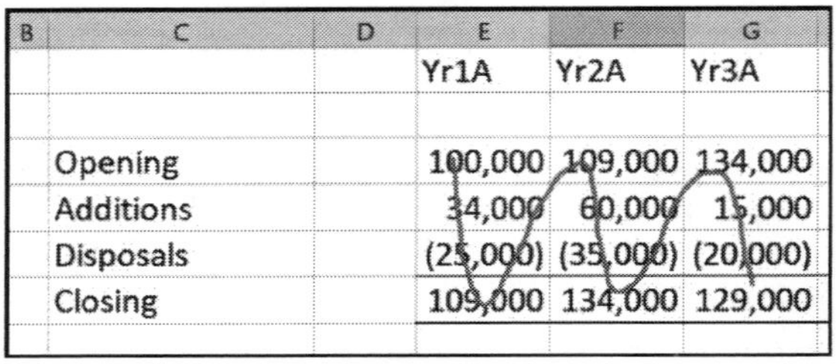

B	C	D	E	F	G
			Yr1A	Yr2A	Yr3A
	Opening		100,000	109,000	134,000
	Additions		34,000	60,000	15,000
	Disposals		(25,000)	(35,000)	(20,000)
	Closing		109,000	134,000	129,000

Figure 7.2 – Corkscrew formation

This creates a corkscrew effect, as seen in the previous screenshot.

Asset schedule

A quick recap of our agenda is as follows:

- Record the historical profit and loss accounts and balance sheet
- Calculate the historical growth drivers
- Project the growth drivers for the profit and loss accounts and balance sheet
- Build up the projected profit and loss accounts and the balance sheet
- Prepare the asset and depreciation schedule
- Prepare the debt schedule
- Prepare the cash flow statement
- Ratio analysis
- DCF valuation
- Other valuations
- Scenario analysis
- Fixed assets including plant and machinery, land and buildings, equipment, motor vehicles, furniture, and fixtures

Any asset from which the company will derive economic value over a period of more than one year falls into the category of fixed assets. The period of producing economic value is called the *useful life* of the asset. Since the asset will be in use for over a year, it would be unfair to charge the entire cost of such an asset to the period in which it was acquired; instead, the cost should be spread over the useful life of the asset. Please note that depreciation is calculated on all fixed assets except land as it is considered that land does not depreciate.

This annual allocation of cost is a measure of the decrease in value of a fixed asset, through its use or effluxion of time. This is called **depreciation**. It is usually expressed as a percentage and is charged to the profit and loss account for each year. The reduction in the value of the fixed asset is reflected in the balance sheet, where the total **accumulated depreciation** is deducted from the original cost and charged to date. This is referred to as the **net book value**.

The straight line method

If management decides that useful service can be extracted from a fixed asset over a period of 10 years, then the cost of the asset will be spread over 10 years. The simplest way of doing this is to allocate the cost of the asset evenly over 10 years in order to arrive at a fixed annual charge or depreciation rate of 10%. This is referred to as the **straight line method (SLM)** of depreciation.

Depreciation using SLM is calculated as follows:

$$Depreciation = \frac{Cost\ of\ asset}{Useful\ life}$$

The SLM is the simplest and most commonly used method of depreciation:

$$Depreciation = Cost\ of\ asset \times Depreciation\ rate$$

The depreciation rate is usually displayed as a percentage.

The reducing balance method

Another method of calculating depreciation is called the **reducing balance method**. This method is based on the assumption that an asset loses value more quickly early in its life. It is therefore constructed to allocate more depreciation in the early years and less depreciation in the later years of an asset's useful life. In the first year of depreciation, the depreciation rate is applied to the cost of the asset. In subsequent years, the depreciation rate is applied to the net book value brought forward from the previous year.

Since the net book value of the asset reduces from year to year, the depreciation will also reduce because the depreciation rate is being applied to a progressively lower figure. The following screenshot shows the difference between the SLM and the reducing balance method:

Depreciation Rate		10%	Useful Life	10years			
	Straight Line				**Reducing Balance**		
Year1	Cost	100,000,000			Cost	100,000,000	
Year 1	Depreciation	10,000,000			Depreciation	10,000,000	
Year2	Net book value	90,000,000			Net book value	90,000,000	
Year2	Depreciation	10,000,000			Depreciation	9,000,000	
Year 3	Net book value	80,000,000			Net book value	81,000,000	
Year 3	Depreciation	10,000,000			Depreciation	8,100,000	
Year 4	Net book value	70,000,000			Net book value	72,900,000	
Year 4	Depreciation	10,000,000			Depreciation	7,290,000	
Year5	Net book value	60,000,000			Net book value	65,610,000	
Year5	Depreciation	10,000,000			Depreciation	6,561,000	
Year 6	Net book value	50,000,000			Net book value	59,049,000	
Year 6	Depreciation	10,000,000			Depreciation	5,904,900	
Year 7	Net book value	40,000,000			Net book value	53,144,100	
Year 7	Depreciation	10,000,000			Depreciation	5,314,410	
Year 8	Net book value	30,000,000			Net book value	47,829,690	
Year 8	Depreciation	10,000,000			Depreciation	4,782,969	
Year 9	Net book value	20,000,000			Net book value	43,046,721	
Year 9	Depreciation	10,000,000			Depreciation	4,304,672	
Year 10	Net book value	10,000,000			Net book value	38,742,049	
Year 10	Depreciation	10,000,000			Depreciation	3,874,205	
	Net book value	-			Net book value	34,867,844	

Figure 7.3 – Depreciation under SLM versus reducing balance

From the preceding screenshot, we can observe the following:

- Both methods begin with the same charge for depreciation —10,000,000 (100,000,000 x 10%).

- From the second year on, the depreciation for the year using the reducing balance method begins to drop from 10,000,000 to 9,000,000 in the second year, to 8,100,000 in the third year, and so on.

- By the tenth year, the depreciation charge has dropped to 3,874,205.

- With the SLM, the annual depreciation charge for the year remains constant at 10,000,000, up until the tenth year.

- The net book value at the end of the tenth year with the SLM is zero, compared to 34,867,844 with the reducing balance method.

The following is a graphical representation of the effect of the two depreciation methods on depreciation and net book value:

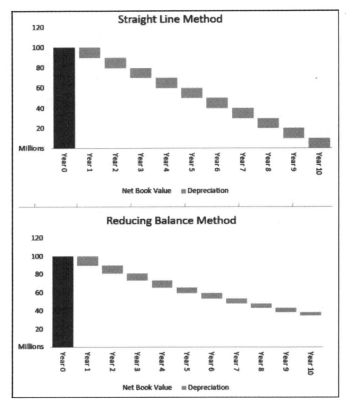

Figure 7.4 – Depreciation by SLM versus reducing balance

You should recognize that no matter how old or utilized an asset becomes, it will always have a residual or scrap value. The **residual value** is an estimate of how much the asset would fetch if it were sold for scrap. With this in mind, you should ensure that you don't depreciate any assets down to zero, but rather down to their residual value, so that in the final year of depreciation, the depreciation charge will be the net book value minus the residual value. The following screenshot shows the annual depreciation for an asset with a residual value of 1,000:

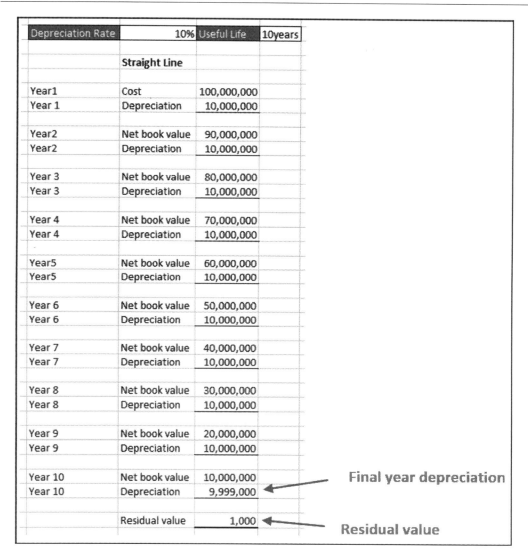

Depreciation Rate		10%	Useful Life	10years
	Straight Line			
Year1	Cost	100,000,000		
Year 1	Depreciation	10,000,000		
Year2	Net book value	90,000,000		
Year2	Depreciation	10,000,000		
Year 3	Net book value	80,000,000		
Year 3	Depreciation	10,000,000		
Year 4	Net book value	70,000,000		
Year 4	Depreciation	10,000,000		
Year5	Net book value	60,000,000		
Year5	Depreciation	10,000,000		
Year 6	Net book value	50,000,000		
Year 6	Depreciation	10,000,000		
Year 7	Net book value	40,000,000		
Year 7	Depreciation	10,000,000		
Year 8	Net book value	30,000,000		
Year 8	Depreciation	10,000,000		
Year 9	Net book value	20,000,000		
Year 9	Depreciation	10,000,000		
Year 10	Net book value	10,000,000		Final year depreciation
Year 10	Depreciation	9,999,000		
	Residual value	1,000		Residual value

Figure 7.5 – Calculation of depreciation over useful life using the SLM

Apart from being more realistic, an asset with a residual value as its net book value is less likely to physically "disappear" than one with a residual value of nil. Although the SLM and reducing balance method are the two most common methods of depreciation, there are other methods, such as sum-of-years digits and units of production.

Approaches to modeling assets

There are two approaches to modeling fixed assets, which are as follows:

- The detailed approach
- The simple approach

The detailed approach

The **detailed approach** is a more precise method than the simple method that looks at the components of fixed assets—the costs of the assets, additions, disposals, depreciation, and accumulated depreciation. Your discussions with management will give you an idea of their CapEx plans over the next five years. Where there is a disposal or sale, a fixed asset has to be removed from the books. The net book value (cost less accumulated depreciation) of that asset will be transferred to a disposal account as a debit and the proceeds of the sale will be transferred to the same account as a credit. The difference between the two will either be a profit—where the *sale's proceeds* exceed the net book value—or a loss—where the net book value is greater than the sale's proceeds—on the disposal of assets and will be transferred from this disposal account to the profit and loss account at the end of the period. The following diagrams show the different scenarios associated with this.

The first diagram shows what happens when there is a profit on the disposal of assets:

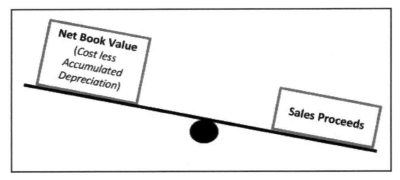

Figure 7.6 – Sales proceeds greater than net book value

This means that you have sold the asset for an amount that is greater than its value, according to the books.

The second diagram shows what happens when you make a loss on the disposal of assets:

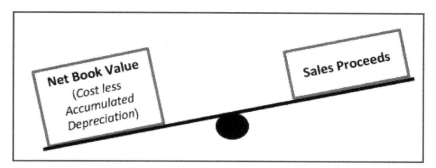

Figure 7.7 – Sales proceeds less than net book value

In this case, you have sold the asset for less than its value, as shown in the books, resulting in a loss on the disposal of assets. All of this is best captured in an asset and depreciation schedule, which should be prepared for each class of fixed assets and then consolidated into a general fixed asset schedule.

Asset and depreciation schedule

The following figure is an illustration of an asset schedule and its various components:

A	B	C	D	E	F	G	H	I	J
3		ASSET SCHEDULE		Yr1A	Yr2A	Yr3A	Yr4A	Yr5A	Yr6E
4		Depreciation Method	SLM						
5		Asset Life	Years	10	10	10	10	10	
6		Disposal of Assets	N Mn	-	-	-	-	-	
7									
8		Capex	N Mn	100,000	-	-	200,000	-	
9									
10		Depreciation Schedule							
11		Yr1A		10,000	10,000	10,000	10,000	10,000	
12		Yr2A			-	-	-	-	
13		Yr3A				-	-	-	
14		Yr4A					20,000	20,000	
15		Yr5A						-	
16		Yr6E							
17		Yr7E							
18		Yr8E							
19		Yr9E							
20		Yr10E							
21		Total Depreciation		10,000	10,000	10,000	30,000	30,000	
22									
23		Cost							
24		Opening Balance		-	100,000	100,000	100,000	300,000	
25		Add: Capex		100,000	-	-	200,000	-	
26		Less: Assets Sold/ Disposed		-	-	-	-	-	
27		Closing Balance		100,000	100,000	100,000	300,000	300,000	
28									
29		Accumulated Depreciation							
30		Opening Balance		-	10,000	20,000	30,000	60,000	
31		Add: Depreciation during current year		10,000	10,000	10,000	30,000	30,000	
32		Less: Depreciation on assets sold							
33		Closing Balance		10,000	20,000	30,000	60,000	90,000	
34									
35		Net Book Value		90,000	80,000	70,000	240,000	210,000	
36									
37									
38		Disposal Of Assets							
39		Cost of assets sold		-	-	-	-	-	
40		Depreciation on assets sold		-	-	-	-	-	
41		Net book value of assets sold		-	-	-	-	-	
42		Proceeds from sale of assets		-	-	-	-	-	
43									
44		(Profit)/loss on sale of assets							

Figure 7.8 – Full depreciation schedule

This is the full asset and depreciation schedule that should be prepared for each asset class. A description of the various parts of the asset schedule follows.

The first section contains the following information:

SCHEDULE		Yr1A	Yr2A	Yr3A	Yr4A	Yr5A	Yr6E
Depreciation Method	SLM						
Asset Life	Years	10	10	10	10	10	10
Disposal of Assets	N Mn	-	-	-	-	-	
Capex	N Mn	100,000	-	-	200,000	-	

Figure 7.9 – First section of depreciation schedule

Here, we have several keywords, such as `Depreciation Method` and `Asset Life`. We will look at what they are for this particular schedule:

- **Depreciation Method**: In our case, it is the SLM.

- **Asset Life**: This is used to represent the useful life of the asset, which, in our case, is 10 years.

- **Disposal of Assets**: This section is for the proceeds of the sale of fixed assets, if any are present.

- **Capex**: This row shows how much was—and is projected to be—spent on fixed assets in each year.

The next section is the `Depreciation Schedule`:

					fx	=$E$8/$E$5				
SUM			×	✓						

▲	A	B	C	D	E	F	G	H	I	J
3	ASSET SCHEDULE				Yr1A	Yr2A	Yr3A	Yr4A	Yr5A	Yr6E
4		Depreciation Method		SLM						
5		Asset Life		Years	10	10	10	10	10	
6		Disposal of Assets		N Mn	-	-	-	-	-	
7										
8		Capex		N Mn	100,000	-	-	200,000	-	
9										
10		Depreciation Schedule								
11		Yr1A			=$E$8/$E$5		10,000	10,000	10,000	
12		Yr2A				-	-	-	-	
13		Yr3A					-	-	-	
14		Yr4A						20,000	20,000	
15		Yr5A							-	
16		Yr6E								
17		Yr7E								
18		Yr8E								
19		Yr9E								
20		Yr10E								
21		Total Depreciation			10,000	10,000	10,000	30,000	30,000	

Figure 7.10 – Depreciation Schedule

Depreciation is in rows **11-20** and across columns **E-N**. The annual depreciation charge on fixed asset additions is the CapEx of the year divided by the asset life. For `Yr1A`, this is **E8** divided by **E5**, which is `10,000`, as shown in the preceding screenshot. The depreciation charge for `Yr1A` additions starts in **E11** and continues along row **11** at `10,000` each year for another 9 years, as shown in the following screenshot:

		A	B	C	D	E	F	G	H	I	J
3	ASSET SCHEDULE					Yr1A	Yr2A	Yr3A	Yr4A	Yr5A	Yr6E
4				Depreciation Method	SLM						
5				Asset Life	Years	10	10	10	10	10	
6				Disposal of Assets	N Mn	-	-	-	-	-	
7											
8				Capex	N Mn	100,000	-	-	200,000	-	
9											
10				Depreciation Schedule							
11				Yr1A		10,000	10,000	10,000	10,000	10,000	
12				Yr2A			-	-	-	-	
13				Yr3A				-	-	-	
14				Yr4A					20,000	20,000	
15				Yr5A						-	

Figure 7.11 – Annual depreciation charge

Depreciation on additions in `Yr2A` is calculated as **F8** divided by **F5** and will be charged annually for 10 years along row **12**—the next row down—starting from **F12**. In the same way, depreciation on `Yr3A` additions will start from **G13** and will be charged for 10 years along row **13**.

The total depreciation charge for each year is the sum of all depreciation in rows **11-20** of the column for that year. For `Yr1A`, this will be the sum of all depreciation in rows **11–20** of column **E**; for `Yr2A`, this will be the sum of all depreciation in rows **11-20** of column **F**. In our example, only `Yr1A` and `Yr4A` have `Capex` additions during the year, as seen in the following screenshot:

SUM	▾	:	✕	✓	*fx*	=SUM(E11:E20)				

	A	B	C	D	E	F	G	H	I	J
3	ASSET SCHEDULE				Yr1A	Yr2A	Yr3A	Yr4A	Yr5A	Yr6E
4			Depreciation Method	SLM						
5			Asset Life	Years	10	10	10	10	10	
6			Disposal of Assets	N Mn	-	-	-	-	-	
7										
8			Capex	N Mn	100,000	-	-	200,000	-	
9										
10		Depreciation Schedule								
11			Yr1A		10,000	10,000	10,000	10,000	10,000	
12			Yr2A			-	-	-	-	
13			Yr3A				-	-	-	
14			Yr4A					20,000	20,000	
15			Yr5A						-	
16			Yr6E							
17			Yr7E							
18			Yr8E							
19			Yr9E							
20			Yr10E							
21			Total Depreciation		=SUM(E11:E20)		10,000	30,000	30,000	

Figure 7.12 – How depreciation is aggregated

The next two sections are summaries of the cost and accumulated depreciation of the fixed assets, which are presented in the base and corkscrew layouts. The closing balance of costs for each year represents the total original or historical costs of fixed assets existing in the business at the end of each year. The following screenshot shows the Cost, Accumulated, Depreciation, and Net Book Value:

SUM	▾	:	✕	✓	*fx*	=E27-E33				

	A	B	C	D	E	F	G	H	I	J
3	ASSET SCHEDULE				Yr1A	Yr2A	Yr3A	Yr4A	Yr5A	Yr6E
22										
23		Cost								
24			Opening Balance		-	100,000	100,000	100,000	300,000	
25			Add: Capex		100,000	-	-	200,000	-	
26			Less: Assets Sold/ Disposed		-	-	-	-	-	
27			Closing Balance		100,000	100,000	100,000	300,000	300,000	
28										
29		Accumulated Depreciation								
30			Opening Balance		-	10,000	20,000	30,000	60,000	
31			Add: Depreciation during current year		10,000	10,000	10,000	30,000	30,000	
32			Less: Depreciation on assets sold							
33			Closing Balance		10,000	20,000	30,000	60,000	90,000	
34										
35		Net Book Value			=E27-E33	80,000	70,000	240,000	210,000	

Figure 7.13 – Cost, accumulated depreciation, and net book value

Accumulated depreciation is the total amount of depreciation charged to date on fixed assets. Fixed assets are carried in the balance sheet at their net book value, which is cost less accumulated depreciation.

This detailed approach relies on information from the client on projected expenditure and disposal of assets over the next 5 years. Where such information is not available, you will need to adopt a less precise but simpler approach.

The simple approach

The simple approach to projecting fixed assets is to model them using a fixed assets turnover ratio based on historical results, as illustrated in the following formula:

$$Fixed\ asset\ turnover\ =\ \frac{Turnover...}{Fixed\ assets}$$

As in our previous examples, we start with historical data and calculate the fixed asset and turnover ratio for each of the historical years. The following screenshot shows the calculation of the Fixed assets turnover Ratio field:

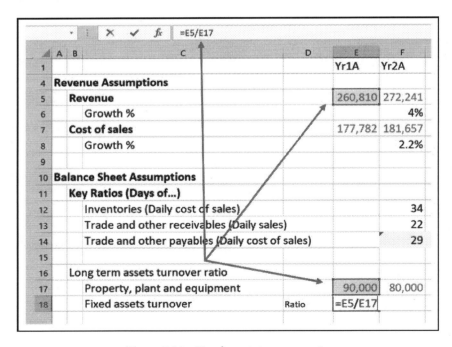

Figure 7.14 – Fixed assets turnover ratio

We calculate the average of the historical fixed assets turnover ratios over `Yr1A-Yr5A`, and then use this average as the projected driver for the next five years. The following screenshot illustrates the calculation of the average of the historical fixed asset turnover ratios:

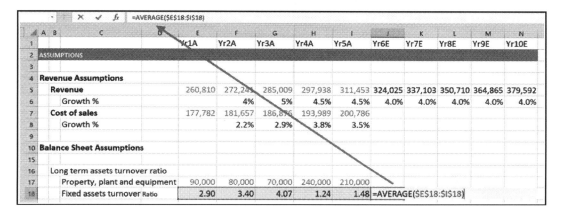

Figure 7.15 – Projected driver for fixed assets

Depreciation can be derived as follows:

1. Divide the historical cost of fixed assets for each year by the depreciation charge for their respective year in order to arrive at the average useful life of assets for that year:

	C	D	E	F
1			Yr1A	Yr2A
54				
55				
56	Cost		90,000	80
57	Depreciation		10,000	20
58	Useful life		=E56/E57	
59				

Figure 7.16 – Calculation of asset's useful life

2. You then calculate the average for the useful life values of the past five historical years:

			Yr1A	Yr2A	Yr3A	Yr4A	Yr5A	Yr6E	Yr7E
Cost			90,000	80,000	70,000	240,000	210,000	123,702	128,695
Depreciation			10,000	20,000	30,000	60,000	90,000		
Useful life			9.0	4.0	2.3	4.0	2.3	=AVERAGE($E$58:$I$58)	

fx =AVERAGE($E$58:$I$58)

Figure 7.17 – Projection of calculated useful life

3. Now, enter the *Useful life* value into the following equation in order to arrive at the *Depreciation* charge for the year:

$$Depreciation = \frac{Cost\ of\ asset}{Useful\ life}$$

The preceding step will result in the following value:

fx =J56/J58

			Yr1A	Yr2A	Yr3A	Yr4A	Yr5A	Yr6E	Yr7E
Cost			90,000	80,000	70,000	240,000	210,000	123,702	128
Depreciation			10,000	20,000	30,000	60,000	90,000	=J56/J58	
Useful life			9.0	4.0	2.3	4.0	2.3	4.3	

Figure 7.18 – Calculation of projected depreciation

4. Now, extend the formula for each of the projected years:

fx =J56/J58

			Yr1A	Yr2A	Yr3A	Yr4A	Yr5A	Yr6E	Yr7E	Yr8E	Yr9E	Yr10E
Cost			90,000	80,000	70,000	240,000	210,000	123,702	128,695	133,890	139,294	144,916
Depreciation			10,000	20,000	30,000	60,000	90,000	28,547	29,699	30,898	32,145	33,442
Useful life			9.0	4.0	2.3	4.0	2.3	4.3	4.3	4.3	4.3	4.3

Figure 7.19 – Projected depreciation for the next five years

This gives us the projected depreciation charge for each of the next 5 years.

You would use the simple approach when you are unable to get information about a company's CapEx plans or you just want a quick simple estimate.

We will now look at long-term debt and how it is dealt with.

Debt schedule

A company's capital is made up of debt and equity, and most businesses try to maintain a steady ratio between debt and equity (a leverage ratio). The debt schedule is part of our forecast of capital structure.

The following list shows our current agenda:

- Record the historical profit and loss accounts and balance sheet
- Calculate the historical growth drivers
- Project the growth drivers for the profit and loss accounts and balance sheet
- Build up the projected profit and loss accounts and balance sheet
- Prepare the asset and depreciation schedule
- Prepare the debt schedule
- Prepare the cash flow statement
- Ratio analysis
- DCF valuation
- Other valuations
- Scenario analysis

As with fixed assets, forecasting debt can be done in one of two ways: a detailed, complex, more accurate method, or a quick and simple less accurate method.

In addition, we need to consider the treatment of interest. The question is, do we take interest on the opening or closing balance of debt or do we apply the interest rate to the average debt for the year?

The complex approach

If your model requires a high level of precision, you will start by getting as much information as possible from published historical accounts and management discussions. You will look out for plans to obtain additional finance and liquidate existing loans, and you will also consider additions to fixed assets that will require finance.

In addition, companies often publish information about maturing loans. You would use this to project annual repayments and ensure that these repayments are stopped once the loan has been paid off. The following screenshot is an illustration of what a debt schedule looks like:

A B	C	D	E	F	G	H	I	J	K	L	M	N
1			Yr1A	Yr2A	Yr3A	Yr4A	Yr5A	Yr6E	Yr7E	Yr8E	Yr9E	Yr10E
61	DEBT SCHEDULE											
62												
63	Unsecured Loans											
64	Opening		-	40,000	35,000	30,000	275,000	245,000	215,000	185,000	155,000	125,000
65	Additions		40,000	-	-	250,000	-	-	-	-	-	-
66	Repayments On 40M	8 yrs		5,000	5,000	5,000	5,000	5,000	5,000	5,000	5,000	-
67	Repayments On 250M	10 yrs					25,000	25,000	25,000	25,000	25,000	25,000
68	Closing		0	=E64+E65-E66-E67	30,000	275,000	245,000	215,000	185,000	155,000	125,000	100,000

Figure 7.20 – Debt schedule

We prepare a debt schedule using the BASE and corkscrew layouts.

In our example, there was a loan of 40 million taken out in Yr1A, at 10% interest, repayable over 8 years, and a loan of 250 million taken out in Yr4A, also at 10% interest, repayable over 10 years. The loan of 40 million is repaid over 8 years, from Yr2A to Yr9E. Repayment of the loan of 250 million does not start until Yr5A and will continue for another 9 years.

In this complex model, you will calculate interest on the average loan outstanding. The average loan outstanding is the opening outstanding plus closing debts divided by two, but in Excel, you can simply use the AVERAGE function, as shown in the following screenshot:

A B	C	D	E	F	G	H	I	J	K	L	M	N
1			Yr1A	Yr2A	Yr3A	Yr4A	Yr5A	Yr6E	Yr7E	Yr8E	Yr9E	Yr10E
61	DEBT SCHEDULE											
62												
63	Unsecured Loans											
64	Opening		-	40,000	35,000	30,000	275,000	245,000	215,000	185,000	155,000	125,000
65	Additions		40,000	-	-	250,000	-	-	-	-	-	-
66	Repayments On 40M	8 yrs		5,000	5,000	5,000	5,000	5,000	5,000	5,000	5,000	-
67	Repayments On 250M	10 yrs					25,000	25,000	25,000	25,000	25,000	25,000
68	Closing		0	40,000	35,000	30,000	275,000	245,000	215,000	185,000	155,000	125,000	100,000
69												
70	Interest rate		10%	10%	10%	10%	10%	10%	10%	10%	10%	10%
71	Interest		=AVERAGE(E64,E68)*E70		15,250	26,000	23,000	20,000	17,000	14,000	11,250

Figure 7.21 – Calculation of interest

The interest is calculated as follows:

$$Interest = \frac{(opening\ debt + closing\ debt)}{2} \times interest\ rate$$

The closing debt is calculated as follows:

$$Closing\ debt = opening\ debt + interest$$

For ease of understanding, let's assume that there's no repayment. The closing debt will be the opening debt plus accrued interest. The following screenshot shows the debt schedule with a closing balance, including accrued interest:

16	Unsecured Loans											
17	Opening		-	40,000	35,000	30,000	275,000	270,000	265,000	260,000	255,000	250,000
18	Additions		40,000	-	-	250,000	-	-	-	-	-	-
19	Repayments On 40M	8 yrs		5,000	5,000	5,000	5,000	5,000	5,000	5,000	5,000	5,000
20	Repayments On 250N	10 yrs										
21	Interest											
22												
23	Closing		0	=E17+E18-E19-E20+E21			275,000	270,000	265,000	260,000	255,000	250,000	245,000
24												
25	Interest rate			10%	10%	10%	10%	10%	10%	10%	10%	10%
26												

Cover   Financial Model   scenarios   Sheet1   comps   (+)

Edit

Figure 7.22 – Closing balance including interest

The following screenshot shows the formula to calculate interest by including both opening and closing debt balances:

16	Unsecured Loans											
17	Opening		-	40,000	35,000	30,000	275,000	270,000	265,000	260,000	255,000	250,000
18	Additions		40,000	-	-	250,000	-	-	-	-	-	-
19	Repayments On 40M	8 yrs		5,000	5,000	5,000	5,000	5,000	5,000	5,000	5,000	5,000
20	Repayments On 250N	10 yrs										
21	Interest		=AVERAGE(E17,E23)*E25									
22												
23	Closing		0	40,000	35,000	30,000	275,000	270,000	265,000	260,000	255,000	250,000	245,000
24												
25	Interest rate		10%	10%	10%	10%	10%	10%	10%	10%	10%	10%
26												

Cover   Financial Model   scenarios   Sheet1   comps   (+)

Point

Figure 7.23 – Closing balance with interest calculated using average debt

In the previous two screenshots, we can see how the formula to calculate the closing balance includes interest and the formula to calculate interest includes the closing debt balance. If left as they are, the formulas will attempt to keep calculating in a loop. This creates a circular reference, which is flagged as an error by Excel.

The following screenshot shows how Excel flags a circular reference:

16	Unsecured Loans						
17	Opening			-	40,000	35,000	30,000	275
18	Additions		40,000	-	-	250,000	
19	Repayments On 40M	8 yrs		5,000	5,000	5,000	5
20	Repayments On 250	10 yrs					
21	Interest			-			
22							
23	Closing		0	40,000	35,000	30,000	275,000	270,
24							
25	Interest rate			10%	10%	10%	10%
26							

Cover | Financial Model | scenarios | Sheet1 | comps | ⊕

Circular References: £23

Circular reference flagged by Excel

Figure 7.24 – Circular reference flagged by Excel

In order to stop the iterations or the continuous calculation of such a formula, Excel flags the formula as a circular reference.

Sometimes, however, you create a circular reference on purpose to achieve a certain result. In our case, we wish to use the most accurate method at our disposal to forecast the interest—utilizing average interest instead of opening or closing debt.

Closing debt is used to calculate interest, which is then used to calculate closing debt. This represents one iteration. This latter closing debt will result in a value that is slightly different from the original closing debt used in the calculation of interest. After the second iteration, the difference is reduced, and it continues to reduce with each successive iteration until it becomes negligible and the two values for closing debt are effectively equal.

In order to allow this to happen without Excel picking it up as an error, you will need to enable iterative calculations under **Excel Options | Formulas**. The following screenshot demonstrates how to enable iterations:

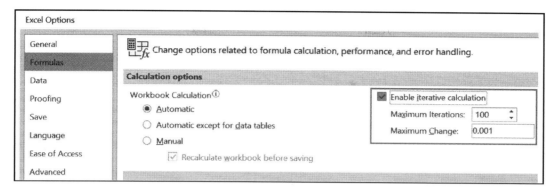

Figure 7.25 – Option to allow circular reference

In Excel 2016, click **File | Options**. This will launch the Excel options dialog box. Then, click on **Formulas** and check the **Enable iterative calculation** box. Accept the default **Maximum Iterations** of **100**. This means that Excel believes that after 100 iterations, the difference generated by each additional iteration becomes negligible or immaterial.

You should always remember to go back and uncheck the **Enable iterative calculation** box. Otherwise, an unintended circular reference may go undetected and could cause Excel to crash, resulting in a loss of information.

The simple approach

If that level of precision is not required, you could adopt a simpler approach, using the leverage ratio:

$$leverage\ ratio\ = \frac{Debt}{Equity}$$

Generally, companies do not frequently change their share capital. It is therefore reasonable to assume that the share capital will remain the same, and that equity will only be affected by retained earnings. Thus, leverage ratio multiplied by equity will give us our debt. For interest, you simply apply the interest rate to the opening debt balance. This will avoid any circular references.

An even simpler method is to consider that, as companies repay old debts, they generally take on new debt. You could therefore assume that the debt balance stays the same. You will forecast the interest charge for the year by applying the interest rate to the opening balance of long-term debt.

Once we have updated our balance sheet and profit and loss accounts with our calculations, the only outstanding item that is needed to complete the three-statement model will be cash.

Now that we have learned everything about historical data, let's apply it to create a loan amortization schedule in the next section.

Creating a simple loan amortization schedule

As mentioned in *Chapter 1, An Introduction to Financial Modeling and Excel*, a loan amortization schedule is a type of financial model. The overall financial decision to be made is whether or not to accept the bank's terms and take the loan.

You will build a set of assumptions made up of interconnected variables. The model will be set up to perform calculations on those variables to eventually arrive at the periodic (usually monthly) repayment. This is the amount to be paid monthly until the loan is fully repaid. It is now left to the customer to decide whether they can afford the periodic repayment now and throughout the term of the loan.

The following is a more detailed step-by-step guide to creating an amortization schedule:

1.   Assumptions: The first step is to prepare a list of assumptions.

Assumptions	
Cost of Asset	20,000,000
Customer's Contribn	20%
Loan Amount	16,000,000
Interest Rate (Annual)	18%
Tenor (Years)	7
Payment periods per year	12
Interest Rate (Periodic)	1.50%
Total periods	84
Periodic Repayment (PMT)	336,285.41

Figure 7.26 – Assumptions

2.   The list, as shown in *Figure 7.26*, is as follows:

   - Cost of the Asset: This is the total cost of the asset you wish to purchase. In this illustration, it is 20,000,000.

   - Customer's contribution: This is the portion that the bank requires the customer to contribute towards the cost of the asset, often referred to as equity contribution; the bank will then make up the difference as a loan. In this example, the customer's contribution is 20% and the loan from the bank is 80% of the cost of the asset.

- Loan amount: This is the loan required from the bank. It is the cost of the asset less the customer's contribution. In this example, it is 16,000,000.

- Interest rate (Annual): This is the per annum interest rate charged by the bank. In this example, it is 18%.

- Tenor (Years): This is the tenor of the loan. In this example, it is 7 years.

- Payment periods per year: Monthly = 12, quarterly = 4, and bi-annually = 2 periods per year. In this example, it is 12.

- Interest Rate (Periodic): This is the interest rate per period. Interest rate divided by the number of periods. In this example, it is 1.50%.

- Total periods: This is the number of payment periods per year multiplied by the number of years. In this example, it is 7 years and 12 periods per year, giving 12 x 7 = 84.

- Periodic Repayment: This is calculated using the PMT function, as shown in the following screenshot:

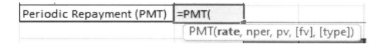

Figure 7.27 – PMT function

The arguments of the PMT function will be taken from our assumptions list and can be explained as follows:

- Rate: This refers to the periodic interest rate.

- Nper: This refers to the total number of payment periods.

- Pv: This is the loan amount (not the cost of the asset).

These are the mandatory arguments. The others are optional, and we will not be using them.

3. Now that we have set up our assumptions list, we can proceed with the amortization schedule proper. Due to space constraints, we will show the schedule in two parts. The first part is a screenshot of the top portion of the schedule up to period 18:

Periods	PMT	Interest Paid	Principal Reduction	Balance
0				16,000,000.00
1	336,285.41	240,000.00	96,285.41	15,903,714.59
2	336,285.41	238,555.72	97,729.69	15,805,984.90
3	336,285.41	237,089.77	99,195.63	15,706,789.27
4	336,285.41	235,601.84	100,683.57	15,606,105.70
5	336,285.41	234,091.59	102,193.82	15,503,911.88
6	336,285.41	232,558.68	103,726.73	15,400,185.15
7	336,285.41	231,002.78	105,282.63	15,294,902.52
8	336,285.41	229,423.54	106,861.87	15,188,040.65
9	336,285.41	227,820.61	108,464.80	15,079,575.85
10	336,285.41	226,193.64	110,091.77	14,969,484.08
11	336,285.41	224,542.26	111,743.15	14,857,740.93
12	336,285.41	222,866.11	113,419.29	14,744,321.64
13	336,285.41	221,164.82	115,120.58	14,629,201.06
14	336,285.41	219,438.02	116,847.39	14,512,353.67
15	336,285.41	217,685.30	118,600.10	14,393,753.56
16	336,285.41	215,906.30	120,379.10	14,273,374.46
17	336,285.41	214,100.62	122,184.79	14,151,189.67
18	336,285.41	212,267.85	124,017.56	14,027,172.11

Figure 7.28 – Amortization schedule top part

The bottom part of the schedule shows that we have 84 periods in this scenario:

70	336,285.41	67,307.02	268,978.39	4,218,156.1
71	336,285.41	63,272.34	273,013.07	3,945,143.1
72	336,285.41	59,177.15	277,108.26	3,668,034.8
73	336,285.41	55,020.52	281,264.89	3,386,769.9
74	336,285.41	50,801.55	285,483.86	3,101,286.0
75	336,285.41	46,519.29	289,766.12	2,811,519.9
76	336,285.41	42,172.80	294,112.61	2,517,407.3
77	336,285.41	37,761.11	298,524.30	2,218,883.0
78	336,285.41	33,283.25	303,002.16	1,915,880.9
79	336,285.41	28,738.21	307,547.19	1,608,333.7
80	336,285.41	24,125.01	312,160.40	1,296,173.3
81	336,285.41	19,442.60	316,842.81	979,330.5
82	336,285.41	14,689.96	321,595.45	657,735.0
83	336,285.41	9,866.03	326,419.38	331,315.6
84	336,285.41	4,969.74	331,315.67	-0.0

Figure 7.29 – Amortization schedule bottom part

Figure 7.28 shows the top half of the amortization table. The headers are as follows:

- `Periods`: This represents the payment periods. In this example, it's 1 to 84. Since we will want the total number of periods to be flexible to accommodate changes in our variables, we use one of the new Excel 365 `SEQUENCE` formulas, as illustrated here:

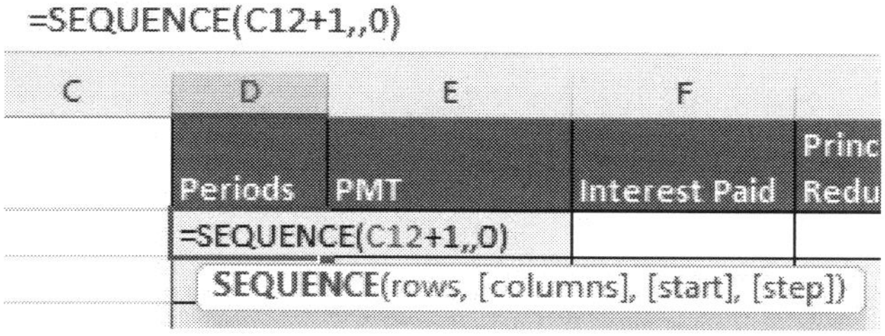

Figure 7.30 – The new SEQUENCE function

In the `SEQUENCE` function, `rows` means the number of rows to be populated; this is the same as the total number of periods. That value is in the assumptions list in cell **C12**, so we point to that cell and add `1`, since we are actually starting from `0` and we need to stop at period `84`. `columns` refers to the number of columns you wish to populate. It is optional and can be overlooked by just typing a second comma to move to the next argument. If you don't enter any value for columns, it defaults to `1`. `start` refers to the starting point of your sequence. In this case, we are starting from `0`. `step` refers to the increment from one row to the next. This argument is also optional and defaults to `1`.

This is one of the new formulas in Excel 365 that can handle arrays. Regular formulas in Excel, no matter how complex they are, will give a single result in a single cell. Array formulas can deliver an array of results in several cells. So even though we only enter the formula once, it returns multiple values, 0 to 84 in this example:

- `PMT`: This refers to fixed periodic payments. It is made up of interest and principal repaid for the period.

- `Interest Paid`: This refers to the periodic interest charge calculated as the periodic interest rate multiplied by loan balance outstanding at the end of the previous period.

- `Principal Reduction`: This refers to the amount of principal repaid in each period. It is arrived at by subtracting interest paid from the fixed periodic interest.

- `Balance`: This is the principal balance left at the end of each period. It is equal to the balance at the end of the previous period less the principal reduction.

There are a number of things to observe about the amortization schedule. The fixed periodic payment is divided between interest and principal in every period. In other words, part interest charge and part repayment of the loan. In period 1, the interest portion is over two and a half times the principal repayment portion.

As you go down the periods, the balance outstanding reduces, the interest charge gets progressively smaller, and the principal repayment portion gets progressively larger until period 84, when over 98% of the final payment is attributable to the principal repayment and the balance is zero.

4. Now that the amortization schedule is set up, we can set about sensitizing the model. We can set up the customer's contribution, interest rate (annual), and number of years variables to accept different values.

We do this with the use of the data validation feature of Excel.

With the cursor in cell **C9** on the value of the `Tenor` (which is currently 7), go to **Data Validation** in the **Data Tools** group of the **Data** ribbon, as shown in the following screenshot:

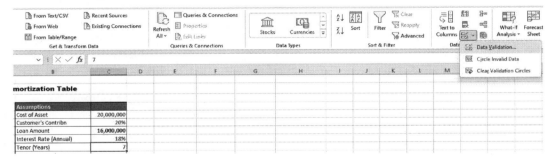

Figure 7.31 – Data Validation option

This opens the **Data Validation** dialog box, as shown in the following screenshot:

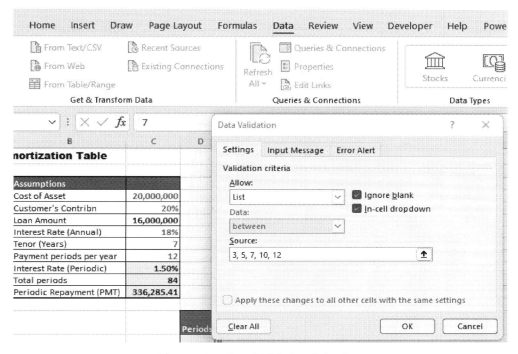

Figure 7.32 – Data Validation dialog box

Click in the **Allow** selection box and a drop-down menu appears with a list of options to choose from, as shown in the following screenshot:

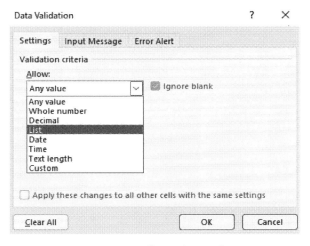

Figure 7.33 – Allow selection box

Select **List**. Then, in the **Source** selection bar, type the following options: 3, 5, 7, 10, 12, as shown in *Figure 7.34*. Click **OK**.

A downward-pointing arrow appears beside cell **C9**, which, when clicked, reveals a drop-down list of the values you typed in the source selection bar of the **Data Validation** dialog box, as shown in the following screenshot:

Assumptions	
Cost of Asset	20,000,000
Customer's Contribn	20%
Loan Amount	16,000,000
Interest Rate (Annual)	18%
Tenor (Years)	7 ▼
Payment periods per year	3
	5
Interest Rate (Periodic)	7
	10
Total periods	12
Periodic Repayment (PMT)	336,285.41

Figure 7.34 – Source selection

In this way, you can substitute any of the other values in the list for Tenor and observe the effect on the schedule.

For example, if we set Tenor to 5 years, view the following figure:

Assumptions	
Cost of Asset	20,000,000
Customer's Contribn	20%
Loan Amount	16,000,000
Interest Rate (Annual)	18%
Tenor (Years)	5
Payment periods per year	12
Interest Rate (Periodic)	1.50%
Total periods	60
Periodic Repayment (PMT)	406,294.84

Figure 7.35 – 5-year tenor parameters

Periodic interest rate, total periods, and periodic repayment all change. The following screenshot illustrates the change in values:

50	406,294.84	61,377.65	344,917.19	3,746,925.99
51	406,294.84	56,203.89	350,090.95	3,396,835.04
52	406,294.84	50,952.53	355,342.31	3,041,492.72
53	406,294.84	45,622.39	360,672.45	2,680,820.28
54	406,294.84	40,212.30	366,082.53	2,314,737.74
55	406,294.84	34,721.07	371,573.77	1,943,163.97
56	406,294.84	29,147.46	377,147.38	1,566,016.59
57	406,294.84	23,490.25	382,804.59	1,183,212.00
58	406,294.84	17,748.18	388,546.66	794,665.34
59	406,294.84	11,919.98	394,374.86	400,290.48
60	406,294.84	6,004.36	400,290.48	-0.00

Figure 7.36 – End of amortization table for a 5-year tenor

You can see that at the end of the 60th period, the balance is now zero. The new SEQUENCE function automatically converts the period to 60 years. The periodic repayments are now 406,294.84.

In the same way, you can sensitize other variables, such as customer's contribution and interest rate, using data validation.

Summary

In this chapter, we have seen the importance of fixed asset and debt schedules. We have illustrated how they affect balance sheets, profit and loss accounts, and cash flow statements. We have learned about the base and corkscrew methods, as well as complex and simple approaches to preparing fixed assets, depreciation, and debt schedules.

It is important to note also that even outside of modeling, it is good practice for asset and debt schedules to be maintained by all companies as part of their accounting procedures. This helps to keep track of non-current assets and liabilities.

We have learned how to prepare a simple loan amortization table and also introduced one of the new functions of Excel 365, the SEQUENCE function, and we have seen how we can combine this with our amortization table to produce a dynamic numbered list of the number of repayment periods.

In the next chapter, we will perform our final calculations and prepare the cash flows in order to arrive at an accurate statement, which should cause our balance sheets to balance and conclude the three-statement model.

8
Preparing a Cash Flow Statement

A wise man once said *Turnover is vanity, profit is sanity, but cash is reality*. An entity's **profit and loss (P&L)** account gives the result (profit or loss) of revenue activities during the year, and the balance sheet gives a snapshot of the assets, liabilities, and equity at the balance sheet date. However, both of these statements are affected by the accruals basis of accounting that seeks to ensure that all transactions that belong to the period under review are brought into the accounts for that period, irrespective of whether or not cash has changed hands. This means that you are likely to have turnover or sales or income that is not supported by cash inflow because some sales would have been made on credit and may would not yet have been paid for by the period end. This also affects purchases, inventory, and expenses that are either prepaid (such as rent and insurance) or accrued (such as electricity). Since the ability to settle its debts as they fall due is essential to the continued existence of an entity, the true cash position and impact on the transactions must be known. This is particularly pertinent in this post-pandemic era when the continued existence of so many entities is hanging by a thread.

The cash flow statement strips everything down to the inflow and outflow of cash, starting with an opening cash position and ending with a closing cash balance. In true accounting fashion, this closing cash balance is equal to the closing cash balance in the balance sheet, providing us with a means of confirming that the sometimes intricate calculations we have performed to extract the cash position are accurate.

In this chapter, you will learn how to prepare a cash flow statement. You will understand the difference between the direct and indirect methods of preparing the statement. You will also learn what makes up each of the sections of a cash flow statement and how to extract each of these items from the P&L account and balance sheet. You will learn how to interpret the cash flow statement and how to troubleshoot if it does not balance.

The following topics are covered in this chapter:

- Introduction to the cash flow statement
- Cash flow from operations
- Cash flow from investing activities
- Cash flow from financing activities
- Balancing the balance sheet
- Troubleshooting
- Circular references

Introduction to the cash flow statement

Following our agenda, the next stage is the preparation of the cash flow statement:

- Record the historical P&L and Balance Sheet.
- Calculate the historical growth drivers.
- Project the growth drivers for P&L and Balance Sheet.
- Build up projected P&L and Balance Sheet.
- Prepare asset and depreciation schedule.
- Prepare debt schedule.
- Prepare cash flow statement.
- Ratio analysis.
- DCF valuation.
- Other valuations.
- Scenario analysis.

You will recall that we created a visual check in *Chapter 2, Steps for Building a Financial Model*, to indicate when the balance sheets are in or out of balance. If they are out of balance, the check cells will be red, but the moment they fall in balance, the cells will turn green, as shown in the following diagram.

Figure 8.1 illustrates the position with the forecast years out of balance. The historical balance sheets will of course be in balance:

	Balance Check		TRUE	TRUE	TRUE	FALSE	FALSE	FALSE	FALSE	FALSE
6	(Unless otherwise specified, all financials an Units		Y01A	Y02A	Y03A	Y04F	Y05F	Y06F	Y07F	Y08F
113	**CASH FLOW STATEMENT**									
115	**Cashflow from Operating Activities**									
116	PAT		13,787	1,850	13,309	13,318	23,312	33,684	44,449
117	Add: Depreciation		10,000	10,000	30,000	30,000	30,000	30,000	30,000
118	Add: Interest Expense		3,750	3,250	15,250	26,000	23,000	20,000	17,000
120	**Net Change in Working Capital**								
121	Add: Increase in Accounts payable		3,524	(223)	(1,759)	1,865	(1,758)	1,866	(1,758)
122	Less: Increase in Inventory		(2,462)	(3,724)	7,201	(7,331)	7,201	(7,331)	7,201
123	Less: Increase in Account Receivables		(10,704)	(4,333)	2,089	(5,252)	1,946	(5,402)	1,789
124	**Net Change in Working Capital**		(9,642)	(8,280)	7,532	(10,717)	7,389	(10,867)	7,232
126	**Cashflow from Operations**		17,895	6,820	66,091	58,600	83,701	72,816	98,681

Figure 8.1 – Balance sheet check

The cash flow statement is divided into three main sections: **Cash flow from Operations**, **Cash flow from Investing activities**, and **Cash flow from Financing activities**.

There are two methods of preparing the cash flow statement, the **direct method** and the **indirect method**. The difference between the two is in the treatment of cash flow from operations. Investing and financing activities are treated the same in both methods. The direct method is the preferred but less popular method. In this method, cash flow from operations is arrived at by considering the following:

- Cash received from customers
- Cash paid to suppliers
- Cash paid to employees
- Cash paid for selling and distribution
- Cash paid for taxes
- Cash paid for other overheads

The reason why this is the less popular method is because of the difficulty in obtaining the information required to arrive at the cash received or paid in respect of these items.

The indirect method starts with the accounting profit after tax. From this, you deduct items not involving the movement of cash that have been considered in arriving at the accounting profit, such as depreciation. You then adjust this with movements in working capital, as detailed in the *Working capital movements* section.

The cash flow statement shows the inflow and outflow of cash from operations, investing activities, and financing activities. The net inflow or outflow of cash is then added to or subtracted from the opening balance of cash to arrive at the closing balance of cash and cash equivalents, which should agree with the corresponding figure on the balance sheet. For the forecast years, there is no cash figure on the balance sheet, so we need to take advantage of this balance sheet/cash flow relationship and arrive at projected cash for the forecast years.

We will now take a closer look at cash flow from operations.

Cash flow from operations

Cash flow from operations is the cash flow from operating activities. If the accounts were prepared on a cash basis, it would simply be the turnover less all expenses.

However, the P&L account is different from the cash flow statement in that it does not wait for the cash implications of a transaction to be settled before the transaction is recognized. For example, if you make a sale of N100,000 and the customer has received the goods or services but has not yet paid, there is no cash movement. However, both you and the customer recognize that a sale has been made; indeed, ownership and custody of the goods have been transferred. So, the P&L account will record this as a credit sale, increasing turnover by 100,000, and to complete the double entry, a receivable is created under that customer's name to signify that they owe you 100,000.

This is the accrual basis of accounting that says that income should be recorded in the period in which it is earned, and expenses should be matched with the income they have helped generate. This permeates throughout the accounts, affecting things such as rent paid in advance (only the rent for this year should go through the P&L), electricity used but the bill has not yet arrived (charge the electricity in the P&L), and purchases must be adjusted by opening and closing stock so that only the cost of goods sold is reflected in the P&L account.

In all these examples, the actual cash flow will differ from the amount taken to profit and loss. This makes good economic sense and is essential in order to arrive at the true profit or loss for each period. However, as quoted earlier, turnover is vanity, profit is sanity, but cash is reality. No matter how much profit a company records, if it is not backed up by cash, sooner or later the company will go bust. This is why the cash flow statement is so important.

So, the cash flow from operating activities is derived as follows:

1. Accounting profit for the year, **profit after tax (PAT)**: Add back items not involving the movement of cash that would have been included in the calculation of profit for the year, for example, depreciation. Since it has been deducted as an expense in arriving at our profit, we need to add it back to the PAT, as shown in the following screenshot.

2. We also add back interest charges to PAT. Although this is a cash flow, it is the cost of debt finance and thus, more appropriately, treated under financing activities.

6	(Unless otherwise specified, all financials a	Units	Y01A	Y02A	Y03A
113	**CASH FLOW STATEMENT**				
114					
115	**Cashflow from Operating Activities**				
116	PAT			13,787	1,850
117	Add: Depreciation			10,000	10,000
118	Add: Interest Expense			3,750	3,250
119					

Figure 8.2 – Cash flow from operating activities

We now move on to the effect on cash of movement in working capital.

Working capital movements

This last adjustment is to account for the effect of the accrual basis of accounting. A simplistic explanation is that if there has been an increase in debtors (which is part of working capital) over the last year, this implies that an equivalent amount has been included in turnover as credit sales, which *is not* a movement of cash and should, therefore, be deducted. On the other hand, if there had been a decrease in debtors, this implies that some of the debtors had settled their debts, which *is* a movement of cash. Similarly, if there has been an increase in creditors, this implies that an equivalent amount has been included in purchases as credit purchases, which *is not* a movement of cash. So, a decrease in creditors would mean the company had made a payment to suppliers, which is the cash portion of that transaction.

Figure 8.3 gives an illustration of the calculation of changes in working capital:

6	(Unless otherwise specified, all financials a Units	Y01A	Y02A	Y03A	Y04F
119					
120	**Net Change in Working Capital**				
121	Add: Increase in Accounts payable			3,524	(223)
122	Less: Increase in Inventory			(2,462)	(3,724)
123	Less: Increase in Account Receivables			(10,704)	(4,333)
124	**Net Change in Working Capital**			(9,642)	(8,280)

Figure 8.3 – Movement in working capital

This is the section that many analysts and accountants find most problematic. You are comparing the closing balance sheets of this year and last year. The difference between the two gives us the movement in that component of working capital. Components of working capital include **Inventory**, **Debtors or Accounts receivable**, **Creditors or Accounts payable**, and all other accounts that can fall into any of these categories. Note that all these are short-term balances. The difficulty is in determining whether the difference computed represents an inflow or an outflow of funds. The movement can only be one of four things: an increase or decrease in debtors and inventory (we consider these together since they are both debit balances) or an increase or decrease in creditors. The trick is to consider the movements that have obvious cash inferences. So, a decrease in debtors infers that some debtors have made a payment, which is clearly an inflow of cash. The opposite would, therefore, be true for the contrary position. An increase in debtors is, therefore, an outflow of cash.

Conversely, a decrease in creditors infers that you have settled some supplier bills and is, therefore, an outflow. This means that an increase in creditors is an inflow. The profit (adjusted for items not involving the movement of cash) is then added to the movement in working capital to arrive at cash flow from operations. This movement in working capital effectively converts our profit from the accruals basis to a cash-based profit. It is usually here that the cash effect of tax transactions is treated. Balances that affect tax are opening and closing tax payable (balance sheet), and the tax charge for the year (P&L account). Cash flow from taxation matters is usually tax paid. This is calculated as opening tax payable, plus tax charge for the year, less closing tax payable. The next section considers **investing activities**.

Cash flow from investing activities

Cash flow from investing activities will include cash generated or utilized in the following:

- The sale or purchase of **property, plant, and equipment (PPE)**: Purchase of PPE is straightforward and can be obtained from the additions in the fixed assets schedule. The sale of PPE would have been reflected in the accounts as profit or loss on the disposal of assets. This is arrived at by comparing the proceeds of the sale to the net book value (cost less accumulated depreciation) of the assets sold. The profit on disposal will be reversed from operating profit along with depreciation as not involving the movement of cash. The **proceeds of sale** is the cash element of the transaction and is calculated as profit on the sale of assets plus the net book value of assets sold.

- Sale or purchase of investments: Cash utilized in the purchase of investments will simply be an increase in investments after considering any sale. Cash generated from the sale of investments will be profit on the sale of investments plus the cost of investments sold.

- Distributions received from investments: To include these here, you must ensure that they are excluded from profit for the year, where they may have been included as other income.

Figure 8.4 gives an example of how cash flow from investments is calculated:

6	*(Unless otherwise specified, all financials a* Units	Y01A	Y02A	Y03A	Y04F
128	**Cashflow from Investment Activities**				
129	Less: Capex			-	-
130	Add: Proceeds from Disposal of Assets				
131	Less: Increase in WIP				
132	Less: Increase in Investments			648	(6,557)
133	**Cashflow from Investment Activities**			**648**	**(6,557)**

Figure 8.4 – Cash flow from investing activities

Finally, we consider financing activities in the next section.

Cash flow from financing activities

Cash flow from financing activities will include cash generated or utilized in the following activities:

- Increase/decrease in long term debt.

- Increase in share capital.

- Payment of interest on long-term debt. Again, to include this here, it must be excluded from the computation of profit for the year.

An illustration of cash flow from financing activities can be seen in *Figure 8.5*:

6	(Unless otherwise specified, all financials a Units	Y01A	Y02A	Y03A	Y04F
134					
135	**Cashflow from Financing Activities**				
136	Add: New Equity Raised				
137	Add: New Unsecured Loans Raised			-	-
138	Less: Unsecured Loans Repaid			(5,000)	(5,000)
139	Less: Dividends Paid				
140	Less: Interest Expense			(3,750)	(3,250)
141	**Cashflow from Financing Activities**			**(8,750)**	**(8,250)**

Figure 8.5 – Cash flow from financing activities

You will then aggregate the cash flows from the different sources to arrive at net cash inflow/outflow:

| M | ⌄ | : | ✕ ✓ fx | =F126+F133+F141 | | | | | | | | |

	A B	C	D	E	F	G	H	I	J	K	L
1											
2											
3											
4	Balance Check				TRUE	TRUE	TRUE	TRUE	TRUE	TRUE	TRUE	TRUE
5											
6	(Unless otherwise specified, all financials Units	Y01A	Y02A	Y03A	Y04F	Y05F	Y06F	Y07F	Y08F		
139	Less: Dividends Paid										
140	Less: Interest Expense			(3,750)	(3,250)	(15,250)	(26,000)	(23,000)	(20,000)	(17,000)
141	Cashflow from Financing Activities			(8,750)	(8,250)	229,750	(56,000)	(53,000)	(50,000)	(47,000)
142											
143	Net Cashflow			=F126+F133+F141		55,841	2,600	30,701	22,816	51,681
144											
145	Cash Balance										
146	Opening Balance			7,459	17,252	9,265	65,106	67,707	98,408	121,224
147	Net Cashflow			9,793	(7,987)	55,841	2,600	30,701	22,816	51,681
148	Closing Balance			17,252	9,265	65,106	67,707	98,408	121,224	172,905
149											

Figure 8.6 – Net cash flow and closing balance of cash

Prepare the cash flow statement, as usual, ending with a figure for the closing cash balance. Then, post this figure to the balance sheet as cash and cash equivalents for the projected years.

If the balance sheet now balances, this indicates that our model up to this stage is mathematically correct. Otherwise, we will begin the tedious process of troubleshooting to trace the error.

	Balance Check	TRUE	TRUE	TRUE	TRUE	TRUE	TRUE	TRUE	TRUE
	(Unless otherwise specified, all financials an Units	Y01A	Y02A	Y03A	Y04F	Y05F	Y06F	Y07F	Y08F
	CASH FLOW STATEMENT								
	Cashflow from Operating Activities								
	PAT		13,787	1,850	13,309	13,318	23,312	33,684	44,449
	Add: Depreciation		10,000	10,000	30,000	30,000	30,000	30,000	30,000
	Add: Interest Expense		3,750	3,250	15,250	26,000	23,000	20,000	17,000
	Net Change in Working Capital								
	Add: Increase in Accounts payable		3,524	(223)	(1,759)	1,865	(1,758)	1,866	(1,758)
	Less: Increase in Inventory		(2,462)	(3,724)	7,201	(7,331)	7,201	(7,331)	7,201
	Less: Increase in Account Receivables		(10,704)	(4,333)	2,089	(5,252)	1,946	(5,402)	1,789
	Net Change in Working Capital		(9,642)	(8,280)	7,532	(10,717)	7,389	(10,867)	7,232
	Cashflow from Operations		17,895	6,820	66,091	58,600	83,701	72,816	98,681
	Cashflow from Investment Activities								
	Less: Capex		-	-	(200,000)	-	-	-	-
	Add: Proceeds from Disposal of Assets								
	Less: Increase in WIP								
	Less: Increase in Investments		648	(6,557)	(40,000)	-	-	-	-
	Cashflow from Investment Activities		648	(6,557)	(240,000)	-	-	-	-
	Cashflow from Financing Activities								
	Add: New Equity Raised								
	Add: New Unsecured Loans Raised		-	-	250,000	-	-	-	-
	Less: Unsecured Loans Repaid		(5,000)	(5,000)	(5,000)	(30,000)	(30,000)	(30,000)	(30,000)
	Less: Dividends Paid								
	Less: Interest Expense		(3,750)	(3,250)	(15,250)	(26,000)	(23,000)	(20,000)	(17,000)
	Cashflow from Financing Activities		(8,750)	(8,250)	229,750	(56,000)	(53,000)	(50,000)	(47,000)
	Net Cashflow		9,793	(7,987)	55,841	2,600	30,701	22,816	51,681
	Cash Balance								
	Opening Balance		7,459	17,252	9,265	65,106	67,707	98,408	121,224
	Net Cashflow		9,793	(7,987)	55,841	2,600	30,701	22,816	51,681
	Closing Balance		17,252	9,265	65,106	67,707	98,408	121,224	172,905

Figure 8.7 – Cash flow statement

This is the completed cash flow statement; the closing cash balances will now be posted to the appropriate balance sheets, and the balance check, which is visible from all schedules, will show that they are all now in balance.

Balancing the balance sheet

The closing cash balance will be posted to the balance sheet as cash and cash equivalent under current assets. However, it is important to note that the balance could be negative, in which case it should be reflected as an overdraft under current liabilities. Since you don't know which it is going to be, especially as it may change as a result of subsequent modifications, you need to build your model in such a way that the cash balance is posted to cash and cash equivalents if it is positive, and to overdraft if it is negative.

Usually, when you need to model a situation that depends on a logical question (one that results in a true or false answer), the first thing that springs to mind is the IF statement. For example, say the cursor is in cell J35, cash and cash equivalents, and you wish to relate this to the calculated cash balance from the cash flow statement in cell J86, you would type = J86 and the cash balance would appear in cell J35 when you press *Enter*.

To incorporate the uncertainty explained above with the IF statement, you would type =IF(J86>0,J86,""). This states that if the cash balance is positive, greater than 0, then put the cash balance in cell J35, otherwise leave the cell blank.

In the corresponding overdraft cell, say cell J45, you would type =IF(J86>0,"",-J86). This states that if the cash balance is positive, greater than 0, then leave the cell blank; otherwise, change the cash balance sign from negative to positive and put it in cell J45. However, there is a more elegant way to handle this using the MIN and MAX formulas. In cell J35, you would simply type = MAX(J86,0). This formula will ensure that the maximum of the cash balance and 0 will always go in cell J35. If you think about it, a positive number is always greater than 0 and will, therefore, always be treated as cash and cash equivalents. In cell J45, overdraft, you would type - MIN(J86,0). This will ensure that whenever the cash balance is negative, it will always be posted in cell J45; otherwise, the cell will be 0. Once this posting has been done, the balance sheets should balance and our balance check cells should all have turned green. If this is not the case, then you will need to troubleshoot to locate the source of the error.

Troubleshooting

The first step is to check the accuracy of your cash flow statement. Since the historical years will already have a cash or overdraft balance, you can check your cash flow and cash balances for those years against the balance sheet cash.

If the balances do not agree, you will need to check your cash flow entries again:

1. First of all, check your totals for any casting errors.

2. Next, determine what the difference is and divide by two. Look through your cash flow to see whether there is an amount equal to this figure. This test checks to see whether you have wrongly posted a figure as negative instead of positive, or vice versa.

3. Scan through the balance sheet and P&L account for an amount equal to the whole difference calculated in *Step 1*. This test checks to see whether you have omitted an amount from the cash flow.

4. Scan through the balance sheet and P&L account to see whether there are any accounts or balances that have not been accounted for in your cash flow. This often happens where you have irregular accounts or movements, for example, share premium, special reserves, and prior year adjustments.

5. Once you have reconciled your historical cash flow statements to the historical balance sheets, your balance checks should now all be green. If they are not, then you will need to widen your troubleshooting to the rest of the model.

The cash flow statement is not only about generating cash balances for the projected years. Interpretation of the statement can give useful insights into the company's liquidity.

A positive cash flow is obviously a good sign for the company's health. Positive cash flow from operations indicates that the company is generating enough cash to cover its running costs. On the other hand, negative cash flow from operations indicates that the company is having to look to investing and/or financing activities to cover the shortfall.

Negative cash flow is not an immediate sign to panic. However, if the loss is sustained over a number of years, then the company is in danger of becoming insolvent.

Circular references

Say you have data in cells A1 to A4 and you type = SUM(A1:A6) in cell A5. This will be flagged by Excel as a circular reference error because you have included the answer cell, A5, in your sum range.

In complex models, you may wish to deliberately create a circular reference for the following reasons.

In the general scheme of things, a company would invest any surplus cash to earn interest. On the other hand, when cash is in overdraft, it will incur interest. If we wanted to expand our model to include this scenario, we would need to extend our cash flow statement to include interest earned or charged on the cash balance. This interest is then subtracted from or added to the existing interest charge in the P&L account, which changes the PAT. Since the PAT is linked to the cash flow statement, this will also result in a change in the closing cash balance, which will affect the interest earned or charged on that balance and the cycle continues, creating a circular reference. With each cycle or iteration, the change in the interest charged or earned on the closing cash balance of the cash flow statement gets smaller and smaller and ultimately tends towards zero.

> **Note**
>
> In order to create a circular reference on purpose, you need to ask Excel to allow it by going to **Options** under **Formulas** and checking **Enable iterative calculation**. You can leave the maximum number of iterations at **100**.

I do not recommend this for anyone other than expert users, and even then, only when you will not be sharing your model with other users, for the reasons mentioned as follows.

Unfortunately, circular references, when enabled, are notoriously unreliable and can cause Excel to become unstable. When this happens, Excel populates the worksheet with errors. You would then need to spend time combing through the model to manually zero out the cells that are the source of the circularity. Alternatively, you could restore a backup that does not contain the circularity. This can be quite alarming to all except for expert users of Excel and can lead to the loss of hours of modeling time. The best way around this is to include a *circuit breaker* from the onset.

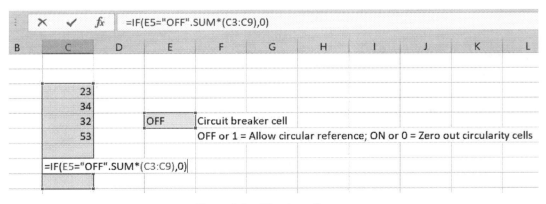

Figure 8.8 – Circular reference

To do this, designate an empty cell, say cell E5, as a circuit breaker, then type in OFF or 1. To allow the circular reference, type ON, or 0 to zero out the cells with the circularity. You then enclose the cell(s) containing the circular reference in an IF statement. The logical question would be E5=1. If this is true, then allow the formula with the circular reference, otherwise set the value as 0. The default value of the circuit breaker should be OFF, then if the formula goes rogue, just type ON in the circuit breaker cell to trigger the 0 in the IF statement and clear the circularity. Remember that Excel continuously recalculates formula cells, so this could be a regular occurrence. Once again, this should only be done by expert users who will not be sharing their model.

Summary

In this chapter, you have learned about the importance of the cash flow statement. You have understood the different elements of the statement and how to calculate them. You also learned that cash flow from operations gives an indication of the company's ability to generate sufficient funds for its operations, and movement in working capital makes adjustments to convert accruals-based accounting to cash-based accounting.

We have seen how to extract cash flow from financing and investing activities and finally, we have seen how to arrive at the closing cash balance for the year and use this to balance out the balance sheet.

We have now concluded the three-statement model, and in the next chapter, we will perform some ratio analysis to gain further insight into the projected performance of the company.

9
Ratio Analysis

In order to assess a company, most people immediately look at its profit history. While this is one of the parameters for assessing a company, it could be misleading to take a decision based solely on this criterion. As we have seen in *Chapter 8, Preparing a Cash Flow Statement*, profits do not always equate to cash and even the most profitable company can fold if its profits are not backed up by cash flow.

Ratio analysis looks at the profitability, liquidity, asset management/efficiency, debt management, and market value of a company in order to give a much more reliable basis for making a decision. Each ratio takes two strategic items from the financial statements and examines the relationship between them in order to gain some insight into the profitability, liquidity, and so on of the company – for example, the ratio of turnover to gross profit. These are two significant items in the statement of comprehensive income in financial statements.

A ratio of gross profit divided by turnover tells you what portion of the turnover is retained as gross profit after deducting the cost of sales from turnover. This is a very important ratio and is called the gross profit percentage (when converted to a percentage by multiplying by 100) or gross profit margin if it stays as a fraction.

This chapter will cover the following topics:

- Understanding the meaning and benefits of ratio analysis
- Learning the various classes of ratios
- Interpreting ratios
- Understanding the limitations of ratio analysis

Understanding the meaning and benefits of ratio analysis

A ratio is calculated by dividing one item by another. In our case, we are looking at financial statements, so the items will come from there, such as profit divided by turnover. However, you do not pick items from the financial statements at random and divide them. You select items whose ratio is meaningful and provides information that will aid decision making. In the example of profit divided by turnover, this ratio, otherwise called *profit margin*, tells you how much profit is generated for every Naira of turnover.

Ratios are usually expressed as percentages but also as *times* or *days*, so a profit margin of 20% means that after all relevant deductions, the company retains 20% of turnover as profit. In other words, the profit for the period is 20% of turnover.

The ratios on their own when calculated for one period are useful in directing the attention of management and section heads to areas of concern. However, management has access to other internal information not available to third parties and can therefore extract more meaning from ratios for the year. It would therefore be more useful if the ratios were calculated over a period of time so that a trend can be established. This is particularly important for the company's external interest groups, such as investors. Investors, for example, only have access to published financial statements. Ratios, which are prepared from the financial statements, are therefore of particular significance to investors and other external interest groups. Ratios should be calculated over a number of years in order to ensure that the results are a true reflection of the company's performance and potential. The results can then be compared with similar companies and the norm for the industry in which the company operates. They can also be used as a basis for forecasting.

Learning the various classes of ratios

There are thousands of ratios and we could easily get carried away with them. However, ratios can be classified into five broad categories:

- Profitability
- Liquidity
- Efficiency
- Debt management
- Market ratios

We will examine a few examples from each of these categories in the following sections.

Profitability

These ratios measure how capable a company is at converting turnover into profit. Profitability ratios are usually referred to as *margin*, which generally means divided by turnover. So, we have the *gross profit margin*, calculated as follows:

$$\frac{Gross\ Profit\ \%}{Turnover}$$

Gross profit is the turnover less cost of sales. Sometimes, when a company makes a loss, you can still take some comfort if there is a gross profit. This means that the direct costs have been covered and there is some contribution toward overheads or administrative expenses. Once a company has been in business for a number of years, the gross profit margin will tend to be fairly constant from one year to another, as it often reflects the company's markup policy, which does not usually change frequently. If the gross profit margin (or simply gross margin) is very low or even negative, then it is fair to conclude that the company is in trouble and efforts should be made to improve this ratio to avoid the company going bust. This ratio is of particular importance to management, who set the markup policy of the company.

There are other categories of profit whose margin can be calculated. The relevance of the profit margins will depend on which interest group you belong to.

Providers of debt expect repayment of the principal debt plus interest. They will therefore be interested in the profit before interest, referred to as **Earnings Before Interest and Tax (EBIT)**. The EBIT margin is calculated as follows:

$$\frac{EBIT\ \%}{Turnover}$$

The higher the margin, the more confident the investors are that the company can repay principal and interest as they fall due. Equity holders, shareholders, are the last to be considered for distribution of a company's profits. Only after depreciation, interest, and taxation do you arrive at profit available for distribution to shareholders in the form of dividends, for example. Equity holders will therefore be particularly interested in **Profit After Tax** (**PAT**). The profitability ratio they will be most interested in is the PAT margin, which is calculated as follows:

$$\frac{PAT \ \%}{Turnover}$$

Earnings Before Interest, Taxation, Depreciation and Amortization (EBITDA) is popular among some analysts as they feel that it allows the user to observe the company's performance before it is influenced by the **Capital Expenditure (CAPEX)** policy in the form of depreciation, debt appetite in the form of interest, and government policy in the form of taxation. EBITDA is therefore considered a purer indicator of a company's financial health. The EBITDA margin is calculated as follows:

$$\frac{EBITDA \ \%}{Turnover}$$

The larger the margin the more financially healthy the company.

Liquidity ratios

Liquidity is one of the most important indicators of whether a company will be able to meet its obligations as they fall due – in other words, whether it is a growing concern and will continue to exist for the foreseeable future. Liquidity ratios compare a company's current assets with its current liabilities.

If the short-term liabilities are not sufficiently covered by short-term assets, that is the first sign that management needs to take action to prevent the company from facing issues. The current ratio is calculated as follows:

$$\frac{Current \ Assets}{Current \ Liabilities}$$

It is difficult to specify what figure represents a good current ratio. However, a ratio of 1.5 to 2 is generally considered to be adequate. A much lower figure would indicate the company may be struggling to meet its liabilities as they fall due. On the other hand, a very high ratio would indicate that cash is being tied up, which could be used to earn income. Current assets are made up broadly of inventory, trade receivables, and cash.

The quick ratio recognizes that inventory is not as readily convertible to cash as the other current assets and compares current assets less inventory with current liabilities. The quick ratio is calculated as follows:

$$\frac{Current\ Assets\ -\ Inventory}{Current\ Liabilities}$$

The strictest test of liquidity is the acid test, which compares cash with current liabilities. The acid test is as follows:

$$\frac{Cash}{Current\ Liabilities}$$

This ratio looks at a worst-case scenario. It shows how well a company is able to meet an immediate demand for settlement of its short-term creditors.

Efficiency ratios

Efficiency ratios measure how well a company uses its assets and manages its liabilities in order to generate income.

These ratios are also discussed in *Chapter 6, Understanding Project and Building Assumptions*. Let's look at some examples of efficiency ratios in the following sections.

Inventory days

This is one of the key ratios we use in modeling:

$$\frac{Average\ Inventory}{Daily\ Cost\ of\ Goods\ Sold}$$

Average inventory is obtained by taking the average of opening and closing inventory. Daily cost of goods sold is obtained by dividing the cost of goods sold for the year by 365. The result is expressed in days and represents the amount of time inventory stays before it is sold.

The company should keep enough stock to satisfy customer demand without delays. However, keeping too much stock or holding on to stock for too long will lead to additional costs. Management will have to find a balance between the two.

Accounts receivable (debtor) days

This is another very important ratio and is calculated as follows:

$$\frac{Average\ Accounts\ Receivable}{Daily\ Credit\ Sales}$$

Average accounts receivable is obtained by taking the average of opening and closing accounts receivable. The daily sales value is obtained by dividing sales for the year by 365. The result is expressed in days and represents the amount of time it takes the customers to pay for goods bought from the company on credit.

Management needs to give customers enough time to pay for goods and services in order to encourage them to continue doing business with the company. However, the credit terms should not be too liberal as this could result in cash flow problems.

Accounts payable (creditor) days

Another good indicator of management efficiency is creditor days.

$$\frac{Average\ Accounts\ Payable}{Daily\ Cost\ of\ Goods\ Sold}$$

Average accounts payable is obtained by taking the average of opening and closing accounts payable. The daily cost of goods sold is obtained by dividing the cost of goods sold for the year by 365. The result is expressed in days and represents the amount of time it takes the company to pay for goods bought from suppliers on credit. Management should aim to take as much time as possible, without alienating its suppliers, to pay for credit purchases.

Average return on assets

The **Return on Assets** (**ROA**) ratio measures how efficiently the company utilizes its assets to generate profit.

$$\frac{EBIT\ \%}{Average\ Total\ Assets}$$

EBIT is the earnings before interest and tax and average total assets is the average of opening and closing total assets.

This is a very important ratio as it gives context to some of the profitability ratios. Consider the following illustration of ROA:

	Company A	Company B
	N	N
Turnover	20,000,000	10,000,000
EBIT	2,000,000	1,000,000
Opening Total Assets	80,000,000	15,000,000
Closing Total Assets	100,000,000	30,000,000
Average Total Assets	90,000,000	22,500,000
Return on Total Assets	2.2%	4.4%

Figure 9.1 – Return on total assets

At first glance, company A appears to be the more attractive, with double the turnover and double the EBIT. However, a closer look shows that company A has utilized assets of N90 million to generate a profit of N2 million, while company B has generated a profit of N1 million with assets of only N22.5 million.

In other words, company B has been more efficient in the use of its assets, giving a return on average assets of 4.4% compared to only 2.2% by company A.

Average return on capital employed

Return on Capital Employed (ROCE) is calculated as follows:

$$ROCE = \frac{EBIT \, \%}{Average \; Capital \; Employed}$$

This ratio determines how efficiently a company utilizes its capital. Capital employed refers to debt and equity capital and can be calculated as follows:

$$Capital \; Employed = Total \; Assets - Current \; Liabilities$$

This is one of the most popular ratios and is used to compare how economically different companies utilize their capital. The higher the ROCE, the more efficiently capital is employed. There is no absolute figure you should target for ROCE and as with other ratios, it is more meaningful when calculated over a number of periods. However, you would expect the ROCE to be higher than the cost of capital.

Average return on equity

Return on Equity (ROE) is calculated as follows:

$$ROE \; = \; \frac{PAT \; \%}{Average \; Equity}$$

PAT is profit after tax. This ratio uses net income or PAT rather than EBIT since interest and tax have to be paid before arriving at the profit attributable to the equity holders.

Rearranging the accounting equation *Assets = Liabilities + Equity*, you get *Equity = Assets – Liabilities*. This is an alternative way of determining equity. ROE measures how efficiently and profitably the company uses its equity capital.

Debt management ratios

Debt management ratios measure the long-term solvency of a company. Leverage or debt to equity is calculated as follows:

$$Leverage \; = \; \frac{Debt}{Equity}$$

This ratio measures the extent to which a company depends on debt financing as opposed to equity financing. The higher the ratio, the more dependent the company is on external debt. A highly leveraged company must ensure it meets the expectation of the long-term debt holders to keep them from calling in their debts early, which could cripple the company.

Interest cover

This ratio is of great importance to the debt holder:

$$Interest \; cover \; = \; \frac{EBIT}{Interest}$$

This ratio measures whether the company is generating enough profit to comfortably cover the cost of external debt, that is, interest.

Market value ratios

These ratios are very useful for investment analysts.

$$Earnings\ per\ Share\ (EPS) = \frac{Profit\ After\ Tax}{Number\ of\ Ordinary\ Shares}$$

If there are preference shares, preference dividends will be deducted from PAT before dividing by the number of ordinary shares.

The EPS ratio can also be classed as a profitability ratio. It is being discussed here because it is a popular market indicator of how much of a company's profit is retained for each ordinary share.

$$Price\ to\ Earnings\ (P/E)\ ratio = \frac{Market\ Price}{EPS}$$

The P/E ratio is a measure of how much investors are willing to pay for the company's profit or earnings.

Interpreting ratios

Investors and other external interest groups of a company usually only have access to the financial statements of a company. However, the financials on their own are of limited use when trying to assess a company. Ratios are a valuable tool for such interest groups, giving them the opportunity to assess companies in a standardized manner using widely accepted parameters.

It is usually very subjective to try and compare companies of different sizes, geographical locations, fiscal jurisdictions, and nature. Ratio analysis provides a level playing field by placing emphasis on performance rather than the absolute size of turnover or profit. Efficiency, profitability, and liquidity are more or less independent of the absolute size of the individual parameters involved, such as turnover, assets, profit, and liabilities.

Ratio analysis allows the comparison of diverse companies, and also allows analysts to set benchmarks for the different ratios so that upcoming companies can assess their performance against these benchmarks and identify areas where they need to improve as well as those areas where they are doing well.

Management can use ratio analysis to monitor the performance of department heads. They could use them to set targets and thresholds for rewards or bonuses. If ratios are calculated over several periods, they may reveal a trend that could highlight impending difficulties that can then be addressed before they crystallize.

Understanding the limitations of ratio analysis

It is important to realize that ratios do not actually solve any problems. They merely highlight trends and exceptions that can then be acted upon. Definitions of ratios often vary from one analyst to another. Examples of this are the quick ratio and the acid test. Some analysts refer to the ratio of current assets less inventory divided by current liabilities as the quick ratio while some others refer to that as the acid test.

One school of thought uses the year-end balances for assets in ROA and equity and long-term debt in ROCE. Another school of thought recognizes that companies can manipulate this ratio by posting significant transactions at the year-end, only to reverse them in the new year. They therefore use the average of those balances, which will counter such practices. These differences in approach can lead to vastly different results.

Another criticism of ratio analysis is that it uses historical values and does not consider changes in market value.

Finally, ratio analysis by its nature only looks at quantitative results, the monetary implications of the ratios, and trends. An assessment of a company cannot be complete without considering qualitative features such as social responsibility, business models, market share, the quality of management, and the effect of operations on the environment.

Summary

In this chapter, we have taken a detailed look at ratio analysis in order to understand why it is a useful exercise, how to select and prepare ratios, how to interpret ratios, and when it might be necessary to take action on certain trends. In *Chapter 10, Valuation*, we will conclude the DCF method of valuation and arrive at values for the enterprise and for each ordinary share.

10
Valuation

After understanding the three-statement model and ratio analysis in *Chapter 9, Ratio Analysis*, we can now proceed with the valuation of the company using the absolute method (**Discounted Cash Flow (DCF)**) and the relative method (comparatives).

Whatever the reason for establishing and running a company, you will at some stage want to know the value of the business. This could be to identify weaknesses, determine whether the business is growing, stagnant, or deteriorating, apply for a loan, attract investors, establish a reference point as a platform for driving future growth, or prepare for divesting from the company. There are several methods of valuation, but the three main methods will be discussed in this chapter.

By the end of the chapter, you will know the differences between the two valuation methods. You will understand the elements that make up the DCF method of valuation and how they are calculated.

The following topics are covered in this chapter:

- Understanding absolute valuation
- Understanding relative valuation
- Interpreting the results

Understanding absolute valuation

It is widely accepted that the most accurate way to value an enterprise is by absolute valuation using the DCF method. Crucially, this method considers the time value of money. It also considers results throughout the life of the enterprise. This is the closest to the definition that an enterprise is worth the total cash flow it can generate.

The DCF method includes technical concepts and calculations. We will attempt to simplify those concepts; nevertheless, you will not have to repeat the complex computations required to derive some of the more complex formulas necessary for the valuation. They are readily discoverable in textbooks and over the internet.

The DCF method continues from where the three-statement method ends. It begins with the concept of free cash flow. The goal is to determine the cash flows generated by the company. However, you need to recognize that some of the cash generated is committed, *inter alia*, to satisfying the debt holders and capital expenditure plans. We will therefore need to adjust the cash generated for these items to arrive at the free cash flow. Generally, you would calculate **Free Cash Flow to the Firm** (**FCFF**) or enterprise as a whole and adjust this to arrive at **Free Cash Flow to the Equity holders (FCFE)**.

The first, FCFF, will lead us to the **Enterprise Value** (**EV**) and the second, FCFE, will lead us to the share price for the company's ordinary shares. Much like the cash flow statement, you will start with the operating profit, **Earnings before Interest and Taxes** (**EBIT**). You then adjust for taxation, then add back items not involving the movement of funds, such as depreciation. An increase in working capital signifies a net outflow of cash, which should be deducted. If it is a decrease in working capital, signifying a net inflow of cash, that should be added to your total. Finally, deduct any planned CAPEX and increase in work in progress to arrive at FCFF.

When a company undertakes a project to build or construct a fixed asset, the project sometimes extends beyond the year end. Since at that stage the project is not yet complete, it would be misleading to allocate the costs incurred so far to the asset account. The normal practice is to create a work in progress account and post all expenditures on unfinished projects to this account. As soon as the projects are concluded, the balance on the account is transferred to the appropriate property, plant and equipment, or fixed asset account. The following figure shows the calculation of FCFF, projected over 5 years:

A	B	C	J	K	L	M	N
1							
2	(Unless otherwise specified, all financials are		**Y06F**	**Y07F**	**Y08F**	**Y09F**	**Y10F**
3							
4	**DCF Valuation using FCFF**						
5							
6	EBIT		55,658	66,822	78,542	90,844	103,754
7	Tax Rate (%)						
8	EBIT*(1-t)		38,961	46,776	54,980	63,591	72,628
9	Add: Depreciation		30,000	30,000	30,000	30,000	30,000
10	Change in Working Capital		(15,107)	12,028	(15,245)	11,883	(15,396)
11	Less: Capex and increase in WIP		-	-	-	-	-
12	**Free Cashflow to the Firm (FCFF)**		53,854	88,803	69,734	105,474	87,232
13							

Figure 10.1 – Calculation of FCFF

In *Chapter 1, An Introduction to Financial Modeling and Excel*, we saw that funds today are potentially worth more than a year from now. This is because you could invest those funds and in a year's time receive them back along with interest. N1,000 invested at 10% will give you back N1,100 in a year's time.

This can be illustrated as follows:

```
1,000 + (1,000 x 10%) = 1,100
Year1 cash + 10% of Year1 cash = Year2 cash
```

Consider the following example:

```
M1   = Year1 cash
r    = interest rate
M2   = Year2 cash

M2 = M1 + (M1 x r)
M2 = M1 (1 + r)
```

Conversely, N1,100 discounted back to today will be worth N1,000. Re-arranging the previous equation, we get the following:

```
M1 = M2 x 1/(1 + r)
```

In other words, in order to arrive at today's cash value, we need to discount tomorrow's cash value using a discount factor. So, today's cash value equals tomorrow's cash value multiplied by a discount factor:

- In our example, the discount factor after the first year is *1/(1 + r)*.
- After the second year, the discount factor is *1/(1 + r) x 1/(1 + r) = [1/(1 + r)]2*.
- After the third year, it is *1/(1 + r) x 1/(1 + r) x 1/(1 + r) = [1/(1 + r)]3*.

This leads us to a discount factor after year *n* of *[1/(1 + r)]n*.

The idea is that we have now calculated free cash flows for 5 years into the future and obtained monetary value for cash flow each of those years. We now need to discount each of those cash flows back to today's value before we obtain an aggregate of the DCFs to arrive at the EV.

The discount factor for the DCF model is the **Weighted Average Cost of Capital (WACC)**. A company typically has different sources of capital, debt, and equity, with each source having its own cost or expectation from the company. For example, the cost of debt capital would be an interest charge. The tax saved by the interest is recognized by using the after-tax cost of capital arrived at, as follows:

```
Cost of debt x (1 - tax rate)
```

WACC is the average cost of the different types of capital owned by the company. The contribution of each source of capital to the WACC is weighted to account for the fraction of the overall capital it represents. For example, if the debt-to-equity ratio is 2:1, then the cost of debt will have double the effect on overall capital as the cost of equity and the weight of the cost of debt in WACC will reflect this.

```
WACC = (Cost of Debt x Weight of Debt) + (Cost of Equity x
Weight of Equity)
```

This is widely referred to as the **Capital Asset Pricing Model (CAPM)**. Calculating the cost of equity is a more complex exercise. Equity carries more risk than debt. This is because the debt holders are assured of their interest as long as the company is a growing concern. Equity holders, however, have to rely on an ordinary dividend, which may or may not be declared. Equity holders, therefore, have a higher expectation of reward and consequently a higher cost.

```
Cost of Equity = Rf + Premium
```

Here, Rf is the risk-free rate. The rate for government securities is usually taken as the risk-free rate.

```
The premium = β x (Rm - Rf)
```

Here, Rm is the premium for the entire stock market and β is the volatility or risk of the company's shares compared to the market. So, the premium can be said to be the difference between the market premium and the risk-free rate, adjusted to accommodate the specific volatility of the company's shares compared to the market.

A β value of 1.0 signifies that the shares exactly match market volatility. For every 1% movement in the market, the shares will also move by 1%. A higher β value signifies that the shares are more volatile than the market. They carry more risk but also more reward than the market. A lower β value signifies the shares are less volatile than the market, while a negative β value indicates a negative correlation with the market. Negative correlation, in other words, means that when the market price increases, the share price will decrease and vice versa. The following figure shows the equation as well as the parameters required to calculate the cost of equity and the WACC:

13				
14	Risk free rate	8.0%		
15	Beta	0.70		
16	Expected return from market	15.0%		
17	Cost of equity	12.9%	⬅	RFR + BETA * (MR-RFR)
18	Cost of debt	10.0%		
19	Post tax cost of debt	7.0%		
20	Target debt: capital ratio	40.0%		
21	**WACC**	10.5%	⬅	cost of equity * Wt + cost of debt * wt
22				
23	Terminal Growth Rate	5.0%		

Figure 10.2 – Calculation of cost of equity and WACC

In your model, you have projected figures for the next 5 years. However, the company does not cease to exist at the end of 5 years but continues to generate income for the foreseeable future. The DCF method attempts to quantify all future cash flows beyond the projected years using the concept of a **terminal value**. At the end of the projected 5 years, it is assumed that the company has reached a position of stability and will continue to experience stable growth for the rest of its existence. The rate of this stable growth is called the **Terminal Growth Rate (TGR)**. With this assumption, formulas can be drawn up to simulate the growth to infinity and then mathematically rearranged to arrive at a terminal value that represents the sum of all future cash flows, starting from the end of the fifth projected year to perpetuity. The equation for the terminal value is as follows:

```
Terminal value = (1+TGR)/(WACC-TGR)
```

The terminal value is typically the largest contributing factor to the valuation by DCF and tends to ensure that the value obtained using this method is usually higher than the valuation by other methods. The following figure shows the calculation of the terminal value:

	A	B	C	D		I	J	K	L	M	N
1											
2		(Unless otherwise specified, all financials are in N '000)					Y05F	Y06F	Y07F	Y08F	Y09F	Y10F
3											
4		**DCF Valuation using FCFF**									
10		Change in Working Capital					(15,107)	12,028	(15,245)	11,883	(15,396)
11		Less: Capex and increase in WIP					-	-	-	-	-
12		**Free Cashflow to the Firm (FCFF)**					53,854	88,803	69,734	105,474	87,232
13											
14		Risk free rate		8.0%							
15		Beta		0.70							
16		Expected return from market		15.0%							
17		Cost of equity		12.9%							
18		Cost of debt		10.0%							
19		Post tax cost of debt		7.0%							
20		Target debt: capital ratio		40.0%							
21		**WACC**		10.5%							
22											
23		Terminal Growth Rate	5.0%	5.0%							
24											
25		**Terminal Value**					FINAL YEAR FCFF * (1+TGR)/(WACC-TGR) ➡				1,653,309

Figure 10.3 – Calculation of terminal value

Using the WACC as the discount factor, discount the cash flows for the projected 5 years and the terminal value. This will give you the present values for the cash flow of each year and the terminal value, as shown in the following figure:

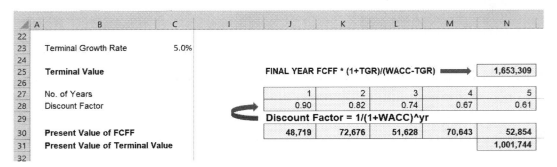

Figure 10.4 – Calculation of the present value of future cash flows

The EV is the sum of all present values of future cash flows.

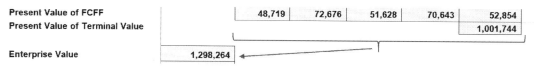

Present Value of FCFF		48,719	72,676	51,628	70,643	52,854
Present Value of Terminal Value						1,001,744
Enterprise Value	1,298,264					

Figure 10.5 – Calculation of EV

In order to get the equity value, you need to pay off the debt holders. You do this by deducting net debt (debt – cash) and any contingencies from EV, as shown in the following figure:

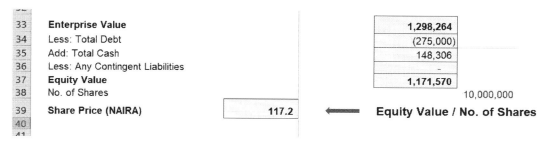

33	Enterprise Value		1,298,264
34	Less: Total Debt		(275,000)
35	Add: Total Cash		148,306
36	Less: Any Contingent Liabilities		-
37	Equity Value		1,171,570
38	No. of Shares		10,000,000
39	Share Price (NAIRA)	117.2	Equity Value / No. of Shares

Figure 10.6 – Calculation of equity value and share price

You then divide **Equity Value** by the number of shares to arrive at **Share Price**.

Understanding relative valuation – comparative company analysis

Relative valuation relies on the theory that, in general, similar companies will produce similar results. This may be a bit simplistic, but in a discipline that involves a lot of assumptions and estimates, relative valuation is popular among analysts as it provides a plausible way to arrive at the value of a business that is quick and simple. The actual calculations are straightforward. The difficulty is in identifying comparable companies. The main criteria to consider are as follows:

- **Industry** – With reference to your major source of income, identify the appropriate industry to which the company belongs and look for examples within that industry class.

- **Size** – The relationship between size and profits is not exactly linear. A company with twice the asset base will not necessarily make twice as much profit. There may be economies of scale and access to restricted benefits as a result of size. You should, therefore, look for companies similar in size that may be subject to the same economic influences.

- **Capital structure** – A company that relies heavily on debt puts its shareholders at greater risk. This is because the debt holders must always be settled before the equity holders, for example, in the event of bankruptcy. You should look for companies with similar debt-to-equity ratios.

- **Geographical location** – This is very important as location can have a significant effect on a company's operations. Economic climate, tax, tariffs, and other relevant legislation could differ and this could have a significant effect on the bottom line. You should look for companies within the same geographical location.

- **Growth rate** – A faster-growing company will be more attractive to potential investors. You should therefore look for companies with a similar growth rate.

It will be impossible to find companies that meet all these criteria. You will, therefore, have to use your judgment to select those that are most similar to the company you are modeling. Once you have identified four or five companies, you will then need to obtain a number of multiples, which will be used in your comparative valuation. The most common multiples used for this purpose are as follows:

- **EV/sales** – EV by sales

- **EV/EBITDA** – EV by EBITDA

- **P/E** – Price-to-earnings ratio

There are two approaches to relative valuation, **trading comparatives** and **precedent transaction comparatives**. Let's look at each of these in detail in the following sections.

Trading comparatives

The following figure shows the relevant parameters required for valuation by trading comparatives, set out in tabular form. Trading comparatives concentrate on similar companies in the same industry:

Trading Comparatives					
Company	EV	Mkt Cap	EV/ Sales	EV/ EBITDA	P/ E (x)
			FY06F	FY06F	FY06F
Company A	2,141.0	2,670.3	2.4x	9.1x	18.2x
Company B	1,321.0	3,385.8	2.3x	10.3x	22.1x
Company C	1,456.0	3,623.4	3.1x	11.3x	23.7x
Company D	1,289.0	3,866.4	1.9x	10.1x	21.4x
Company E	987.0	2,970.0	2.2x	9.3x	15.1x
Mean			2.4x	10.0x	20.1x
Median			2.3x	10.1x	21.4x

Figure 10.7 – Example of trading comparatives for five companies

The mean and median of the multiples are taken. Usually, the median is used in order to remove the effect of outliers. Say you have a set of figures, as follows: 3, 5, 4, 3, 22. The mean (or average) would be 7 and the median 4. Looking at the set, the number 22 is clearly an outlier; for one reason or another, it is much larger than the other members of the set. It has clearly influenced the mean to return a figure that does not appear to be in line with most of the numbers in the set. The median, however, by its nature, has neutralized the effect of the outlier and returned a figure more representative of the set. The following figure shows the medians of the selected multiples used to calculate a share price for the company:

Trading Comparatives

Company	EV	Mkt Cap	EV/ Sales	EV/ EBITDA	P/ E (x)
			FY06F	FY06F	FY06F
Company A	2,141.0	2,670.3	2.4x	9.1x	18.2x
Company B	1,321.0	3,385.8	2.3x	10.3x	22.1x
Company C	1,456.0	3,623.4	3.1x	11.3x	23.7x
Company D	1,289.0	3,866.4	1.9x	10.1x	21.4x
Company E	987.0	2,970.0	2.2x	9.3x	15.1x
Mean			2.4x	10.0x	20.1x
Median			2.3x	10.1x	21.4x

	Multiple (x)	Sales	EV	Net Debt	Mkt Cap	Share Price
FY06F EV/ Sales (x)	2.3x	325,582	748,838	126,694	622,144	62.2
	(Median)					

	Multiple (x)	EBITDA	EV	Net Debt	Mkt Cap	Share Price
FY06F EV/ EBITDA (x)	10.1x	58,908	594,971	126,694	468,277	46.8
	(Median)					

	Multiple (x)	PAT	Mkt Cap	Share Price
FY06F P/ E (x)	21.4x	20,236	433,042	43.3

Figure 10.8 – Calculation of EV and share price using trading comparatives

The EV is derived as follows:

```
Multiple = EV/Sales
EV = Sales x Multiple
```

The median for the multiple, EV/Sales, is 2.3.

The sales for the company you are reviewing is 325.582 (N'thousands).

```
EV = 325,582 x 2.3
EV = 748,838
```

To get the equity value, we need to deduct a net debt of 126,694:

```
Equity = 748,838 - 126,694 = 622,144 (N'thousands)
```

The number of shares is 100 million.

```
Share price = 622,144/100,000,000 x 10³
```

```
Share price = N62.2
```

Using EV/EBITDA, the share price is N46.8.

```
Using P/E ratio Share price = N43.3
```

Precedent transaction comparative

This method looks at similar-sized companies that have recently undertaken similar transactions and assumes the price at which the securities changed hands. The following figure shows a table of similar transactions with their multiples:

Transaction Comparatives					
Transaction	Year	EV/sales (x)	EV/EBITDA (x)	P/E (x)	% stake
Acquisition	FY03	2.7x	11.7x	23.0x	100.0%
Acquisition	FY03	1.5x	7.2x	13.3x	60.0%
Investment	FY03	3.0x	10.0x	17.5x	22.0%
Investment	FY02	1.8x	5.9x	11.7x	10.0%
Investment	FY01	2.8x	12.2x	19.5x	35.0%
Mean		2.4x	9.4x	17.0x	
Median		2.7x	10.0x	17.5x	

Figure 10.9 – EV by EBITDA multiples

The share price computations are shown in the following figure:

Transaction Comparatives

Transaction	Year	EV/sales (x)	EV/EBITDA (x)	P/E (x)	% stake
Acquisition	FY03	2.7x	11.7x	23.0x	100.0%
Acquisition	FY03	1.5x	7.2x	13.3x	60.0%
Investment	FY03	3.0x	10.0x	17.5x	22.0%
Investment	FY02	1.8x	5.9x	11.7x	10.0%
Investment	FY01	2.8x	12.2x	19.5x	35.0%
Mean		2.4x	9.4x	17.0x	
Median		2.7x	10.0x	17.5x	

	(Median) Multiple (x)	Sales	EV	Net Debt	Mkt Cap	Share Price
FY05F EV/ Sales (x)	2.7x	325,582	879,071	126,694	752,377	75.2

	(Median) Multiple (x)	EBITDA	EV	Net Debt	Mkt Cap	Share Price
FY05F EV/ EBITDA (x)	10.0x	58,908	589,080	126,694	462,386	46.2

	(Median) Multiple (x)	PAT	Mkt Cap	Share Price
FY05F P/ E (x)	17.5x	20,236	354,123	35.4

Figure 10.10 – EV and share price using transaction comparatives

Here are the values of EV and share price:

- Using EV/Sales, share price = N75.2.
- Using EV/EBITDA, share price = N46.2.
- Using the P/E ratio, share price = N35.4.

This results in a range of share price values from N35.4 to N75.2.

Interpreting the results

A summary of the results is shown in the following figure:

Summary of Results		
Method	**Lowest (N)**	**Highest (N)**
DCF	117.2	117.2
Trading Comparatives	43.3	62.2
Transaction Comarativ	35.4	75.2

Figure 10.11 – Summary of valuation results

These results can be displayed in graphical form in what is referred to as a "football field." It gets its name from the way the different valuations are scattered around the chart like football players. To do this, we start by expanding our previous table, as follows:

Summary of Results			
Method	**Lowest (N)**	**Highest (N)**	**Difference**
DCF	117.2	117.2	0
Trading Comparatives	43.3	62.2	18.9
Transaction Comparatives	35.4	75.2	39.8

Figure 10.12 – Data for chart

Highlight the table and select **Insert | 2-D Bar | Stacked Bar**. The following figure shows how to select the chart from the ribbon:

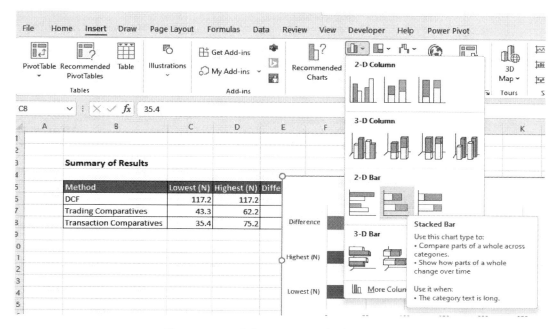

Figure 10.13 – Selecting 2D stacked bar chart

A 2D stacked bar chart is created from the information in the table selected, as shown in the following figure:

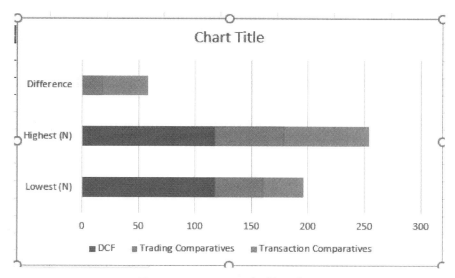

Figure 10.14 – 2D stacked bar chart

We will need to make a number of formatting changes to the chart:

1. First of all, we will select **Switch Row/Column** in order to put the categories on the vertical axis.

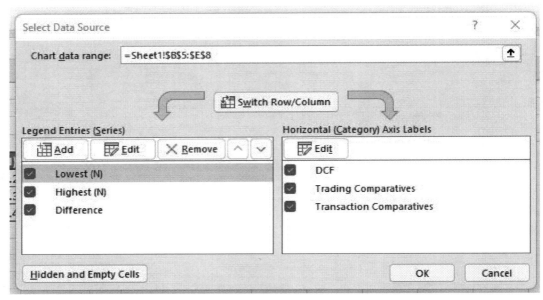

Figure 10.15 – Switch axes

Press the button that says **Switch Row/Column** to swap the axes around so that the categories are now on the vertical axis and the amounts on the horizontal axis.

2. We also want to show the DCF valuation at the top as there is only one DCF value. To do this, right-click on the edge of the vertical axis and select **Format Axis**. On the **Format Axis** sidebar, scroll down and check **Categories in reverse order**. This will produce the chart shown in *Figure 10.15*:

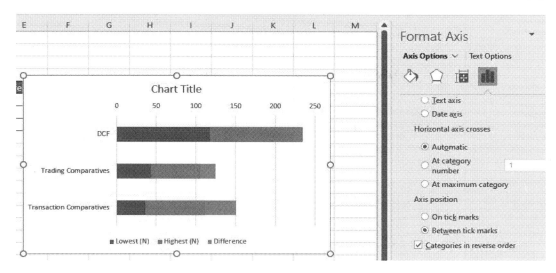

Figure 10.16 – Categories in reverse order

3. Next, remove the **Highest** series. Select any of the bars of the **Highest** series, then press **Delete**.

4. Then, click on any of the grid lines and press **Delete** to remove the gridlines and make the chart less cluttered.

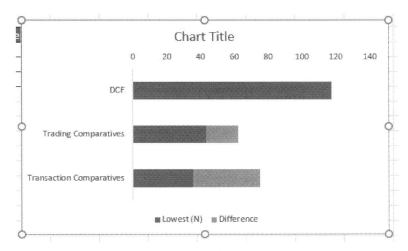

Figure 10.17 – Gridlines and Highest series removed

5. Right-click on the **Lowest** series and select **Format Series**. Then, select **No line**.

6. Now, right-click again, then select **Add Data Labels**. Do this for the **Difference** series as well.

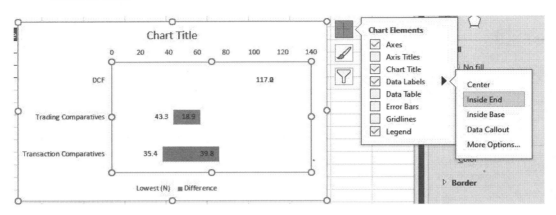

Figure 10.18 – Remove the fill color and add data labels

7. As shown in *Figure 10.17*, select **Inside End** as the position for the data labels.

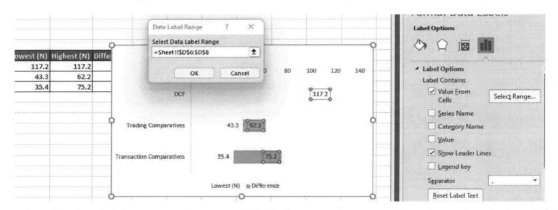

Figure 10.19 – Label values from different range

8. Select the **Difference** series, click the right mouse button, and then click **Format Series**. From the sidebar, under **Label Options**, select **Label Contains Value From Cells**, then return to your table and select the values under the **Highest** column. In this way, you force Excel to display labels for the lowest and highest values for each category.

The chart now displays a splattering of figures like football players on a field, hence the name football field chart. You can also now see that the lowest amount is **35.4** and the highest is **117.2**. From these results, we can make the following deductions:

- If shares of the company are quoted at below N35.4, they are undervalued, and you would be advised to **buy**.

- If shares of the company are quoted at over N117.2, they are overvalued, and you would be advised to **sell**.

Let's summarize the learnings of this chapter in the next section.

Summary

This chapter included a lot of new and varied concepts, and you are encouraged to review it more than once. It is a very important chapter as it represents the final step before we present our recommendations to the decision-maker.

In this chapter, we have looked at absolute and relative methods of valuing a company. We have explained the time value of money and the different formulas used in calculating the EV and share price of a company. We have understood the concepts of free cash flow, WACC, and terminal value. We have also seen how to represent our results in a chart, which can be used as a simple visual aid for decision making.

In the next chapter, we will look at why it is necessary to test your model and how to apply a number of tools to test your model.

11
Model Testing for Reasonableness and Accuracy

In *Chapter 10, Valuation*, we built a complete **Discounted Cash Flow (DCF)** valuation model and obtained alternative valuations with trading and transaction comparatives. We also prepared a football field chart to interpret our results.

In the process of building our model, we made a number of assumptions based on our experience, historical financials, and discussions with management. We recognize that we could have selected a different set of assumptions from the same information so it is only right that we test our model as it is for reasonableness and accuracy.

In order to reduce the effects of the subjectivity inherent in your model, you will need to adopt certain procedures, some of which we have already mentioned, and carry out certain tests designed to highlight the most volatile assumptions and give direct attention to the inputs to which the model is most sensitive.

By the end of the chapter, you will understand why it is necessary to test your model and how to apply a number of tools to test your model.

In this chapter, we will cover the following topics:

- Incorporating built-in tests and procedures
- Troubleshooting
- Understanding sensitivity analysis
- Using direct and indirect methods
- Understanding scenario analysis
- Creating a Monte Carlo simulation model

Incorporating built-in tests and procedures

A financial model, by its nature, is full of formulas and calculations. Although most of them are simple, their volume and repetitiveness create exposure to errors that could cause the most accomplished modeler nightmares trying to track them down.

The following are some of the procedures to adopt in your model to reduce this exposure:

- Hardcoded cells
- Balance checks
- Cash and cash equivalents
- Entering values only once
- Using one formula per row

Let's look at each of these procedures in detail:

- **Hardcoded cells**: Hardcoded cells should be distinguished by using a blue font. The significance of hardcoded cells is that they are the primary input number cells, which contain data that is fixed and will not change (unless it is to correct an error or modify an assumption) and should therefore be formatted in such a way that the cells are easily identified. An example of this is historical information. All other number cells will contain a formula and should be in black font.

The following illustration shows hardcoded cells in blue font, distinguished from calculated cells, which are in the normal black font.

55							
56	**BALANCE SHEET**						
57							
58	**ASSETS**			Hard coded cells in blue font			
59	Non current assets						
60	Property, plant and equipment	90,000	80,000	70,000	240,000	210,000	180,000	1
61	Investments	12,197	11,549	58,106	63,106	58,106	58,106	
62	Total non current assets	102,197	91,549	128,106	303,106	268,106	238,106	
63	Current assets			Calculated cells in normal black font			
64	Inventories	15,545	18,007	21,731	14,530	14,530	20,274	
65	Trade and other receivables	20,864	31,568	35,901	28,054	28,054	39,026	
66	Cash and cash equivalents	7,459	17,252	9,265	110,863	148,306	178,435	
67	Total current assets	43,868	66,827	66,897	153,447	190,890	237,736	

Figure 11.01 – Hardcoded cells in blue font

If a model has to be modified, it is these hardcoded cells that will need to be adjusted for the required change to take effect. Using the blue font reduces the time it will take to navigate to the cells that need to be modified.

- **Balance checks**: Creating a balance check for the balance sheet ensures that you are able to confirm that it is in balance and quickly identify any action that causes it to go out of balance. The balance check should be conspicuous and differentiate clearly between in-balance and out-of-balance conditions. For the balance sheet to be in balance, *Total assets less current liabilities* must be equal to *Total equity and non-current liabilities*.

Since our model is fully integrated, any adjustment anywhere in the model will filter through to the balance sheet and either maintain the balance or throw it out of balance. If there is a rounding difference that is not displayed, it will still cause an out-of-balance alert. A rounding difference is caused when some cells have numbers with decimal places that are not displayed because of formatting.

This is why you should use the **Round** function to make sure Excel ignores the decimal figures when comparing the two totals.

The following illustration shows an example of a balance check:

		=ROUND(E76,0)=ROUND(E87,0)			

	A B	C	D	E	F	G
1	**Wazobia Global Limited**					
2						
3	Balance Check			*TRUE*	*TRUE*	*TRUE*
4						
5	(Unless otherwise speci		Units	Y01A	Y02A	Y03A
75						
76	Total Assets less current liabilities			133,535	142,322	179,172
77		Balance Check				
78	Non current liabilities					
79	Unsecured loans			40,000	35,000	30,000
80	Other non current liabilities			5,000	5,000	5,000
81	Total non current liabilities			45,000	40,000	35,000
82	Equity					
83	Share capital			70,000	70,000	70,000
84	Retained earnings			18,535	32,322	74,172
85	Total equity			88,535	102,322	144,172
86						
87	Total equity and non current liabili			133,535	142,322	179,172

Figure 11.02 – illustration of balance check and use of the Round function

- **Cash and cash equivalents**: Cash and cash equivalents on the balance sheet should be the same as the closing cash balance for the corresponding year in the cash flow statement. This gives some assurance that, up to that point, the model is mathematically accurate.

- **Entering values only once**: If there is a need to enter a value again, simply refer to the cell containing the original entry of that value. This reduces the exposure to error and ensures that if that value has to be modified, you would only need to adjust the original entry and all other occurrences will be updated accordingly.

- **Using one formula per row**: Make use of Excel's referencing framework as explained in *Chapter 4, The Referencing Framework in Excel*, to enter a formula once and fill the same formula along the row to the right for the rest of the years.

If done properly, this will greatly reduce the modeling time and reduce the incidence of errors.

We have looked at various practices and procedures to follow in order to reduce the likelihood of errors. Nevertheless, we are aware that errors still occur so we will now look at how to troubleshoot the inevitable errors.

Troubleshooting

It is unprofessional to share a model that is full of errors. You should always check your model for errors and then take steps to correct them.

The following are guidelines to follow when errors are detected in your model:

- **Precedents** are those cells that have been referred to in arriving at the value in a particular cell.

- **Dependents** are those cells that have included the cell in focus in their formula.

The following illustration will be used to explain this further:

	A	B	C	D	J	K	L
1							
2		(Unless otherwise specified, all financials are in N '000)			Y06F	Y07F	Y08F
3							
4		**DCF Valuation using FCFF**					
6		EBIT			55,658	66,822	78,542
7		Tax Rate (%)		30.0%			
8		EBIT*(1-t)			38,961	=K6*(1-$D$7)	
9		Add: Depreciation			30,000	30,000	30,000
10		Change in Working Capital			(15,107)	12,028	(15,245)
11		Less: Capex and increase in WIP			-	-	-
12		**Free Cashflow to the Firm (FCFF)**			53,854	88,803	69,734
13							

Figure 11.03 – Cells connected as dependents or precedents

Look at cell K8. The formula in that cell is =K6*(1-$D$7). The formula relies on the contents of cells K6 and D7, which makes them precedents of cell K8. On the other hand, cell K8 is a dependent of both cells K6 and D7.

On the formula ribbon, in the formula auditing group, selecting trace precedents or trace dependents reveals thin blue arrows linking a cell to either its precedents or its dependents accordingly.

The following illustration shows us how we can use Excel to visualize dependents and precedents. The lines link cell D7 to its dependents.

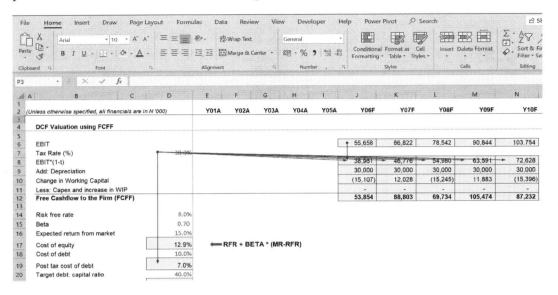

Figure 11.04 – Blue lines connecting to dependent cells

We can see that cell D7 has several dependents. However, since it is a hardcoded entry, it has no precedents. If you have an issue with any cell, tracing precedents and/or dependents can reveal erroneous referencing that may have caused the anomaly.

In the event that there is an error, there are certain techniques you can use to quickly eliminate several possibilities. Let's learn about these techniques in the following subsections.

Show Formulas

There is a useful keyboard shortcut, *Ctrl +* `, that allows you to toggle between displaying the formulas in all relevant cells in a worksheet or leaving them as values. Pressing *Ctrl +* ` once displays all formulas on the worksheet:

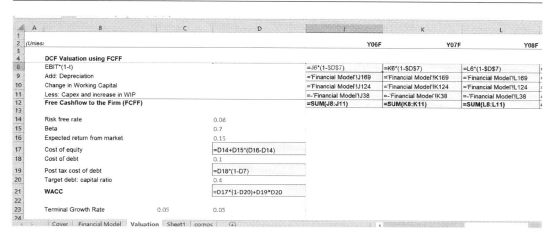

Figure 11.05 – This is the result of using the Show Formulas command

Pressing *Ctrl +* ` again returns the display to values as shown in the following illustration:

	A	B	C	D	J	K	L
1							
2		(Unless otherwise specified, all financials are in N '000)			**Y06F**	**Y07F**	**Y08F**
3							
4		**DCF Valuation using FCFF**					
8		EBIT*(1-t)			38,961	46,776	54,980
9		Add: Depreciation			30,000	30,000	30,000
10		Change in Working Capital			(15,107)	12,028	(15,245)
11		Less: Capex and increase in WIP			-	-	-
12		**Free Cashflow to the Firm (FCFF)**			**53,854**	**88,803**	**69,734**
13							
14		Risk free rate		8.0%			
15		Beta		0.70			
16		Expected return from market		15.0%			
17		Cost of equity		12.9%			
18		Cost of debt		10.0%			
19		Post tax cost of debt		7.0%			
20		Target debt: capital ratio		40.0%			
21		**WACC**		10.5% t * wt			
22							
23		Terminal Growth Ra	5.0%	5.0%			

Figure 11.06 – The same worksheet with the cells restored to show values

This feature is useful in that it allows you to quickly browse through the formulas in a worksheet and spot any obvious errors.

Evaluate Formula

There is an *order of operations* that states the order in which operands (+, -, x, ∴, ^) will be performed by Excel – brackets, then exponents, then multiplication and division (whichever is first from left to right), and then addition and subtraction (whichever is first from left to right).

When you have to write complex formulas with several operands, following the order of operations helps to ensure that the formula executes correctly. Inevitably, there will be times when you arrange a formula incorrectly and get the order wrong, resulting in an erroneous answer. **Evaluate Formula** walks you through the stages followed by Excel, step by step, in executing a formula and arriving at the answer displayed.

For example, the formula to calculate the terminal value is this:

$$FINAL\ YEAR\ FCFF\ *\ (1 + TGR)\ /\ (WACC - TGR)$$

Which, when entered into an Excel cell, becomes =N12*(1+D23)/(D21-D23). With the terminal value cell selected, go to the **Formula** ribbon | **Formula editing** group | **Evaluate Formula**. The **Evaluate Formula** dialog box is launched. The following illustration shows the **Evaluate Formula** dialog box:

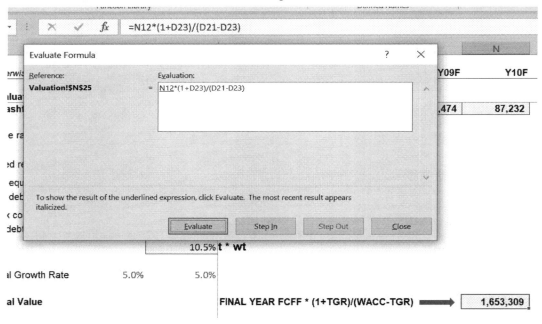

Figure 11.07 – Evaluate Formula dialog box

The **Evaluate Formula** dialog box displays the following:

- The cell with the formula being evaluated (in this case N25)

- The formula itself, which is reproduced in the **Evaluation** box

- Four buttons at the bottom of the dialog box: **Evaluate**, **Step In**, **Step Out**, and **Close**

When the **Evaluation** box is launched, the formula is reproduced in it as shown in *Figure 11.07* and the first item to be evaluated is underlined. This could be an operation (+, -, x, ∴, ^) or converting a cell reference to the value in that cell, or removing brackets from a part of the equation. Excel, by default, will execute a formula from left to right until it gets to a decision point where there is an option to execute an operand of higher rank that will result in a different answer. Excel will then jump to that higher-ranked operand and execute it first before returning to the lower-ranked operand and will continue from left to right.

In the formula in N25, the first step is for Excel to convert the first reference, N12, the **Free Cash Flow to the Firm** (**FCFF**) to the value in that cell. Accordingly, in the preceding illustration, the reference N12 is underlined. The following illustrations continue, step by step, through the execution of the formula.

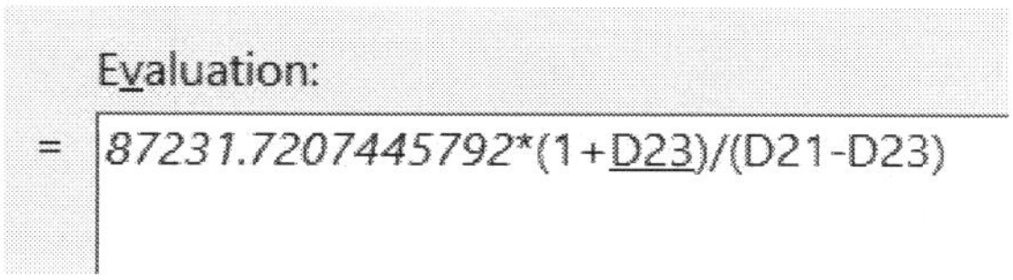

Evaluation:

= 87231.7207445792*(1+D23)/(D21-D23)

Figure 11.08 – Evaluation box with the formula reproduced in it

The reference N12 is now replaced by its value.

Notice how Excel shows the full figure to 10 decimal places, 87231.7207445792, with no formatting rather than the abbreviated amount 87,232, which is a result of formatting. This informs us that Excel ignores formatting and retains the full value of any number that has decimals to 10 decimal places. The formatting is just for presentation purposes.

The next operand in the sequence should be multiplication; however, brackets are ranked higher than multiplication and will therefore take precedence. The contents within the brackets will thus be fully executed before Excel returns to the default left to right sequence.

In the following illustration, the reference D23, within the first set of brackets, is now underlined, signifying that it will be executed next.

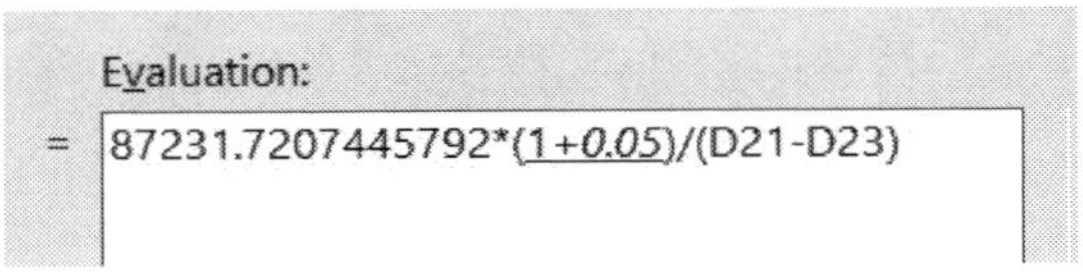

Evaluation:

= 87231.7207445792*(1+_0.05_)/(D21-D23)

Figure 11.09 – Reference D23 replaced by the value in that cell

The reference D23 is now replaced by its value, **0.05 (5%)**, and the line now sits under the contents of the first set of brackets, signifying that the addition, even though it is of lower rank, will be executed next to give (**1.05**).

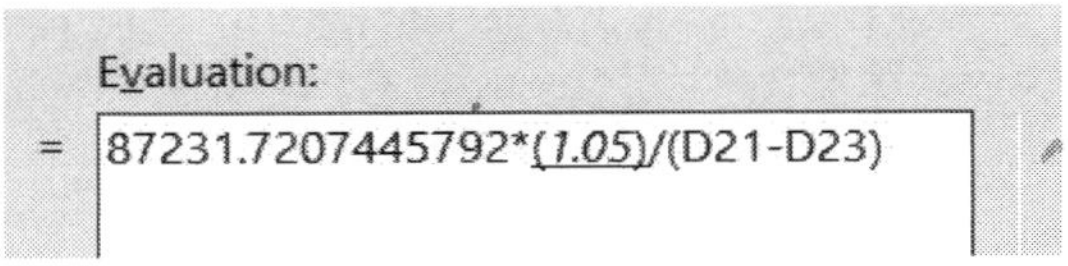

Evaluation:

= 87231.7207445792*(_1.05_)/(D21-D23)

Figure 11.10 – Evaluation box with formula

The first brackets continue to take precedence. The brackets force Excel to elevate the addition to the first rank and execute it before the multiplication.

In the next illustration, the brackets around (**1.05**) are removed, and the line now returns to the normal sequence and sits under the multiplication:

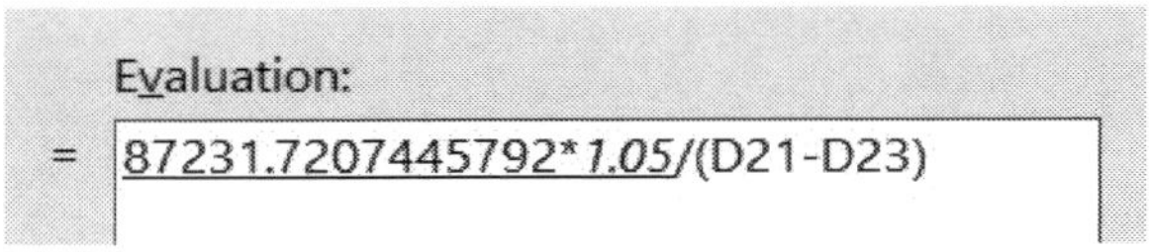

Evaluation:

= 87231.7207445792*_1.05_/(D21-D23)

Figure 11.11 – Brackets are removed and the next operand in line is underlined

The next illustration shows the result of the multiplication still to 10 decimal places.

Evaluation:

= 91593.3067818082/(_D21_-D23)

Figure 11.12 – Result of multiplication and the next in line underlined

The last 2 references, D21 and D23, will then be converted to their values one after the other…

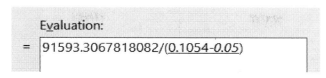

Figure 11.13 – D21 and D23 converted to the values in those cells

With the next two clicks of the **Evaluate** button, the result of the subtraction is displayed then the brackets are removed.

Evaluation:

= 91593.3067818082/0.0554

Figure 11.14 – The result of evaluating the final brackets

Then the final operand, division, is executed to give the result of the formula as displayed in the next illustration.

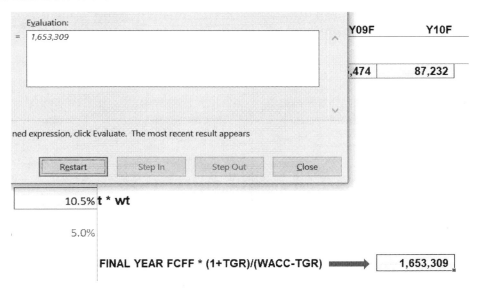

Figure 11.15 – Final result of the evaluated formula

Note that the final result is displayed with the number in the formatted form.

> **Note**
>
> If at any stage an error is detected within the formula, you can click on **Step In** to pause the evaluation, step into the formula, effect the correction, then click **Step Out** to resume the evaluation.

Understanding sensitivity analysis

In *Chapter 10*, *Valuation*, we computed a value for equity share price. As a result of the uncertainty inherent in your model, you should take some steps to mitigate this. One way is to run some tests to see how the share price behaves when you change some of the inputs and drivers utilized in arriving at that value. This process is called **Sensitivity Analysis**. Apart from the volatility of your target value, it also indicates which inputs or drivers have the greatest effect on the target value.

You will need to identify two inputs or drivers that appear to hold prominence in your model:

- **Turnover**: We have already mentioned that turnover is the most prominent figure on the income statement. So we can use the revenue growth driver as one of the items to sensitize.

- **Terminal Value**: Another item of prominence is the terminal value.

We have seen in *Chapter 10*, *Valuation*, how much of an impact this has on your share price valuation. You could use terminal growth rate as the second item to sensitize. The idea is to vary these inputs, see what effect it has on your share price, and plot the results.

Using direct and indirect methods

There are two methods in sensitivity analysis, **direct** and **indirect** methods. Both methods make use of data tables that can be found under **What If?** in the forecast group on the **Data** ribbon in Excel.

In order to make use of the data table, you must structure your data in a particular way. The cell at the top-left corner of the table layout must be related to the target value share price, whose behavior we wish to observe.

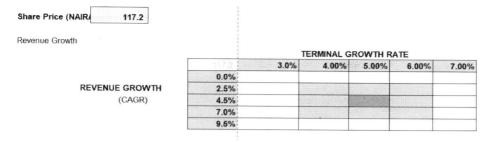

Figure 11.16 – Layout for a data table

That specific position is essential for the data table function to work. However, since it will not be used for anything else, it is shown here in a white font, making it invisible, so as not to cause any distraction. The row input values are entered across the top row of the table. We have selected the terminal growth rate for the row input, with values from 3% with 1% increments up to 7%.

The column input is **revenue growth (Compound Annual Growth Rate (CAGR))** and is entered down the far-left column of the table, with values from 0% in 2.5% increments up to 9.5%. However, the 5% entry is changed to 4.5% to agree with the actual historical CAGR used as the turnover growth driver.

In preparation for the data table function, select the entire table from the cell with the target value at the top left excluding the input/driver values. Then select **Data table** from the **WhatIf?** menu of the forecast group on the **Data** ribbon. This launches the data table dialog box as shown in the following illustration.

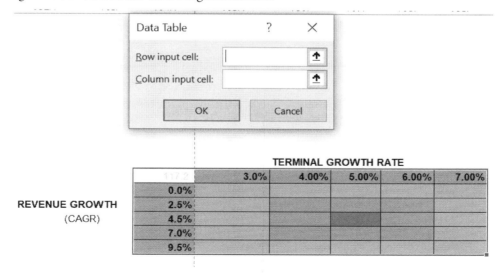

Figure 11.17 – Data selection for the data table and the Data Table dialog box

The **Data Table** dialog box has two inputs, **Row input cell** and **Column input cell**. We will revisit these inputs shortly.

The direct method

In this method, the row and column input cells are linked directly to the model via the cells in which they appear in the model. In this case, the row input cell is the terminal growth rate cell in the valuation section that is linked to your model, cell D265.

The column input cell is the turnover growth driver for Y06F, in the assumptions section, that is linked to your model, J11.

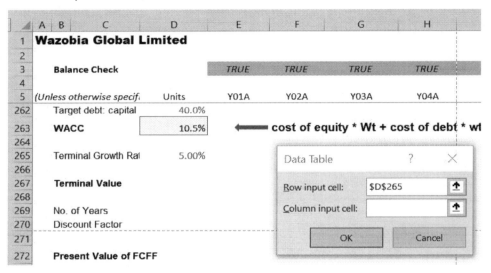

Figure 11.18 – Row input cell

It is important that the row and column input cells are linked to the share price, which is the value we wish to observe. The selected cells, D265 and J11, are connected to the share price by a series of formulas.

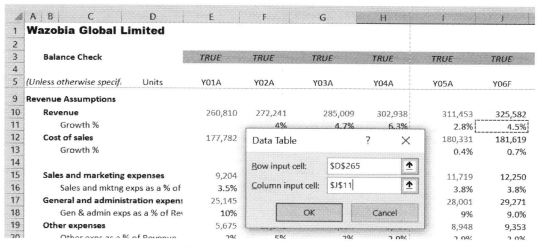

Figure 11.19 – Column input cell

Now press **OK**. When you press **OK**, the data table is filled with the results generated from substituting for terminal growth rate and turnover growth driver in your model, with the alternative values in the data table row and column headers.

	TERMINAL GROWTH RATE				
117.2	3.0%	4.00%	5.00%	6.00%	7.00%
0.0%	80.2	91.1	105.9	127.3	160.7
2.5%	85.2	96.6	112.1	134.5	169.5
4.5%	89.1	101.0	117.1	140.3	176.6
7.0%	94.1	106.4	123.3	147.5	185.4
9.5%	99.0	111.9	129.4	154.7	194.3

REVENUE GROWTH (CAGR)

Figure 11.20 – Completed data table

You can test the accuracy of your data table by looking at the share value at the 5% terminal growth rate and 4.5% turnover growth driver.

Your table has been arranged so that this value is right in the middle of the table, in the cell with the darker green fill. It shows **117.1** compared to your valuation result of 117.2.

This gives you confidence that your data table is set up right and is calculating correctly.

From the table, we see that the lowest share price is N80.2 at a 3% terminal growth rate and 0% revenue growth, and the highest share price is N194.3 obtained with a terminal growth rate of 7% and revenue growth of 9.5%.

The indirect method

This method links the table to formulas that include the variables/drivers we have selected.

1. To do this, we first set up data tables as shown in the following illustration.

Turnover Growth +/-2.5%		Cost of Sales +/-2.5%		Terminal Growth Rate +/-1%	
Change	Share Price (N)	Change	Share Price (N)	Change	Share Price (N)
0.0%	117.2	0.0%	117.2	0.0%	117.2
-2.5%		-2.5%		-1.0%	
2.5%		2.5%		1.0%	

Figure 11.21 – Data for data tables for the indirect method

All three inputs have a change base value of 0.0%, which will be added to formulas that include the inputs we have selected.

Then two additional values of -2.5% and 2.5% for turnover growth and cost of sales and -1.0% and 1.0% for terminal growth rate.

The change values signify the range over which we will be testing the sensitivity of our model with data tables using the indirect method.

2. You then edit the relevant formulas to link the data tables to the model by adding the 0.0% cells.

   For example, the turnover for Y06F, the first year of forecasts, is arrived at by applying the turnover growth driver to the turnover of the previous year, Y05A:

   `Last year's turnover * (1+turnover growth driver)`

   You will edit the formula (`= I10 * (1 + J11)`) to add the base value for the turnover growth driver from your data table, 0.0%, in cell C295: `= I10 * (1 + J11+C295)`.

3. You should then copy the formula across the other forecast years. In this way, you have linked the data table to your model without changing its result.

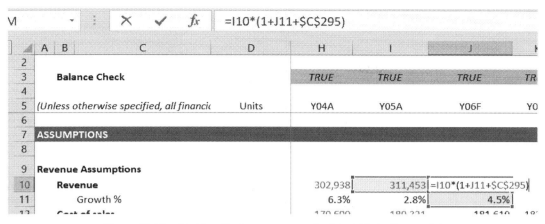

Figure 11.22 – Linking the turnover growth data table to the model

4. In the same way, link the **Cost of sales** data table to the formula in cell J12:

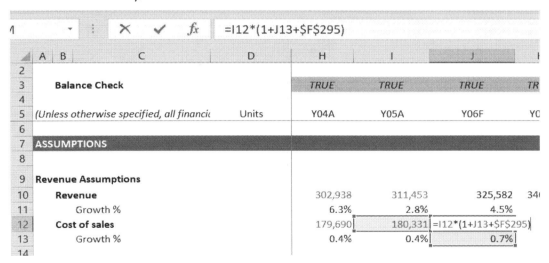

Figure 11.23 – Linking the Cost of sales data table to the model

5. Then link the terminal growth rate data table to cell N267.

    Note that the terminal growth rate appears twice in this formula so the modification has to be to each occurrence of the input.

6. On the valuation worksheet, go to the calculation of **Terminal Value**.

		fx	=N254*(1+D265+$I$295)/(D263-D265-$I$295)							
	A B	C	D	I	J	K	L	M	N	O	P	Q
2											
3	Balance Check			TRUE	TRUE	TRUE	TRUE	TRUE	TRUE		
4											
5	(Unless otherwise specified, all financi	Units	Y05A	Y06F	Y07F	Y08F	Y08F	Y10F		
260	Cost of debt		10.0%								
261	Post tax cost of debt		7.0%								
262	Target debt: capital ratio		40.0%								
263	WACC		10.5%								
264											
265	Terminal Growth Rate		5.00%								
266											
267	Terminal Value				FINAL YEAR FCFF * (1+TGR)/(WACC-TGR)					=N254*(1+D265+$I$295)/(D263-D265-$I$295)
268											

Figure 11.24 – Linking the terminal growth rate data table to the model

You can now go back and populate your data table with the **WhatIf?** data table feature:

1. First, select the entire **Turnover Growth** table.

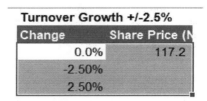

Figure 11.25 – Select the Turnover Growth data table

2. Go to the data table under **Data | WhatIf** or use the keyboard shortcut *Alt* + *A* + *W* + *T* to bring up the **Data Table** dialog box.

The **Data Table** dialog box opens up.

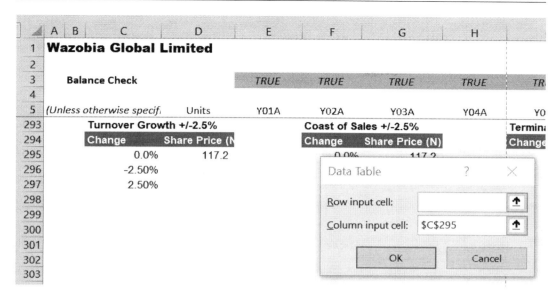

Figure 11.26 – Data Table for Turnover Growth

3. Leave **Row input cell** blank and select the cell with 0.0% for **Column input cell**.

When you click **OK**, the data table will be populated with calculated values for the share price at a turnover growth rate of 2.5% below the original rate and 2.5% above the original rate.

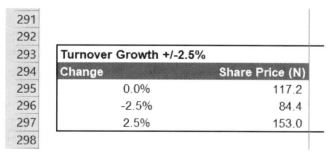

Figure 11.27 – Completed Turnover Growth data table

Following the same steps, prepare data tables for **Cost of Sales** and **Terminal Growth Rate**.

Turnover Growth +/-2.5%		Cost of Sales +/-2.5%		Terminal Growth Rate +/-1%	
Change	Share Price (N)	Change	Share Price (N)	Change	Share Price (N)
0.0%	117.2	0.0%	117.2	0.0%	117.2
-2.5%	84.4	-2.5%	138.3	-1.0%	101.0
2.5%	153.0	2.5%	93.9	1.0%	140.4

Figure 11.28 – Complete data tables using the indirect method

You can check your data table again. 2.5% above the base turnover growth of 4.5% is 7.0%.

At 7% turnover growth and 5% terminal growth rate, using the direct method we get a share price of N123.3, which agrees with the value in our indirect method database for turnover growth.

At a 4% terminal growth rate and 4.5% turnover growth rate, using the direct method we get a share price of N101.0, which agrees with the value in our indirect method database for terminal growth rate.

As they stand, the indirect method data tables are difficult to understand, so you will need to go a step further and prepare a **tornado** chart.

A tornado chart is an effective way of showing the impact of changes in a number of inputs/drivers in one place.

You start off by preparing a table with the information required for the chart, from the indirect method data table:.

1. The first step is to calculate the percentage change in share price from the base value to the value at the negative change.

    We are not interested in whether the change is negative or positive and only require the absolute change. So, we use the following formula:

    ```
    =ABS((new share price - base share price)/base share
    price) %
    ```

    This gives the percentage change in share price with the change in input/driver.

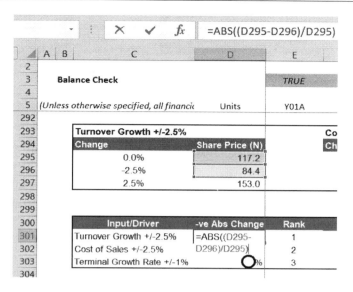

Figure 11.29 – Calculating percentage change in share price

2. Repeat this for **Cost of Sales** and **Terminal Growth Rate**.

3. Now rank the percentage change with the smallest first using the following formula:

```
=SMALL(% change, rank number)
```

4. Copy the formula down the next two rows so that the rank number will change from 1 to 2, then to 3.

   This will result in the percentage changes being ranked smallest to largest. The summary table is updated to show the ranking of the drivers.

			fx	=SMALL($D$301:$D$303,E301)

	A B	C	D	E	F
2					
3	Balance Check			TRUE	TRUE
4					
5	(Unless otherwise specified, all financic	Units	Y01A	Y02A	
299					
300	Input/Driver	-ve Abs Change	Rank	Output	
301	Turnover Growth +/-2.5%	28%	1	14%	
302	Cost of Sales +/-2.5%	18%	2	18%	
303	Terminal Growth Rate +/-1%	14%	3	28%	
304					
305					

Figure 11.30 – Ranking of absolute change from smallest to largest in the summary table

5. Using the INDEX and MATCH functions, which were explained in *Chapter 3, Formulas and Functions - Completing Modeling Tasks with a Single Formula*, enter the appropriate input/driver name beside the ranked output (absolute change). These will serve as horizontal axis labels.

| | | fx | =INDEX($C$301:$C$303,MATCH(F301,$D$301:$D$303,0)) |

	A	B	C	D	E	F	G	H	I
2									
3			**Balance Check**		*TRUE*	*TRUE*	*TRUE*	*TRUE*	*TRUE*
4									
5			*(Unless otherwise specified, all financi(*	Units	Y01A	Y02A	Y03A	Y04A	Y05A
299									
300			Input/Driver	-ve Abs Change	Rank	Output	Input/Driver	+ve	-ve
301			Turnover Growth +/-2.5%	28%	1	14%	=INDEX($C$301:$C$303,MATCH(F301,$D$301:$D$303,0))		
302			Cost of Sales +/-2.5%	18%	2	18%	Cost of Sales +/-2.5%	18%	-18%
303			Terminal Growth Rate +/-1%	14%	3	28%	Turnover Growth +/-2.5%	28%	-28%
304									

Figure 11.31 – Match input name with output

Instead of INDEX and MATCH, you could use XLOOKUP, in which case, the syntax would be as follows:

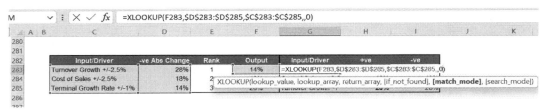

Figure 11.32 – Match input name with output using XLOOKUP

The new XLOOKUP formula effectively replaces the INDEX and MATCH combo.

6. Bring the output to the right of the labels and form two series, one positive and the other negative, of the same figures.

The resulting table is now ready for use in building the tornado chart.

Input/Driver	-ve Abs Change	Rank	Output	Input/Driver	+ve	-ve
Turnover Growth +/-2.5%	28%	1	14%	Terminal Growth Rate +/-1%	14%	-14%
Cost of Sales +/-2.5%	18%	2	18%	Cost of Sales +/-2.5%	18%	-18%
Terminal Growth Rate +/-1%	14%	3	28%	Turnover Growth +/-2.5%	28%	-28%

Figure 11.33 – Data for tornado chart

7. Now create a chart by going to **Insert column or bar chart**, then select **2-D stacked bar chart**. A blank chart will be placed on your worksheet.

8. From the context-sensitive chart design menu, click on **Select data** and the **Select Data Source** dialog box opens up.

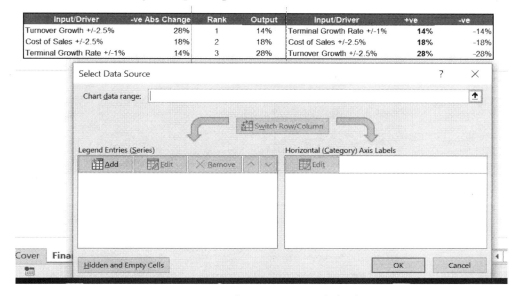

Figure 11.34 – Select Data Source dialog box

9. Now add the two series one after the other by selecting **Add** under **Legend Entries (Series)**. The **Edit Series** dialog box opens.

10. Select the positive output column as the first series.

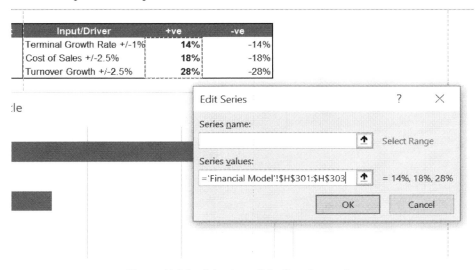

Figure 11.35 – Selection of the first data series

11. Repeat the procedure to add the second series:

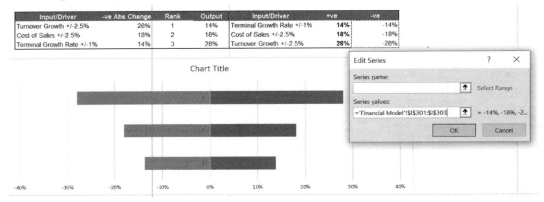

Input/Driver	-ve Abs Change	Rank	Output	Input/Driver	+ve	-ve
Turnover Growth +/-2.5%	28%	1	14%	Terminal Growth Rate +/-1%	14%	-14%
Cost of Sales +/-2.5%	18%	2	18%	Cost of Sales +/-2.5%	18%	-18%
Terminal Growth Rate +/-1%	14%	3	28%	Turnover Growth +/-2.5%	28%	-28%

Figure 11.36 – Selecting the second data series

12. Now select the horizontal axis labels. Click **Edit**, then select the column with the input/driver names.

    This imports the **Input/Driver** names as labels:

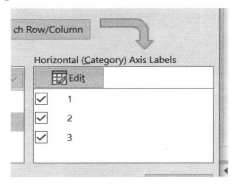

Figure 11.37 – Editing the horizontal axis labels (step 1)

The driver names are now the labels.

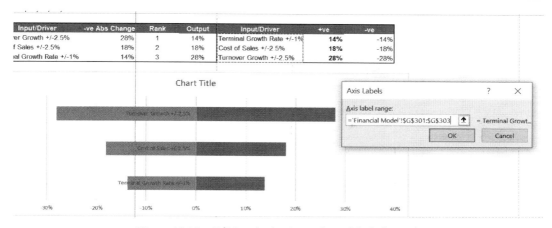

Input/Driver	-ve Abs Change	Rank	Output	Input/Driver	+ve	-ve
er Growth +/-2.5%	28%	1	14%	Terminal Growth Rate +/-1%	14%	-14%
f Sales +/-2.5%	18%	2	18%	Cost of Sales +/-2.5%	18%	-18%
ial Growth Rate +/-1%	14%	3	28%	Turnover Growth +/-2.5%	28%	-28%

Figure 11.38 – Editing the horizontal axis labels (step 2)

The labels will appear against the horizontal axis, within the negative series data.

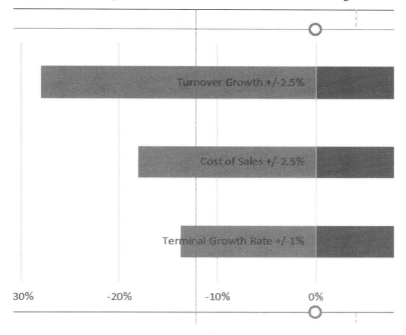

Figure 11.39 – Display horizontal axis labels

Remember that your chart is a stacked bar chart and is therefore flipped on its side so that the horizontal axis is actually vertical.

13. Double-click on the horizontal axis to launch the **Format Axis** dialog box.

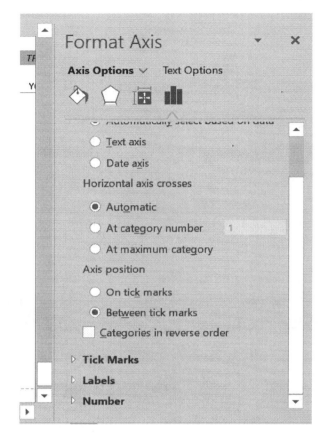

Figure 11.40 – Format Axis dialog box

14. Scroll down to reveal the **Labels** option and click on **Labels**. Change **Label Position** to **Low**.

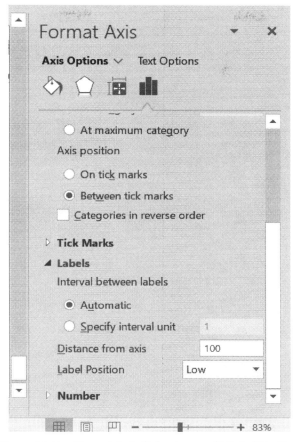

Figure 11.41 – Format Axis dialog box – edit Label Position

15. Select the position for the horizontal axes labels.

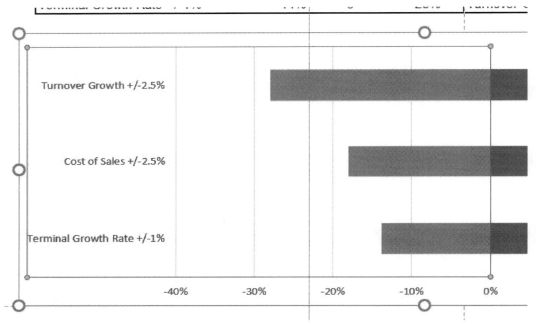

Figure 11.42 – Horizontal label position – Low

Now click on the colored series one after the other and change the color to a more suitable one of your choice unless you are happy with the default color, in which case skip this step.

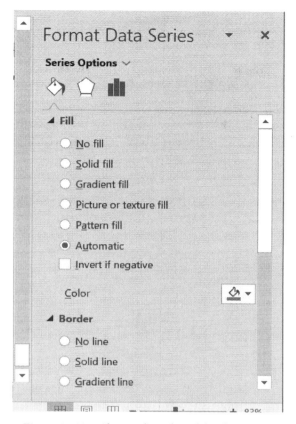

Figure 11.43 – Change the color of the data series

16. Add a chart title and edit it to give it appropriate prominence.

This is the completed tornado chart:

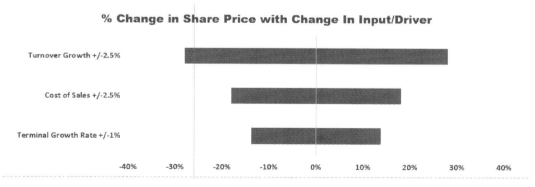

Figure 11.44 – Full completed tornado chart

The chart clearly shows that changing the turnover growth driver has the most significant effect on the share price, followed by the cost of sales and finally the terminal growth rate.

Understanding scenario analysis

In sensitivity analysis, we have selected a few inputs/drivers and changed them while keeping all other variables the same. This has shown us the isolated effect that each of the selected inputs has on the share price. However, in practice, this is rarely the case. Variables do not change in isolation. What you generally have is a number of variables changing as a result of a certain set of circumstances or a scenario.

Scenario analysis usually looks at two or three sets of circumstances, most likely, worst-case and best-case scenarios. For each scenario, you would assume alternative values for selected variables. In selecting the variables, you would concentrate on those inputs or drivers that are the most subjective. Scenario analysis involves substituting all the selected variables for a given scenario in your model and examining the effect this has on the share price.

Creating a simple Monte Carlo simulation model

Monte Carlo simulation is a model that calculates probabilities of different results in a process where there is much inherent uncertainty. The model makes use of randomly generated numbers to obtain thousands of possible results from which a most likely outcome can be deduced. We will look at growth in free cash flow, FCFF, as well as the cost of capital and WACC, which are both integral parts of our DCF model.

FCFF Growth rates can be calculated using the following formula:

$$Y02\ Growth\ rate = \frac{Y02FCFF}{Y01FCFF} - 1$$

Here are the steps to create a simple Monte Carlo simulation model:

1. Calculate the FCFF growth rates for the historical years Y02 to Y05.

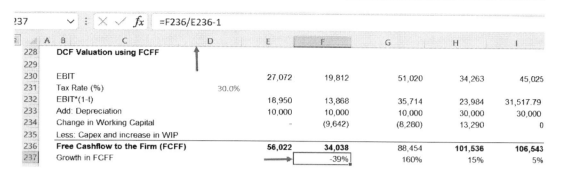

Figure 11.45 – FCFF growth rates 02 to 05

Usually, a Monte Carlo simulation uses thousands of repetitions. However, for illustration purposes, we will limit the number to 100.

2. Take the average of FCFF historical growth to arrive at the (historical) mean growth.

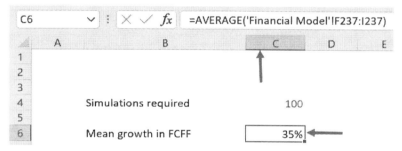

Figure 11.46 – Formula to calculate the average growth in FCFF 02 to 05

3. Now fetch the WACC from the valuation section of our model:

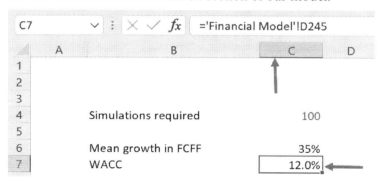

Figure 11.47 – Fetch WACC from the valuation section of our model

We will assume a standard deviation of 1% each.

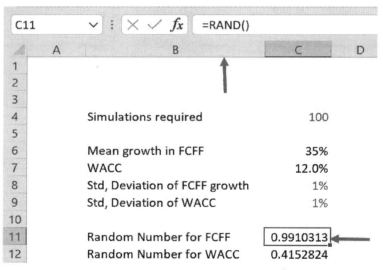

Figure 11.48 – Assume a standard deviation of 1% for FCFF and WACC growth

Standard deviation is a measure of how much we expect our simulations to vary from our starting values for FCFF growth and WACC.

We now create a random number generator for FCFF growth and WACC using the Excel function **RAND** for both FCFF growth and WACC.

Figure 11.49 – Random number generator RAND ()

The **RAND** function generates a random number between 0 and 1. Each time Excel performs a calculation in this or some other cell, the function recalculates and another random number will be regenerated. The number 0.9910313 translates to a 99.10% chance of that value occurring.

With this setup, Excel generates 100 different results for both FCFF growth and WACC. If these results were plotted on a graph, they would follow what is called a **normal distribution**.

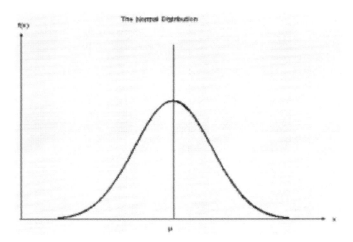

Figure 11.50 – Normal distribution graph

The points are clustered around a central peak. The further away a value is from the peak, the less likely it is for that value to occur. The peak represents the mean of all the values and is the most likely value of the variable.

From the graph, you could select a value from the *x* axis, the horizontal axis, and then trace a vertical line upwards. The point at which it hits the curve gives the probability of that value occurring.

In the scenario we are creating, we are doing the opposite. We are generating random probabilities and we wish to convert these to values for both FCFF growth and WACC. To do this, we use the Excel function **NORMINV**.

This function uses the mean, standard deviation, and probability to calculate a value for the variables growth in FCFF and WACC.

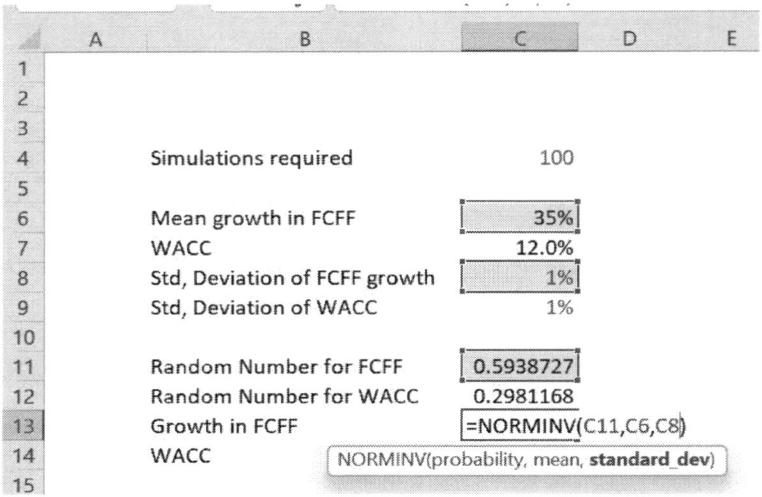

Figure 11.51 – The NORMINV function

> **Note**
> The values in the screenshots are different from one screenshot to the next. This is because new random numbers are constantly being generated as a result of the **RAND** function.

We can manually force Excel to generate a fresh random number by simply pressing *F2* (**Edit**), then *Enter*. Each time new random numbers are generated, new values are created for FCFF growth and WACC. We can copy and paste these new values to another location one after the other in order to tabulate the results. We would have to do this 100 times to cover the number of simulations required by the scenario we are building.

Alternatively, there is a much more efficient way to do this using data tables:

1. Start off by typing 1 in a blank cell.

2. With that cell selected, click the **Fill** icon, which is in the **Edit** group on the **Home** ribbon, then select **Series**.

Figure 11.52 – The Fill Series option

A **Series** dialog box opens up.

3. Select **Columns** for **Series in**, **Columns**, enter 1 for **Step value**, and 100 for **Stop value**.

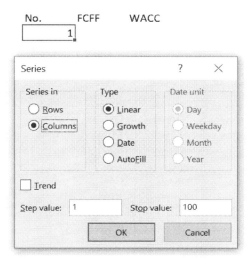

Figure 11.53 – Series dialog box

4. When you click **OK**, a series from 1 to 100 is generated down the column starting with the number 1 you typed earlier.

    Alternatively, you could use the new Excel formula **Sequence** to achieve the same result more quickly.

5. Instead of typing 1, enter the sequence formula shown in *Figure 11.52*.

SUM	∨ : X ✓ fx	=SEQUENCE(E6)						
	D	E	F	G	H	I	J	K
6	Simulations required	100			No.			
7					=SEQUENCE(E6)			
8	Mean growth in FCFF	35%			SEQUENCE(**rows**, [columns], [start], [step])			
9	WACC	12%			3			
10	Std, Deviation of FCFF growth	1%			4			
11	Std, Deviation of WACC	1%			5			
12					6			
13	Random Number for FCFF	0.924493			7			
14	Random Number for WACC	0.309057			8			
15	Growth in FCFF	36.5%			9			
16	WACC	11.5%			10			
17					11			
18	New Growth in FCFF				12			
19	New WACC				13			
20					14			
21					15			
22					16			
23					17			
24					18			
25					19			

Figure 11.54 – The Sequence formula

You only need to enter a value for the rows argument by linking it to the simulations required, which tells Excel that we want the sequence to continue for 100 rows – as simple as that.

The other arguments – columns, start, and step – are all optional and default to 1 (meaning one column, start from the number one, and increment by one), so we can ignore them, close the brackets, and press *Enter*.

6. Now create the first iteration by linking the growth in FCFF to the cell beside the number 1 and link the WACC in the same fashion.

Simulations required	100		No.	FCFF	WACC
			1	35.1%	=C14
Mean growth in FCFF	35%		2		
WACC	10.5%		3		
Std, Deviation of FCFF growth	1%		4		
Std, Deviation of WACC	1%		5		
			6		
Random Number for FCFF	0.511692		7		
Random Number for WACC	0.345056		8		
Growth in FCFF	35.1%		9		
WACC	10.1%		10		
			11		
			12		

Figure 11.55 – Relate FCFF and WACC for data table

We will now use a data table to populate our new table with values for growth in FCFF and WACC.

7. Highlight all the cells in the new table, then go to the **Forecast** group under the **Data** ribbon and select **What-If Analysis**, then **Data Table**.

In the **Data Table** dialog box that opens up, ignore **Row input cell**.

8. For **Column input cell**, select any empty cell outside the table.

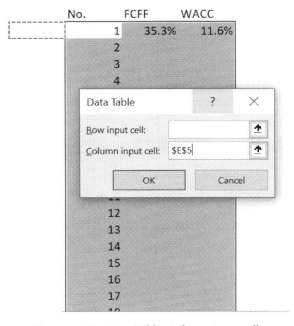

Figure 11.56 – Data Table, Column input cell

9. When you click **OK**, the table is populated with 100 iterations of growth in FCFF and WACC.

10. We then obtain the most likely value for growth in FCFF, given our assumptions, by taking the average of the 100 iterations of FCFF growth.

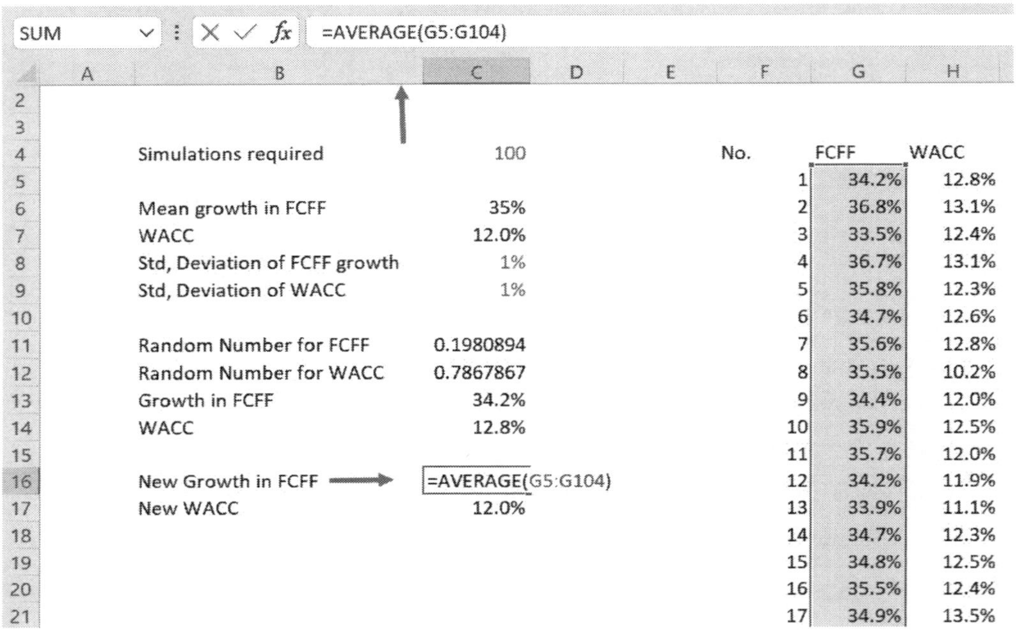

Figure 11.57 – Calculation of new growth in FCFF

11. In a similar way, calculate the most likely value for **New WACC** using the values in column **H** under **WACC**.

12. We will now take our new values for growth in FCFF and WACC and substitute them into our valuation model.

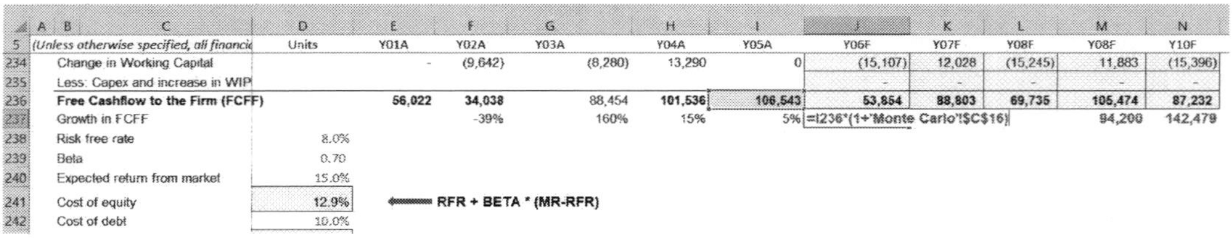

Figure 11.58 – Substitute the new value for FCFF in the valuation model

13. We then substitute WACC in our formula for terminal value.

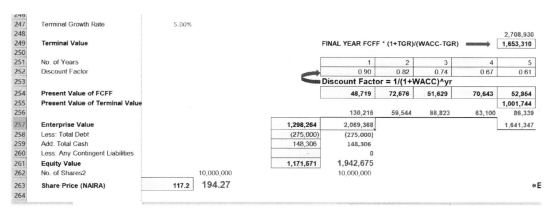

Figure 11.59 – Substitute WACC in our valuation model

We recalculate the present values for the FCFF for the forecast years and the terminal value, the net present value, and so on to arrive at an enterprise value of N'(000)2,069,368 equity value, market capitalization of N'(000) 1,942,675, and eventually, a share price of N194.27.

Summary

In this chapter, we have learned how to build a number of tests and procedures into a model, in order to improve the accuracy of the model. We have learned some basic procedures to follow in order to troubleshoot where errors are revealed in a model. We have understood the meaning of sensitivity analysis and learned how to use direct and indirect methods. We have also learned how to display our results on a chart and to interpret them meaningfully. Finally, we learned about scenario analysis, how it differs from sensitivity analysis, and how to use it, as well as creating a simple Monte Carlo simulation model.

In the next chapter, you will learn how to integrate a trial balance into a 3-statement model of balance sheet, profit and loss account, and cash flow statement.

Part 4 – Case Study

In this part, we will cover case studies on how to build a model to extract a profit and loss account and a balance sheet from raw data. We will also cover a case study on capital budgeting.

This part includes the following chapters:

- *Chapter 12, Case Study 1 – Building a Model to Extract Balance Sheets and Profit and Loss from a Trial Balance*
- *Chapter 13, Case Study 2 – Creating a Model for Capital Budgeting*

12
Case Study 1 – Building a Model to Extract a Balance Sheet and Profit and Loss from a Trial Balance

The task of extracting financial statements from a trial balance can be taxing and prone to error, especially when you then have to incorporate journals and repeat the whole process in subsequent years.

This case study will teach you how to create an integrated template that seamlessly updates the financial statements with audit journals and other adjustments to the original data.

By the end of the chapter, you will have learned how to integrate a trial balance into the three-statement model of the balance sheet, profit and loss account, and cash flow statements.

In this chapter, we will cover the following steps:

1. Introduction – Case study and requirements
2. Preparing a **working trial balance** (**WTB**)
3. Extracting groupings from the WTB
4. Preparing a model template for the **balance sheet** (**BS**) and **profit and loss** (**P&L**), and relevant extracts from notes and schedules
5. Populating the BS, PNL, notes, and schedules from groupings
6. Preparing journal adjustments and linking to the WTB
7. Updating financial statements and troubleshooting to correct errors

Scenario for the case study

Your client, Wazobia Company Limited, commenced business on 1 January, 2021, and has asked you to look at their first set of accounts made up to 31 December, 2021. Wazobia has a competent bookkeeper who prepared a trial balance on 31 December, 2021, and has given you a copy in an Excel file. You are required to perform the following tasks:

1. Create a model template to extract the BS and PNL and relevant notes and schedules from the trial balance. The model should be integrated so that adjustments and updates can be affected in just a few actions.
2. Populate the model from the trial balance making sure that the BS is in balance.
3. Update your model with the following adjustments:

   - It was discovered that the closing inventory had been understated by N10,000,000.
   - You are to make a provision of N10,512,000 for taxation.

Let's begin by preparing a WTB.

Preparing a WTB

You have been given the following trial balance:

		C1		fx	
	A	B	C	D	

	A	B	C	D
1				
2		Wazobia Company Limites		
3				
4		Trial Balance December 2022		
5			DR	CR
6		Furniture & fittings – Cost	10,500,000	
7		Plant & Machinery – Cost	97,500,000	
8		Motor vehicles – Cost	52,250,000	
9		Land	75,750,000	
10		Furniture & fittings – Acc. Deprecn.		1,050,000
11		Plant & Machinery – Acc. Deprecn.		9,750,000
12		Motor vehicles – Acc. Deprecn.		10,450,000
13		Inventory	125,600,500	
14		Trade debtors	195,750,000	
15		Sundry debtors	9,294,000	
16		Prepayments	12,600,000	
17		Cash and bank	57,350,000	
18		Trade creditors		173,060,000
19		Accruals		87,570,500
20		Bank loans		215,500,000
21		Share capital		100,000,000
22		Retained earnings		
23		Turnover		755,800,000
24		Cost of sales	604,640,000	
25		Selling & distribution	37,790,000	
26		Admin & General	52,906,000	
27		Depreciation	21,250,000	
28		Taxation	–	
29				
30			1,353,180,500	1,353,180,500

Figure 12.1 – Client's trial balance

Here are the steps to prepare a WTB:

1. Open a new Excel workbook and copy this worksheet to a worksheet in the new workbook. Rename the worksheet CTB.

   You will notice that the trial balance has separate columns for DR and CR. You will need to combine these into one column, with CR balances shown as negative (in brackets).

   To do this, you will create another column of figures using the IF formula:

	A	B	C	D	E	F	G	H	I
SUM				fx	=IF(C6>0,C6,-D6)				
1									
2		Wazobia Company Limites							
3									
4		Trial Balance December 2022							
5			DR	CR	AMOUNT				
6		Furniture & fittings – Cost	10,500,000		=IF(C6>0,C6,-D6)				
7		Plant & Machinery – Cost	97,500,000		IF(logical_test, [value_if_true], [value_if_false])				
8		Motor vehicles – Cost	52,250,000						
9		Land	75,750,000						
10		Furniture & fittings – Acc. Deprecn.		1,050,000					

Figure 12.2 – Syntax for the IF formula

As you can see from *Figure 12.2*, the IF formula has three arguments. The first argument is logical_test, which is a statement that must evaluate as TRUE or FALSE. In this example, we are using C6 (the DR column or field) > 0.

This DR column contains either positive amounts for DR accounts or blanks for CR accounts. Therefore, our logical test will result in TRUE for DR accounts and FALSE for CR accounts.

So, for the value if true, we will say C6, and for the value if FALSE, we will put -D6.

2. Now, double-click on the **FILL** handle, which is the small square at the bottom right of each cell:

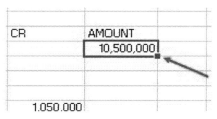

Figure 12.3 – The fill handle

This copies the IF formula you have typed in cell E6 to the rest of the records. Column E is now filled with positive DR values and negative CR values:

E6		f_x	=IF(C6>0,C6,-D6)		
	A	B	C	D	E
1					
2		Wazobia Company Limites			
3					
4		Trial Balance December 2022			
5			DR	CR	AMOUNT
6		Furniture & fittings – Cost	10,500,000		10,500,000
7		Plant & Machinery – Cost	97,500,000		97,500,000
8		Motor vehicles – Cost	52,250,000		52,250,000
9		Land	75,750,000		75,750,000
10		Furniture & fittings – Acc. Deprecn.		1,050,000	(1,050,000)
11		Plant & Machinery – Acc. Deprecn.		9,750,000	(9,750,000)
12		Motor vehicles – Acc. Deprecn.		10,450,000	(10,450,000)
13		Inventory	125,600,500		125,600,500
14		Trade debtors	195,750,000		195,750,000
15		Sundry debtors	9,294,000		9,294,000
16		Prepayments	12,600,000		12,600,000
17		Cash and bank	57,350,000		57,350,000
18		Trade creditors		173,060,000	(173,060,000)
19		Accruals		87,570,500	(87,570,500)
20		Bank loans		215,500,000	(215,500,000)
21		Share capital		100,000,000	(100,000,000)
22		Retained earnings			–
23		Turnover		755,800,000	(755,800,000)
24		Cost of sales	604,640,000		604,640,000
25		Selling & distribution	37,790,000		37,790,000
26		Admin & General	52,906,000		52,906,000
27		Depreciation	21,250,000		21,250,000
28		Taxation	–		–
29					
30			1,353,180,500	1,353,180,500	

Figure 12.4 – DR and CR amounts in one column

3. Rename a new worksheet WTB. Write out field names for the WTB from cell B4 to cell G4, as shown in *Figure 12.5*:

	A	B	C	D	E	F	G
4		GROUP	ACC GRP	ACC DESCRIPTION	2022 UNAUDITED	AUDIT JOURNALS	2022 FINAL
5				Furniture & fittings - Cost			
6				Plant & Machinery - Cost			
7				Motor vehicles - Cost			
8				Land			
9				Furniture & fittings - Acc. Deprecn.			
10				Plant & Machinery - Acc. Deprecn.			
11				Motor vehicles - Acc. Deprecn.			
12				Inventory			
13				Trade debtors			
14				Sundry debtors			
15				Prepayments			
16				Cash and bank			
17				Trade creditors			
18				Accruals			
19				Bank loans			
20				Share capital			
21				Retained earnings			
22				Turnover			
23				Cost of sales			
24				Selling & distribution			
25				Admin & General			
26				Depreciation			
27				Taxation			
28							

Figure 12.5 – WTB field names

4. Copy the trial balance account names to the ACC DESCRIPTION column.

5. Also, copy the amounts from column E in the trial balance to the 2022 UNAUDITED field of the WTB.

6. In the ACC GRP column, enter the appropriate name for each ACC DESCRIPTION, as well as the appropriate group under the GROUP field. The 2022 FINAL field will be the sum of 2022 UNAUDITED and AUDIT JOURNALS.

C11		✓ :	× ✓ fx	Property, Plant & Equipment			
	A	B	C	D	E	F	G
4		GROUP	ACC GRP	ACC DESCRIPTION	2022 UNAUDITED	AUDIT JOURNALS	2022 FINAL
5		BS	Property, Plant & Equipment	Furniture & fittings - Cost	10,500,000		10,500,000
6		BS	Property, Plant & Equipment	Plant & Machinery - Cost	97,500,000		97,500,000
7		BS	Property, Plant & Equipment	Motor vehicles - Cost	52,250,000		52,250,000
8		BS	Property, Plant & Equipment	Land	75,750,000		75,750,000
9		BS	Property, Plant & Equipment	Furniture & fittings - Acc. Deprecn.	(1,050,000)		(1,050,000)
10		BS	Property, Plant & Equipment	Plant & Machinery - Acc. Deprecn.	(9,750,000)		(9,750,000)
11		BS	Property, Plant & Equipment	Motor vehicles - Acc. Deprecn.	(10,450,000)		(10,450,000)
12		BS	Inventory	Inventory	125,600,500		125,600,500
13		BS	Trade debtors	Trade debtors	195,750,000		195,750,000
14		BS	Sundry debtors	Sundry debtors	9,294,000		9,294,000
15		BS	Prepayments	Prepayments	12,600,000		12,600,000
16		BS	Cash and bank	Cash and bank	57,350,000		57,350,000
17		BS	Trade creditors	Trade creditors	(173,060,000)		(173,060,000)
18		BS	Accruals	Accruals	(87,570,500)		(87,570,500)
19		BS	Long term loans	Bank loans	(215,500,000)		(215,500,000)
20		BS	Share capital	Share capital	(100,000,000)		(100,000,000)
21		PNL	Retained earnings	Retained earnings	-		-
22		PNL	Turnover	Turnover	(755,800,000)		(755,800,000)
23		PNL	Cost of sales	Cost of sales	604,640,000		604,640,000
24		PNL	Selling & distribution	Selling & distribution	37,790,000		37,790,000
25		PNL	Admin & General	Admin & General	52,906,000		52,906,000
26		PNL	Depreciation	Depreciation	21,250,000		21,250,000
27		PNL	Taxation	Taxation	-		-
28							

Figure 12.6 – Working trial balance

The GROUP field tells us whether it is a BS or a PNL account, ACC GROUP gives us the appropriate account name for the financial statements for each item, ACC DESCRIPTION is the original title given to each item by the client, 2022 UNAUDITED is the client's trial balance amounts, and the 2022 FINAL field contains the final balances after the audit adjustments.

Extracting groupings from the WTB

The next step is to convert the WTB into an Excel table and then prepare a pivot table to summarize the account descriptions:

1. To convert to a table, place the cursor anywhere inside WTB, then press *Ctrl + T*.

2. The range is highlighted and the **Convert to Table** dialog box is launched. Check the **My Table Has Headers** checkbox, confirm that the correct range is covered, and then click **Ok**.

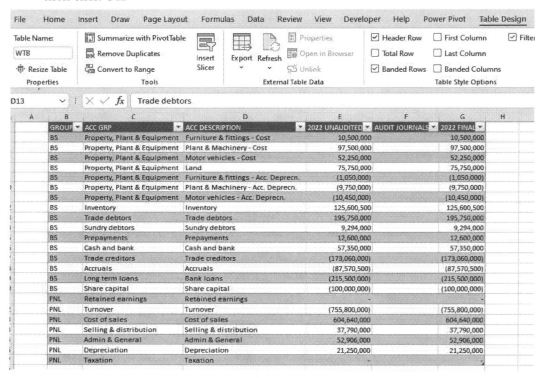

Figure 12.7 – The WTB formatted as a table

3. With the **Table Design** ribbon selected, go to the **Table Name** option at the beginning of the ribbon icons and change the name of the table to WTB.

Formatting the range as a table has several advantages:

-   Type in a formula at the beginning of any field and when you press *Enter*, the formula is filled down the rest of the records of that field.

- You can include the range in formulas simply by typing the WTB table name.

- You can add new records to the bottom of the table and they will be automatically incorporated into the table name without having to first go back and resize the table range.

4. With the cursor anywhere within the table, use the *Alt + N + V* key combination by pressing the keys successively to launch the **PivotTable from table or range** dialog box:

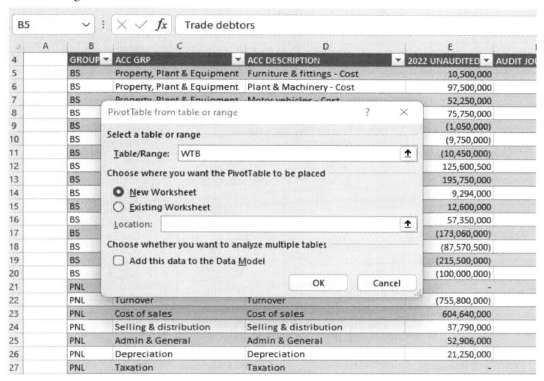

Figure 12.8 – PivotTable from table or range dialog box

Notice how the table name is automatically adopted as the range. Also, we are happy with the default option to place the pivot table on a new worksheet:

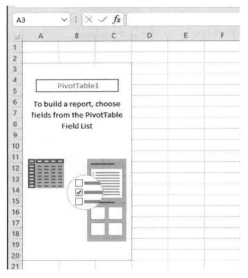

Figure 12.9 – Pivot table outline

A pivot table is launched with the empty table outline. On the right-hand side of the screen, you will see **PivotTable Fields**:

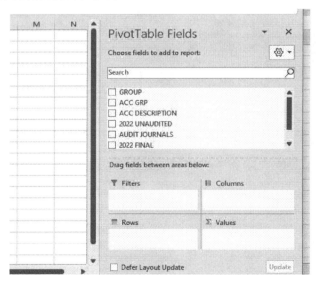

Figure 12.10 – PivotTable Fields

This view is context-sensitive and only appears when the cursor is within the pivot table. Similarly, two additional ribbons are displayed when the cursor is within the pivot table: **PivotTable Analyze** and **Design**.

You should try and envisage a layout for your pivot table, then drag the fields to the appropriate area boxes below **PivotTable Fields**:

Figure 12.11 – PivotTable with data

This layout is ideal for our purposes. It separates the accounts into BS and PNL. It also displays the totals for each group and the grand total, which can be seen to be equal and opposite with the grand total as Nil.

Row Labels	Sum of 2022 FINAL	
⊟ BS	39,214,000	←
Accruals	(87,570,500)	
Cash and bank	57,350,000	
Inventory	125,600,500	
Long term loans	(215,500,000)	
Prepayments	12,600,000	
Property, Plant & Equipment	214,750,000	
Share capital	(100,000,000)	
Sundry debtors	9,294,000	
Trade creditors	(173,060,000)	
Trade debtors	195,750,000	
⊟ PNL	(39,214,000)	←
Admin & General	52,906,000	
Cost of sales	604,640,000	
Depreciation	21,250,000	
Retained earnings	-	
Selling & distribution	37,790,000	
Taxation	-	
Turnover	(755,800,000)	
Grand Total	-	

Figure 12.12 – Pivot table BS and PNL totals equal and opposite

In order to format the numbers, right-click in the **Sum of 2022 Final** column, select **Number Format/Custom**, then in the type box, type #,##0;(#,##0);"-", and click **Ok**. #.##0 indicates that positive numbers should be comma-separated at thousands with no decimal places, (#,##0) indicates that negative numbers should be the same but enclosed in (), and "-" indicates that zero values should be displayed as a hyphen, -.

Preparing a model template for BS and PNL, and relevant extracts from notes and schedules

In order to create the template, rename a new worksheet, BS PL CF Ns. Then, each schedule you prepare will have a banner of light blue with white characters from column A to column E, with the schedule title written in column A. The schedule itself will start with the name of the company from column B with the amounts in column E.

The schedules will be prepared one on top of the other, with each schedule grouped by selecting from the row above the company name to the row after the end of the schedule, and pressing *Shift + Alt + Right Arrow* simultaneously.

When all the groups are collapsed, you get the following effect:

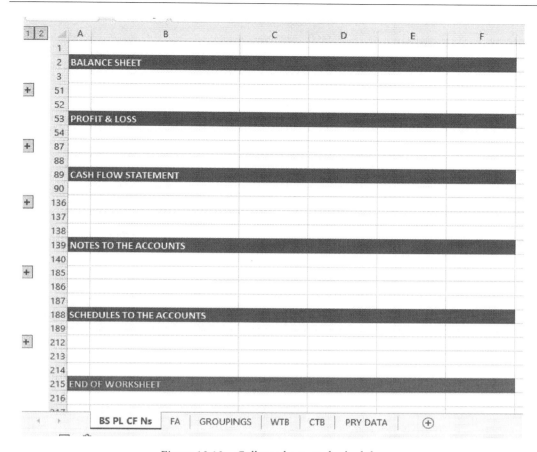

Figure 12.13 – Collapsed grouped schedules

The schedules can be expanded individually by clicking on the plus sign below and to the left of each heading, or all at once by clicking the **2** to the left of the column header A.

Next, rename a new worksheet PRY DATA. Then, type Wazobia Company Limited, 2022, and For the year ended 31st December, 2022 in cells A1, B1, and C1 respectively:

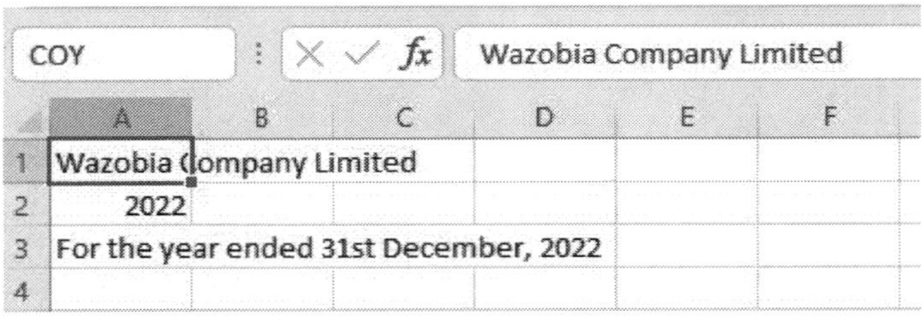

COY		:	✕ ✓ *fx*	Wazobia Company Limited		

	A	B	C	D	E	F
1	Wazobia Company Limited					
2	2022					
3	For the year ended 31st December, 2022					
4						

Figure 12.14 – Cell named COY

Assign names to each of the cells using the **Name** box. With the cursor in cell A1, click in **Name Box** above column header A and type COY. This will name that cell COY so that typing =COY will retrieve the contents of cell A1. In the same way, name cell B1, THISYR, and cell C1, YREND.

Populating BS, PNL, notes, and schedules from groupings

You will now populate the statements from the groupings using the XLOOKUP function. In this function, you will need to specify Lookup Array and Return Array, so to simplify our formula, we will name those ranges as well:

1. On the **Groupings** worksheet, select ACC GRP (Column B) from the first item beneath the header (Row 4) to five rows below the grand total (Row 29). In other words, B4:B29:

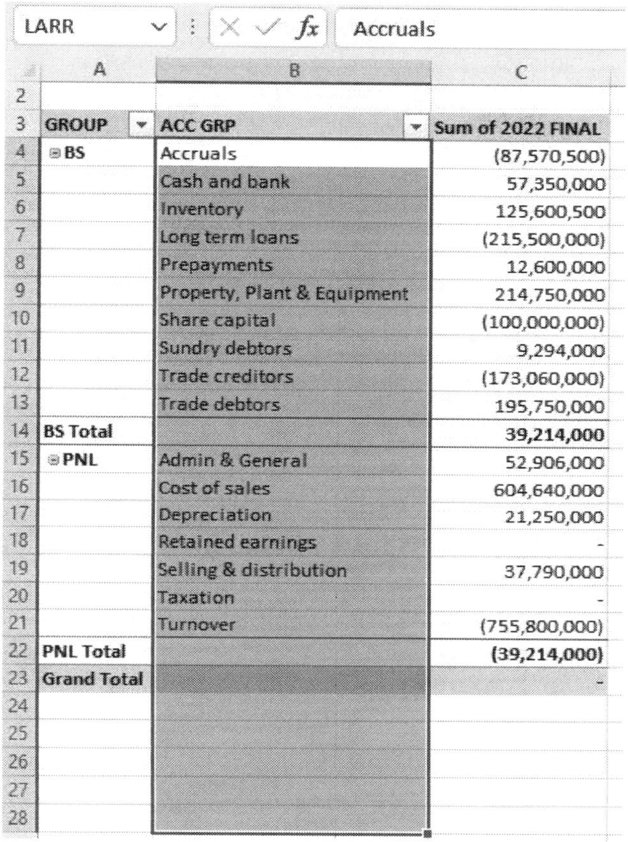

Figure 12.15 – XLOOKUP lookup array

2. Name this range LARR. This is the lookup array. The reason we extend it by five rows is in case we are required to expand our WTB with additional accounts.

3.   Do the same for the `return` array, C4 : C29, and name this range RARR:

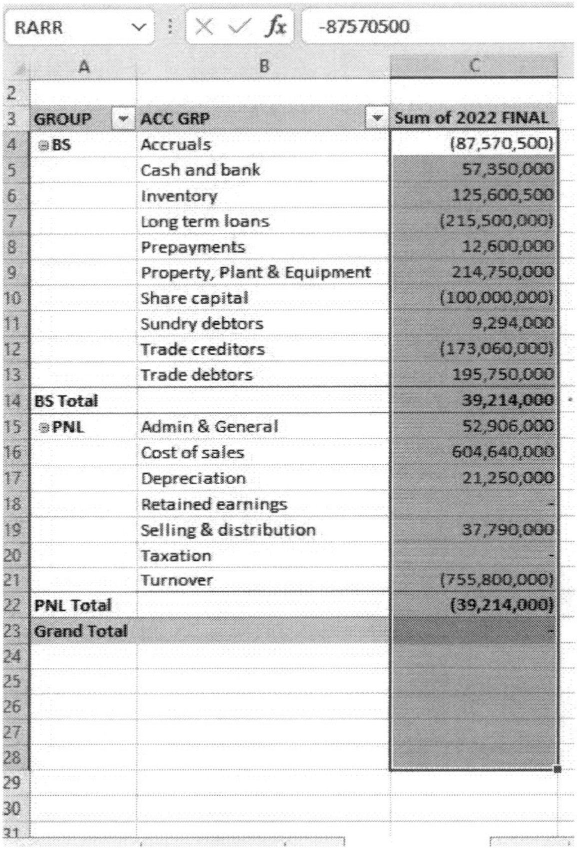

	A	B	C
RARR	⌄ ⋮ ✕ ✓ *fx*	-87570500	
	A	B	C
2			
3	GROUP ⌄	ACC GRP	⌄ Sum of 2022 FINAL
4	⊟ BS	Accruals	(87,570,500)
5		Cash and bank	57,350,000
6		Inventory	125,600,500
7		Long term loans	(215,500,000)
8		Prepayments	12,600,000
9		Property, Plant & Equipment	214,750,000
10		Share capital	(100,000,000)
11		Sundry debtors	9,294,000
12		Trade creditors	(173,060,000)
13		Trade debtors	195,750,000
14	BS Total		39,214,000
15	⊟ PNL	Admin & General	52,906,000
16		Cost of sales	604,640,000
17		Depreciation	21,250,000
18		Retained earnings	-
19		Selling & distribution	37,790,000
20		Taxation	-
21		Turnover	(755,800,000)
22	PNL Total		(39,214,000)
23	Grand Total		-
24			
25			
26			
27			
28			
29			
30			
31			

Figure 12.16 – XLOOKUP return array

We can now populate the statements using XLOOKUP, starting from the schedules to the accounts:

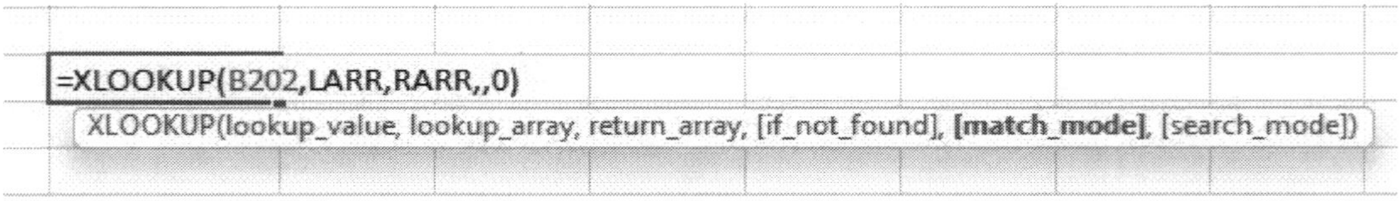

```
=XLOOKUP(B202,LARR,RARR,,0)
XLOOKUP(lookup_value, lookup_array, return_array, [if_not_found], [match_mode], [search_mode])
```

Figure 12.17 – XLOOKUP syntax

When you press *Enter*, the correct value is retrieved from the groupings.

The beauty of this method (which I have coined the **MOCO method**) is that you only have to enter the XLOOKUP formula once and then copy it to any cell where you want to retrieve a value from **Groupings**.

		fx	=XLOOKUP(B204,LARR,RARR,,0)			
	A	B	C	D	E	F
197		Sch				2022
198		1				
199						
200		**Administrative expenses**				
201						
202		Admin & general				52,906,000
203		Selling & distribution				37,790,000
204		Depreciation				21,250,000
205						

Figure 12.18 – Copying the XLOOKUP formula to other cells

This is possible because the lookup array and the return array are the same in all instances, and since your template has fixed the distance between **ACC GROUP** (Column B) and the column with the amounts (Column E), the referencing framework dictates that we can copy a formula with one or more cell references to another location. As long as the relative position of the cell reference/s is maintained, the result will be correct.

In *Figure 12.19*, the original formula is copied down two rows, and if we look at the formula for the **Depreciation** amount as displayed in the formula bar, we see that the cell reference is now looking at cell B204 as the lookup value, which is correct.

You only need to look out for CR balances that are displayed in brackets (). However, all you need to do is put a minus sign immediately after the = sign.

66	5		
67	ACCOUNTS PAYABLE		
68	Trade creditors		=-XLOOKUP(B168,LARR,RARR,,0)
69	Accruals		(87,570,500)
70			

Figure 12.19 – Copying the XLOOKUP formula for negative values

The brackets are then removed and the absolute values are displayed. Continue in this manner to populate the BS and PNL:

	A	B	C	D	E	F
5		**Wazobia Company Limited**				
6						
7		Statement of Financial Position at 31st December 2022				
8						
9						2022
10		NON-CURRENT ASSETS				
11		Property, Plant & Equipment				214,750,000
12						
13		CURRENT ASSETS				
14		Inventory				125,600,500
15		Accounts receivable				217,644,000
16		Cash & cash equivalents				57,350,000
17						
18						400,594,500
19						
20		CURRENT LIABILITIES				
21		Accounts payable				260,630,500
22		Tax liabilities				
23						
24						260,630,500
25						
26		NET CURRENT ASSETS				139,964,000
27						
28						
29		NON-CURRENT LIABILITIES				215,500,000
30						
31		TOTAL ASSETS LESS LIABILITIES				139,214,000
32						
33		EQUITY				
34		Share capital				100,000,000
35		Retained earnings				39,214,000
36						
37						139,214,000

Figure 12.20 – Complete draft BS

You will note that some of the amounts in the BS have not come directly from **Groupings**, but rather via **Notes**, for example, **Accounts Payable** and **Accounts Receivable**.

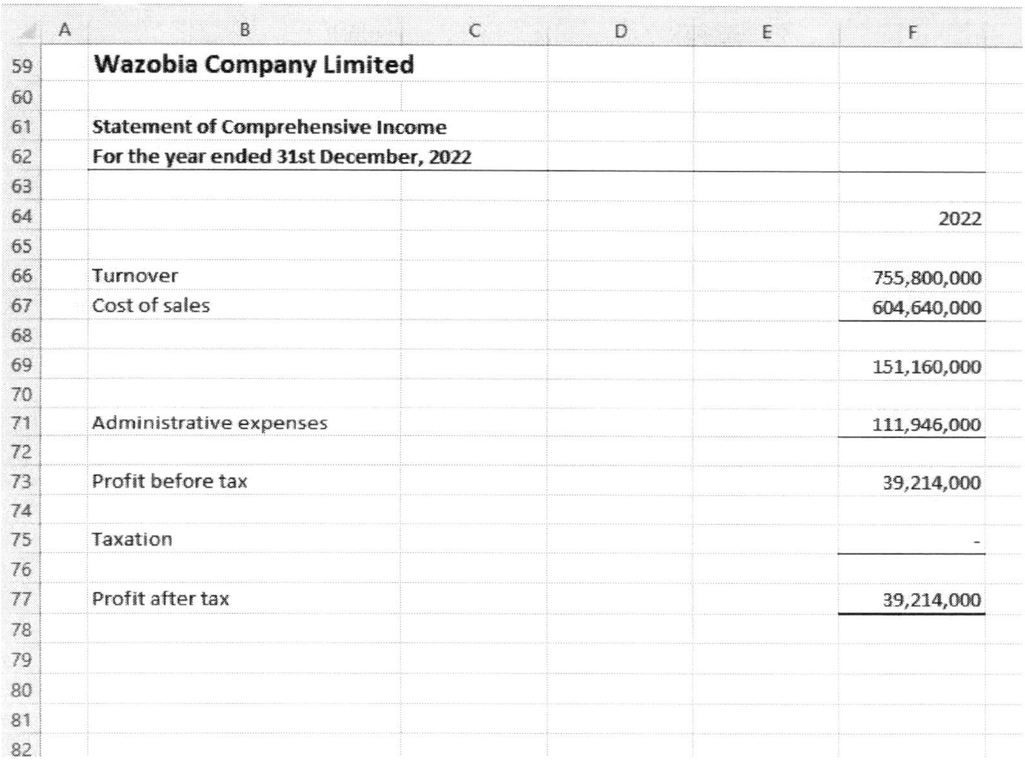

	A	B	C	D	E	F
59		**Wazobia Company Limited**				
60						
61		**Statement of Comprehensive Income**				
62		**For the year ended 31st December, 2022**				
63						
64						2022
65						
66		Turnover				755,800,000
67		Cost of sales				604,640,000
68						
69						151,160,000
70						
71		Administrative expenses				111,946,000
72						
73		Profit before tax				39,214,000
74						
75		Taxation				-
76						
77		Profit after tax				39,214,000
78						
79						
80						
81						
82						

Figure 12.21 – Completed PNL

You now have a complete set of draft accounts.

Preparing journal adjustments and linking to the WTB

You now need to address the adjustments in *Part 3* of the requirements:

1. Create a new worksheet and rename it JNLs. Prepare your journal adjustments in the following manner:

	A	B	C	D	E
1					
2					
3			**Wazobia Company Limited**		
4					
5			Audit Adjustments		
6			For the year ended 31st December, 2022		
7					
8			Account description	DR/(CR)	
9					
10		1	Inventory	10,000,000	
11			Cost of sales	=-D10	
12			Being error in closing inventory now corrected		
13					

Figure 12.22 – Template for journals

2. Enter the DR amount, then for the CR value, enter – (minus) in the cell with the DR value. This way, you reduce the exposure to typographic errors and ensure that your journals balance.

    Note that the account name you use is from **ACC DESCRIPTION** and not **ACC GRP**.

    Now, go to the **AUDIT JOURNAL** column of the WTB and enter the following formula in the first record in a cell:

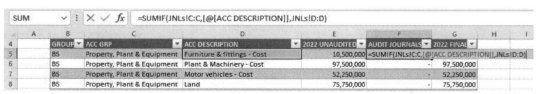

SUM		× ✓ fx	=SUMIF(JNLs!C:C,[@[ACC DESCRIPTION]],JNLs!D:D)					
A	B	C	D	E	F	G	H	I
4	GROUP	ACC GRP	ACC DESCRIPTION	2022 UNAUDITED	AUDIT JOURNALS	2022 FINAL		
5	BS	Property, Plant & Equipment	Furniture & fittings - Cost	10,500,000	=SUMIF(JNLs!C:C,[@[ACC DESCRIPTION]],JNLs!D:D)			
6	BS	Property, Plant & Equipment	Plant & Machinery - Cost	97,500,000	-	97,500,000		
7	BS	Property, Plant & Equipment	Motor vehicles - Cost	52,250,000	-	52,250,000		
8	BS	Property, Plant & Equipment	Land	75,750,000	-	75,750,000		

Figure 12.23 – Syntax for SUMIF

The SUMIF function has three arguments:

- **Range** – This refers to the range Excel will search for records matching the criteria. In this case, all of column C on the JNLs worksheet.

- **Criteria** – All occurrences of this item in the range argument will be aggregated. In this case, Excel will look for every occurrence of **Acc Description** for each record on the WTB, starting with **Furniture & Fittings - Cost**.

- **Sum range** – This contains the actual values to be aggregated for each occurrence of the criteria. In this case, it is all of column D on the JNLs worksheet.

3.   When you press *Enter*, the formula is automatically copied down the rest of the records on the WTB. However, a quick glance at the WTB shows that it is out of balance:

	A	B	C	D	E	F	G
4		GROUP	ACC GRP	ACC DESCRIPTION	2022 UNAUDITED	AUDIT JOURNALS	2022 FINAL
5		BS	Property, Plant & Equipment	Furniture & fittings - Cost	10,500,000	-	10,500,000
6		BS	Property, Plant & Equipment	Plant & Machinery - Cost	97,500,000	-	97,500,000
7		BS	Property, Plant & Equipment	Motor vehicles - Cost	52,250,000	-	52,250,000
8		BS	Property, Plant & Equipment	Land	75,750,000	-	75,750,000
9		BS	Property, Plant & Equipment	Furniture & fittings - Acc. Deprecn.	(1,050,000)	-	(1,050,000)
10		BS	Property, Plant & Equipment	Plant & Machinery - Acc. Deprecn.	(9,750,000)	-	(9,750,000)
11		BS	Property, Plant & Equipment	Motor vehicles - Acc. Deprecn.	(10,450,000)	-	(10,450,000)
12		BS	Inventory	Inventory	125,600,500	10,000,000	135,600,500
13		BS	Trade debtors	Trade debtors	195,750,000	-	195,750,000
14		BS	Sundry debtors	Sundry debtors	9,294,000	-	9,294,000
15		BS	Prepayments	Prepayments	12,600,000	-	12,600,000
16		BS	Cash and bank	Cash and bank	57,350,000	-	57,350,000
17		BS	Trade creditors	Trade creditors	(173,060,000)	-	(173,060,000)
18		BS	Accruals	Accruals	(87,570,500)	-	(87,570,500)
19		BS	Long term loans	Bank loans	(215,500,000)	-	(215,500,000)
20		BS	Share capital	Share capital	(100,000,000)	-	(100,000,000)
21		PNL	Retained earnings	Retained earnings	-	-	-
22		PNL	Turnover	Turnover	(755,800,000)	-	(755,800,000)
23		PNL	Cost of sales	Cost of sales	604,640,000	(10,000,000)	594,640,000
24		PNL	Selling & distribution	Selling & distribution	37,790,000	-	37,790,000
25		PNL	Admin & General	Admin & General	52,906,000	-	52,906,000
26		PNL	Depreciation	Depreciation	21,250,000	-	21,250,000
27		PNL	Taxation	Taxation	-	10,512,000	10,512,000
28							
29					0		10,512,000

Figure 12.24 – WTB out of balance

On reviewing our journals, we realize that there is a new account that was not in the original trial balance and, therefore, not in the WTB – **Tax liabilities**. We, therefore, have to add this to the WTB.

4.   Go to the bottom-right cell of the WTB, cell G27:

	A	B	C	D	E	F	G	H
4		GROUP	ACC GRP	ACC DESCRIPTION	2022 UNAUDITED	AUDIT JOURNALS	2022 FINAL	
5		BS	Property, Plant & Equipment	Furniture & fittings - Cost	10,500,000	-	10,500,000	
6		BS	Property, Plant & Equipment	Plant & Machinery - Cost	97,500,000	-	97,500,000	
7		BS	Property, Plant & Equipment	Motor vehicles - Cost	52,250,000	-	52,250,000	
8		BS	Property, Plant & Equipment	Land	75,750,000	-	75,750,000	
9		BS	Property, Plant & Equipment	Furniture & fittings - Acc. Deprecn.	(1,050,000)	-	(1,050,000)	
10		BS	Property, Plant & Equipment	Plant & Machinery - Acc. Deprecn.	(9,750,000)	-	(9,750,000)	
11		BS	Property, Plant & Equipment	Motor vehicles - Acc. Deprecn.	(10,450,000)	-	(10,450,000)	
12		BS	Inventory	Inventory	125,600,500	10,000,000	135,600,500	
13		BS	Trade debtors	Trade debtors	195,750,000	-	195,750,000	
14		BS	Sundry debtors	Sundry debtors	9,294,000	-	9,294,000	
15		BS	Prepayments	Prepayments	12,600,000	-	12,600,000	
16		BS	Cash and bank	Cash and bank	57,350,000	-	57,350,000	
17		BS	Trade creditors	Trade creditors	(173,060,000)	-	(173,060,000)	
18		BS	Accruals	Accruals	(87,570,500)	-	(87,570,500)	
19		BS	Long term loans	Bank loans	(215,500,000)	-	(215,500,000)	
20		BS	Share capital	Share capital	(100,000,000)	-	(100,000,000)	
21		PNL	Retained earnings	Retained earnings	-	-	-	
22		PNL	Turnover	Turnover	(755,800,000)	-	(755,800,000)	
23		PNL	Cost of sales	Cost of sales	604,640,000	(10,000,000)	594,640,000	
24		PNL	Selling & distribution	Selling & distribution	37,790,000	-	37,790,000	
25		PNL	Admin & General	Admin & General	52,906,000	-	52,906,000	
26		PNL	Depreciation	Depreciation	21,250,000	-	21,250,000	
27		PNL	Taxation	Taxation	-	10,512,000	10,512,000	←
28								

Figure 12.25 – Bottom-right cell of the table

5.   Then, press *Tab*:

26	PNL	Depreciation	Depreciation	21,250,000	-	21,250,000
27	PNL	Taxation	Taxation	-	10,512,000	10,512,000
28					-	-
29						

Figure 12.26 – New table row created

A new table row is formed at the bottom of the table, row 28.

6. Enter the details of the new account.

	A	B	C	D	E	F	G
4		GROUP	ACC GRP	ACC DESCRIPTION	2022 UNAUDITED	AUDIT JOURNALS	2022 FINAL
5		BS	Property, Plant & Equipment	Furniture & fittings - Cost	10,500,000	-	10,500,000
6		BS	Property, Plant & Equipment	Plant & Machinery - Cost	97,500,000	-	97,500,000
7		BS	Property, Plant & Equipment	Motor vehicles - Cost	52,250,000	-	52,250,000
8		BS	Property, Plant & Equipment	Land	75,750,000	-	75,750,000
9		BS	Property, Plant & Equipment	Furniture & fittings - Acc. Deprecn.	(1,050,000)	-	(1,050,000)
10		BS	Property, Plant & Equipment	Plant & Machinery - Acc. Deprecn.	(9,750,000)	-	(9,750,000)
11		BS	Property, Plant & Equipment	Motor vehicles - Acc. Deprecn.	(10,450,000)	-	(10,450,000)
12		BS	Inventory	Inventory	125,600,500	10,000,000	135,600,500
13		BS	Trade debtors	Trade debtors	195,750,000	-	195,750,000
14		BS	Sundry debtors	Sundry debtors	9,294,000	-	9,294,000
15		BS	Prepayments	Prepayments	12,600,000	-	12,600,000
16		BS	Cash and bank	Cash and bank	57,350,000	-	57,350,000
17		BS	Trade creditors	Trade creditors	(173,060,000)	-	(173,060,000)
18		BS	Accruals	Accruals	(87,570,500)	-	(87,570,500)
19		BS	Long term loans	Bank loans	(215,500,000)	-	(215,500,000)
20		BS	Share capital	Share capital	(100,000,000)	-	(100,000,000)
21		PNL	Retained earnings	Retained earnings	-	-	-
22		PNL	Turnover	Turnover	(755,800,000)	-	(755,800,000)
23		PNL	Cost of sales	Cost of sales	604,640,000	(10,000,000)	594,640,000
24		PNL	Selling & distribution	Selling & distribution	37,790,000	-	37,790,000
25		PNL	Admin & General	Admin & General	52,906,000	-	52,906,000
26		PNL	Depreciation	Depreciation	21,250,000	-	21,250,000
27		PNL	Taxation	Taxation	-	10,512,000	10,512,000
28		BS	Tax liabilities	Tax liabilities		(10,512,000)	(10,512,000)
30						0	-

Figure 12.27 – WTB balanced with new account

As soon as **ACC DESCRIPTION** is entered, the **AUDIT JOURNAL** column is updated and the WTB is once again in balance.

Updating financial statements and troubleshooting to correct errors

In order to update the financial statements, we just need to do the following:

1. Refresh the pivot table, and the values will be updated accordingly.

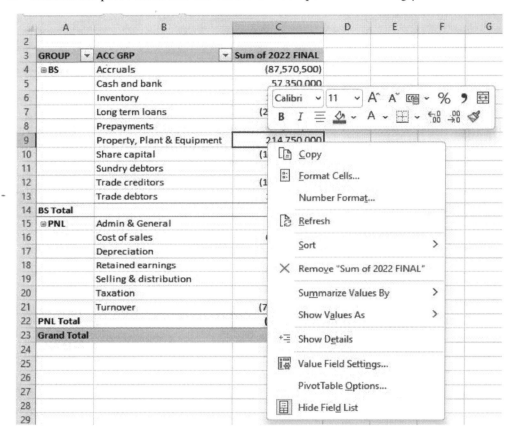

Figure 12.28 – Refreshing the pivot table

2. With the cursor anywhere within the pivot table, right-click on the mouse and select **Refresh** from the drop-down menu. The pivot table is then updated for any adjustment made to the WTB.

	A	B	C
2			
3	GROUP ▼	ACC GRP ▼	Sum of 2022 FINAL
4	⊟BS	Accruals	(87,570,500)
5		Cash and bank	57,350,000
6		Inventory	135,600,500
7		Long term loans	(215,500,000)
8		Prepayments	12,600,000
9		Property, Plant & Equipment	214,750,000
10		Share capital	(100,000,000)
11		Sundry debtors	9,294,000
12		Trade creditors	(173,060,000)
13		Trade debtors	195,750,000
14	➡	Tax liabilities	(10,512,000)
15	BS Total		38,702,000
16	⊟PNL	Admin & General	52,906,000
17		Cost of sales	594,640,000
18		Depreciation	21,250,000
19		Retained earnings	-
20		Selling & distribution	37,790,000
21		Taxation	10,512,000
22		Turnover	(755,800,000)
23	PNL Total		(38,702,000)
24	Grand Total		-

Figure 12.29 – Pivot table updated with new information

The new account is incorporated into the pivot table. We now turn to the BS to confirm that the financial statements have been updated correctly.

The PNL has been updated correctly for **Cost of sales** and **Taxation**. The BS has updated **Inventory**, but is now out of balance.

In this exercise, it is easy to see where the difference is coming from; however, these are the steps you would normally take when the difference is not so obvious:

1. Check the PNL PAT against the PNL total of the pivot table.

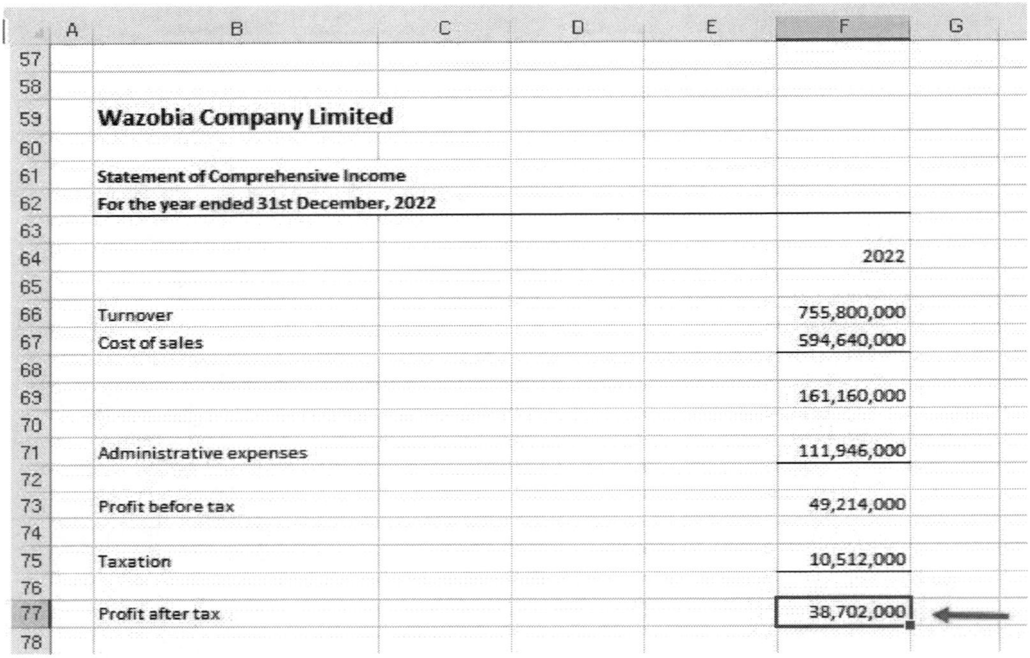

	A	B	C	D	E	F	G
57							
58							
59		**Wazobia Company Limited**					
60							
61		Statement of Comprehensive Income					
62		For the year ended 31st December, 2022					
63							
64						2022	
65							
66		Turnover				755,800,000	
67		Cost of sales				594,640,000	
68							
69						161,160,000	
70							
71		Administrative expenses				111,946,000	
72							
73		Profit before tax				49,214,000	
74							
75		Taxation				10,512,000	
76							
77		Profit after tax				38,702,000	
78							

Figure 12.30 – Profit after tax

Profit after tax amounts to **38,702,000**, as shown in *Figure 12.31*:

	A	B	C	D
2				
3	GROUP ▾	ACC GRP ▾	Sum of 2022 FINAL	
4	⊞ BS	Accruals	(87,570,500)	
5		Cash and bank	57,350,000	
6		Inventory	135,600,500	
7		Long term loans	(215,500,000)	
8		Prepayments	12,600,000	
9		Property, Plant & Equipment	214,750,000	
10		Share capital	(100,000,000)	
11		Sundry debtors	9,294,000	
12		Trade creditors	(173,060,000)	
13		Trade debtors	195,750,000	
14		Tax liabilities	(10,512,000)	
15	BS Total		38,702,000	
16	⊞ PNL	Admin & General	52,906,000	
17		Cost of sales	594,640,000	
18		Depreciation	21,250,000	
19		Retained earnings	-	
20		Selling & distribution	37,790,000	
21		Taxation	10,512,000	
22		Turnover	(755,800,000)	
23	PNL Total		(38,702,000)	⟵
24	Grand Total		-	
25				

Figure 12.31 – PNL total in the pivot table

PNL Total in the pivot table is **38,702,000**, which is the same as the PAT; this indicates that the error is not in the PNL. So, we turn our attention to the BS.

2. The BS shows the new account but no figure is against it. You just need to copy the XLOOKUP formula there, bearing in mind that it is a CR balance.

	A	B	C	D	E	F
2	BALANCE SHEET					
3						
4						
5		Wazobia Company Limited				
6						
7		Statement of Financial Position at 31st December 2022				
8						
9						
10		NON-CURRENT ASSETS				2022
11		Property, Plant & Equipment				
12						214,750,000
13		CURRENT ASSETS				
14		Inventory				135,600,500
15		Accounts receivable				217,644,000
16		Cash & cash equivalents				57,350,000
17						
18						410,594,500
19						
20		CURRENT LIABILITIES				
21		Accounts payable				260,630,500
22		Tax liabilities				10,512,000
23						
24						271,142,500
25						
26		NET CURRENT ASSETS				139,452,000
27						
28						
29		NON-CURRENT LIABILITIES				215,500,000
30						
31		TOTAL ASSETS LESS LIABILITIES				138,702,000
32						
33		EQUITY				
34		Share capital				100,000,000
35		Retained earnings				38,702,000
36						
37						138,702,000

Figure 12.32 – BS now in balance

The correct value is retrieved for the new account, and the BS is once more in balance.

Summary

In this chapter, you have prepared a model to extract financial statements from a trial balance. You have learned how to construct your template so that the model can be updated with a few keystrokes for any adjustments or updates. You have also learned how to systematically approach the task of troubleshooting in the event of an error.

In the next chapter, we will look at capital budgeting with the help of another case study.

13
Case Study 2 – Creating a Model for Capital Budgeting

During its existence, an organization will be faced with critical investment decisions, such as branch expansion, purchase of new equipment, making or buying machinery decisions, the introduction of new products, and research and development projects. All of these require the allocation of crucial financial resources. The management of these investment decisions, including the allocation of scarce resources, is referred to as **capital budgeting**. There are four common concepts developed to assist management with these critical decisions, namely, **Net Present Value (NPV)**, **Internal Rate of Return (IRR)**, **Profitability Index (PI)**, and **Pay Back Period (PBP)**. The first three of these consider the time value of money and the fourth one doesn't. In this chapter, we will discuss and explain these concepts and then put them into practice with a comprehensive case study. The following are the major topics covered in this chapter:

- Introduction
- Understanding NPV
- Understanding IRR

- Understanding PI
- Understanding PBP
- Case study

By the end of the chapter, you will have learned how to calculate each of the techniques mentioned and how to create a model to assist management with capital budgeting, using the four concepts.

Introduction

Throughout this book, we have mentioned the time value of money, that money today is of more value than money tomorrow. This is due to the following reasons:

- Depreciation – Prices always go up, so the spending power of 1 Naira today is greater than the spending power of 1 Naira tomorrow.
- The ability to invest, so with interest, your money grows over time. 1 Naira today = 1 Naira + interest tomorrow.

This brings us to the concepts of **Present Value (PV)**, **Future Value (FV)**, and **opportunity cost** or **discount rate**. The PV is today's value and FV is the value at some time in the future.

When you choose a particular line of action, the benefit you would have derived from other alternatives that you did not choose is referred to as the **opportunity cost**. The opportunity cost is the same as the discount rate and this rate is what is used to convert FV to PV and vice versa.

Understanding NPV

As the name suggests, NPV is a net figure and is obtained as follows:

```
NPV = Present Value of all cash inflows - Present Value of all
cash outflows
```

Usually, the outflow tends to be at the commencement of the project and is thus not discounted. However, where there is additional outflow some time in the future, this has to be discounted to its PV and added to the initial outflow before subtracting from the PV of cash inflows.

For investment decisions, if the NPV of a project is positive, then accept the project. If the NPV is negative, reject the project. The greater the NPV, the more financially rewarding the project.

The relationship between PV and FV is captured as follows:

$$FV = PV \times (1 + K)^n$$

Here, we have the following:

- FV = future value
- PV = present value
- K = discount rate
- n = number of years (assuming that now is year 0 and after one year is year 1)

Rearranging the equation, we get the following:

$$PV = FV \times \frac{1}{(1 + K)^n}$$

The discount factor is $\frac{1}{(1 + K)^n}$.

This is the factor by which the FV is discounted to arrive at the PV. Let's look at an example:

- Assuming a discount rate of 10%, calculate the PV of the following:
  - 100 Naira received after 1 year
  - 100 Naira received after 3 years
  - 100 Naira received after 12 years
- The solution is as follows:

$$PV = FV \times \frac{1}{(1 + K)^n}$$

These are the meanings of the abbreviations:

- FV = 100 Naira at the time specified
- K = 10% or 0.10
- $(1 + K) = (1 + 0.10) = (1.10)$

The time value of money is clearly illustrated here:

- $PV = 100 \times \dfrac{1}{1.1^1} = 90.91$
- $PV = 100 \times \dfrac{1}{1.1^3} = 75.13$
- $PV = 100 \times \dfrac{1}{1.1^{12}} = 31.86$

100 Naira received in 1 years' time is worth 90.91 Naira today, after 3 years is worth 75.13 Naira today, and after 15 years is worth only 31.86 Naira today.

Understanding IRR

The IRR is the discount rate at which the NPV is 0. Where there are several projects, the IRR is used to rank them so that the higher the IRR, the more desirable the project. With all other things being equal, the project with the highest IRR is recommended.

The following are the criteria for accepting the project:

- Where the IRR is greater than the discount rate, accept the project.
- Where the IRR is less than the discount rate, reject the project.

The IRR can be obtained by substituting various amounts for the discount factor while observing the NPV until you arrive at a discount factor that results in an NPV of 0.

Alternatively, we could use the **Goal Seek** function under **What-If Analysis** in the **Data Tools** section of the **Data** ribbon in Excel. We shall illustrate this in the solution to our case study.

Understanding PI

This index measures how much you get in return for every Naira you incur:

$$PI = \frac{Present\ value\ of\ all\ inflows}{Present\ value\ of\ all\ outflows}$$

The PI is calculated as follows:

- If the *PI* is greater than 1, accept the project.
- If the *PI* is less than 1, reject the project.
- If the *PI* = 1, then consider other factors in making a decision.

Understanding PBP

PBP is the number of years it takes to recover the initial investment from project inflows. As mentioned at the beginning of the chapter, this method is usually calculated without considering the time value of money. You would accept projects with PBPs less than the industry average or a standard set by top management. The project with the shortest payback period is the most desirable. The payback period is very important to all projects as it indicates when the invested funds will be available for other projects.

Case study

Wazobia Ventures Ltd is seeking your advice on whether to invest N5,000,000 on a waste recycling project that will yield the following results:

- N300,000 in year 1
- N1,500,000 in year 2
- N2,000,000 in year 3
- N2,000,000 in year 4
- N800,000 in year 5

Wazobia's cost of capital is 9%. Management expects to recover the initial investment within 4 years.

You are to perform the following tasks:

1. Calculate the NPV, IRR, PI, and PBP of the project.
2. For each of these indicators, state whether the project is viable and advise management.
3. Would your answer be different if the cost of capital was 10%?

Let's look at the solution in the following section.

Solution

In accordance with good practice, we must first make some assumptions and put them together in an assumption table:

1. First, build an assumption table.

	A	B	C
	D9	fx	
	A	B	C
3		YEAR (n)	AMOUNT
4	Initial Outlay	0	(5,000,000)
5	Inflow in year	1	300,000
6	Inflow in year	2	1,500,000
7	Inflow in year	3	2,000,000
8	Inflow in year	4	2,000,000
9	Inflow in year	5	800,000
10	Discount rate K		9%

Figure 13.1 – Assumptions table

2. Prepare a layout for the calculations.

	Inflow (FV)	Outflow	$1 + K$	$(1 + K)^n$	$\dfrac{1}{(1 + K)^n}$	$PV = FV \times \dfrac{1}{(1 + k)^n}$
Year 0						
End of year 1						
End of year 2						
End of year 3						
End of year 4						
End of year 5						
					NPV =	
					Profitability Index =	

Figure 13.2 – Layout for calculations

The layout is designed to gradually build up to the NPV using formulas that link to the assumptions.

3. Link the outflow in year 0 to the assumptions.

	A	B	C
	SUM		fx =C4
3		YEAR (n)	AMOUNT
4	Initial Outlay	0	(5,000,000)
5	Inflow in year	1	300,000
6	Inflow in year	2	1,500,000
7	Inflow in year	3	2,000,000
8	Inflow in year	4	2,000,000
9	Inflow in year	5	800,000
10	Discount rate K		9%
11			
12	Calculations		
13			
14		Inflow	Outflow
15	Year 0		=C4

Figure 13.3 – Outflow linked to assumptions

4. Link the inflows to the assumptions.

	A	B	C
	SUM		fx =C5
3		YEAR (n)	AMOUNT
4	Initial Outlay	0	(5,000,000)
5	Inflow in year	1	300,000
6	Inflow in year	2	1,500,000
7	Inflow in year	3	2,000,000
8	Inflow in year	4	2,000,000
9	Inflow in year	5	800,000
10	Discount rate K		9%
11			
12	Calculations		
13			
14		Inflow	Outflow
15	Year 0		(5,000,000)
16	End of year 1	=C5	
17	End of year 2	1,500,000	
18	End of year 3	2,000,000	
19	End of year 4	2,000,000	
20	End of year 5	800,000	

Figure 13.4 – Inflows linked to assumptions

Due to the referencing framework in Excel, we can copy the formula in cell B16 down to the other years' inflows.

5. Populate the 1 + K column.

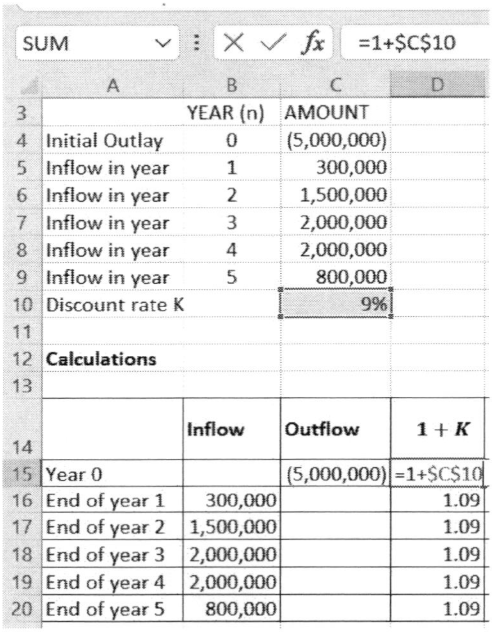

SUM	∨	⋮	× ✓	*fx*	=1+$C$10

	A	B	C	D
3		YEAR (n)	AMOUNT	
4	Initial Outlay	0	(5,000,000)	
5	Inflow in year	1	300,000	
6	Inflow in year	2	1,500,000	
7	Inflow in year	3	2,000,000	
8	Inflow in year	4	2,000,000	
9	Inflow in year	5	800,000	
10	Discount rate K		9%	
11				
12	Calculations			
13				
14		Inflow	Outflow	1 + K
15	Year 0		(5,000,000)	=1+$C$10
16	End of year 1	300,000		1.09
17	End of year 2	1,500,000		1.09
18	End of year 3	2,000,000		1.09
19	End of year 4	2,000,000		1.09
20	End of year 5	800,000		1.09

Figure 13.5 – Populating the 1 + K column

6. Ensure that the value of K is linked to the assumptions table's cell C10.

7. Populate the next column, $(1 + K)^n$.

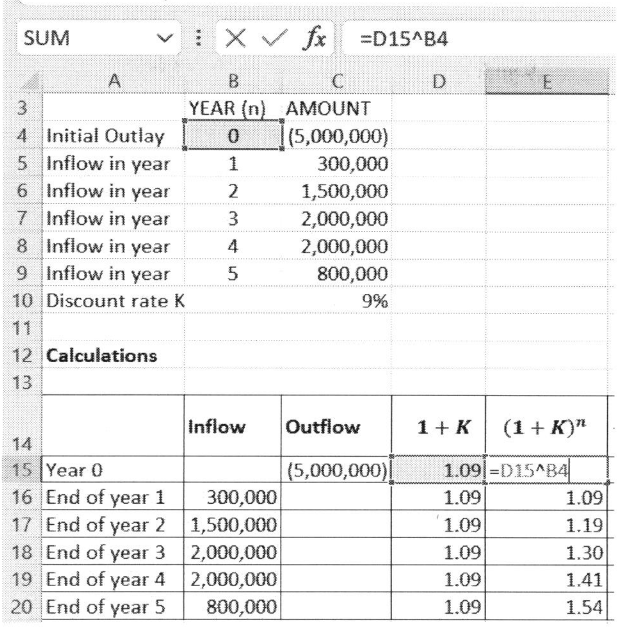

Figure 13.6 – Population of the next column, $(1 + K)^n$

Again, the values should be related to the assumptions. You will notice that the value for the outflow equates to 1. There is no discounting in year 0.

8. Now, populate the discount factor column.

Figure 13.7 – Discount factors calculated

9. Finally, multiply by the appropriate inflow to give the PV for each year.

Figure 13.8 – PVs of inflows

We have now arrived at the PVs of all inflows and outflows.

10. Now, calculate the NPV.

G21		fx	=SUM(G15:G20)			

	A	B	C	D	E	F	G
2	ASSUMPTIONS						
3		YEAR (n)	AMOUNT				
4	Initial Outlay	0	(5,000,000)				
5	Inflow in year	1	300,000				
6	Inflow in year	2	1,500,000				
7	Inflow in year	3	2,000,000				
8	Inflow in year	4	2,000,000				
9	Inflow in year	5	800,000				
10	Discount rate K		9%				
11							
12	Calculations						
13							
14		Inflow (FV)	Outflow	$1+K$	$(1+K)^n$	$\dfrac{1}{(1+K)^n}$	$PV = FV \times \dfrac{1}{(1+k)^n}$
15	Year 0		(5,000,000)	1.09	1.00	1.00	(5,000,000)
16	End of year 1	300,000		1.09	1.09	0.92	275,229
17	End of year 2	1,500,000		1.09	1.19	0.84	1,262,520
18	End of year 3	2,000,000		1.09	1.30	0.77	1,544,367
19	End of year 4	2,000,000		1.09	1.41	0.71	1,416,850
20	End of year 5	800,000		1.09	1.54	0.65	519,945
21						NPV =	18,912

Figure 13.9 – NPV

The NPV of the project is N18,912. The IRR is the discount factor that produces an NPV of 0. We will use Goal Seek to evaluate the IRR.

11. With the cursor on cell G21, the NPV, Go to the **Data** ribbon | **Data Tools** | **What-If Analysis** and select **Goal Seek….**

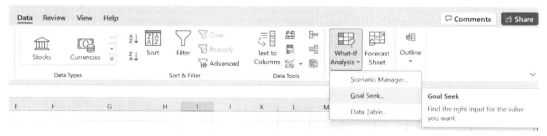

Figure 13.10 – Goal Seek from the Data ribbon

The **Goal Seek** dialog box is launched.

12. In the **Goal Seek** dialog box, select the options as shown in *Figure 13.11*:

	A	B	C	D	E	F	G	H
							G21 ∨ : ✕ ✓ *fx* =SUM(G15:G20)	
2	**ASSUMPTIONS**							
3		YEAR (n)	AMOUNT				Goal Seek ? ✕	
4	Initial Outlay	0	(5,000,000)					
5	Inflow in year	1	300,000				Set cell: G21 ↑	
6	Inflow in year	2	1,500,000				To value: 0	
7	Inflow in year	3	2,000,000				By changing cell: $C$10 ↑	
8	Inflow in year	4	2,000,000					
9	Inflow in year	5	800,000				OK Cancel	
10	Discount rate K		9%					
11								
12	**Calculations**							
13								
14		Inflow (FV)	Outflow	$1 + K$	$(1 + K)^n$	$\frac{1}{(1 + K)^n}$	$PV = FV \times \frac{1}{(1 + k)^n}$	
15	Year 0		(5,000,000)	1.09	1.00	1.00	(5,000,000)	
16	End of year 1	300,000		1.09	1.09	0.92	275,229	
17	End of year 2	1,500,000		1.09	1.19	0.84	1,262,520	
18	End of year 3	2,000,000		1.09	1.30	0.77	1,544,367	
19	End of year 4	2,000,000		1.09	1.41	0.71	1,416,850	
20	End of year 5	800,000		1.09	1.54	0.65	519,945	
21						NPV =	18,912	

Figure 13.11 – Goal Seek parameters

13. Set cell G21 (NPV) to the value 0 by changing cell C10 (discount rate), and then click **OK**.

	A	B	C	D	E	F	G	H
2	**ASSUMPTIONS**							
3		YEAR (n)	AMOUNT					
4	Initial Outlay	0	(5,000,000)					
5	Inflow in year	1	300,000					
6	Inflow in year	2	1,500,000					
7	Inflow in year	3	2,000,000					
8	Inflow in year	4	2,000,000					
9	Inflow in year	5	800,000					
10	Discount rate K		9.13% ⬅					
11								
12	**Calculations**							
13								
14		Inflow (FV)	Outflow	$1 + K$	$(1 + K)^n$	$\frac{1}{(1 + K)^n}$	$PV = FV \times \frac{1}{(1 + k)^n}$	
15	Year 0		(5,000,000)	1.09	1.00	1.00	(5,000,000)	
16	End of year 1	300,000		1.09	1.09	0.92	274,897	
17	End of year 2	1,500,000		1.09	1.19	0.84	1,259,476	
18	End of year 3	2,000,000		1.09	1.30	0.77	1,538,785	
19	End of year 4	2,000,000		1.09	1.42	0.71	1,410,026	
20	End of year 5	800,000		1.09	1.55	0.65	516,816	
21						NPV =	0 ⬅	

Figure 13.12 – Calculated IRR

The arrows point to the NPV at value 0 and the attendant discount rate. The discount rate that gives an NPV of 0 is 9.13%. This is the IRR.

14. Next, calculate the PI, as shown in *Figure 13.13*:

	A	B	C	D	E	F	G	H
10	Discount rate K		9.00%					
11								
12	Calculations							
13								
14		Inflow (FV)	Outflow	$1 + K$	$(1+K)^n$	$\dfrac{1}{(1+K)^n}$	$PV = FV \times \dfrac{1}{(1+k)^n}$	
15	Year 0		(5,000,000)	1.09	1.00	1.00	(5,000,000)	
16	End of year 1	300,000		1.09	1.09	0.92	275,229	
17	End of year 2	1,500,000		1.09	1.19	0.84	1,262,520	
18	End of year 3	2,000,000		1.09	1.30	0.77	1,544,367	
19	End of year 4	2,000,000		1.09	1.41	0.71	1,416,850	
20	End of year 5	800,000		1.09	1.54	0.65	519,945	
21						NPV =	18,912	
22						Profitability Index =	=SUM(G16:G20)/-G15	

Figure 13.13 – Calculation of PI

The PI is calculated as follows:

$$PI = \frac{Present\ value\ of\ all\ inflows}{Present\ value\ of\ all\ outflows}$$

This gives a PI of 1.0038.

128			$\times\ \checkmark\ fx$				
	A	B	C	D	E	F	G
11							
12	Calculations						
13							
14		Inflow (FV)	Outflow	$1 + K$	$(1+K)^n$	$\dfrac{1}{(1+K)^n}$	$PV = FV \times \dfrac{1}{(1+k)^n}$
15	Year 0		(5,000,000)	1.09	1.00	1.00	(5,000,000)
16	End of year 1	300,000		1.09	1.09	0.92	275,229
17	End of year 2	1,500,000		1.09	1.19	0.84	1,262,520
18	End of year 3	2,000,000		1.09	1.30	0.77	1,544,367
19	End of year 4	2,000,000		1.09	1.41	0.71	1,416,850
20	End of year 5	800,000		1.09	1.54	0.65	519,945
21						NPV =	18,912
22						Profitability Index =	1.0038

Figure 13.14 – PI evaluated

The final measure is PBP.

The PBP uses the non-discounted cash flows.

	A	B	C	D
24				
25	**Pay Back Period**			
26				
27	YEAR	INFLOW	CUMULATIVE INFLOW	
28	1	300,000	300,000	
29	2	1,500,000	1,800,000	
30	3	2,000,000	3,800,000	←
31	4	2,000,000	5,800,000	
32	5	800,000	6,600,000	

Figure 13.15 – PBP

The PBP falls between years 3 and 4.

Cumulative inflow at the end of year 3 is N3,800,000, which is N1,200,000 short of the initial outlay of N5,000,000. Inflow in year 4 is N2,000,000; thus, assuming that the inflow is evenly spread through the year, it will take:

$$\frac{1,200,000}{2,000,000} \times 365$$
$$= 219 days\ (approximately\ 7\ months\ 19\ days)\ of\ year\ 4\ \ toget\ to\ 5,000,000$$

PBP is 3 years, 7 months, and (approximately) 19 days.

Here are the answers to the preceding questions:

- **Answer 1**

  - NPV = 18,912

  - IRR = 9.13%

  - PI = 1.0038

  - PBP = 3 years, 7 months, and about 19 days

- **Answer 2**

  - NPV is positive, so accept the project.

  - IRR is greater than the discount rate (9.13% to 9%), so accept the project.

- PI is greater than 1, so accept the project.

- PBP is within management expectations of 4 years, so accept the project.

All four indicators are in agreement, so accept the project.

- **Answer 3**

    - NPV is negative, so reject the project.

    - IRR is less than the discount rate (9.13% to 10%), so reject the project.

    - PI is less than 1 (0.9756), so reject the project.

	A	B	C	D	E	F	G	H
3		YEAR (n)	AMOUNT					
4	Initial Outlay	0	(5,000,000)					
5	Inflow in year	1	300,000					
6	Inflow in year	2	1,500,000					
7	Inflow in year	3	2,000,000					
8	Inflow in year	4	2,000,000					
9	Inflow in year	5	800,000					
10	Discount rate K		10.00% ⟵────					
11								
12	Calculations							
13								
14		Inflow (FV)	Outflow	$1+K$	$(1+K)^n$	$\dfrac{1}{(1+K)^n}$	$PV = FV \times \dfrac{1}{(1+k)^n}$	
15	Year 0		(5,000,000)	1.10	1.00	1.00	(5,000,000)	
16	End of year 1	300,000		1.10	1.10	0.91	272,727	
17	End of year 2	1,500,000		1.10	1.21	0.83	1,239,669	
18	End of year 3	2,000,000		1.10	1.33	0.75	1,502,630	
19	End of year 4	2,000,000		1.10	1.46	0.68	1,366,027	
20	End of year 5	800,000		1.10	1.61	0.62	496,737	
21						NPV =	(122,210) ⟵────	
22						Profitability Index =	0.9756 ⟵────	

Figure 13.16 – Discount rate of 10%

PBP is within management expectations of 4 years, so accept the project. Since three out of four indicators say reject, the project should be rejected.

Summary

In this chapter, we have understood the meaning and importance of capital budgeting. We have discussed and illustrated the time value of money and the concepts of NPV, IRR, PI, and PBP. You can now face any capital budgeting assignment with ease. We have also seen how these concepts can assist in deciding the viability of projects.

Index

Packt.com

Subscribe to our online digital library for full access to over 7,000 books and videos, as well as industry leading tools to help you plan your personal development and advance your career. For more information, please visit our website.

Why subscribe?

- Spend less time learning and more time coding with practical eBooks and Videos from over 4,000 industry professionals

- Improve your learning with Skill Plans built especially for you

- Get a free eBook or video every month

- Fully searchable for easy access to vital information

- Copy and paste, print, and bookmark content

Did you know that Packt offers eBook versions of every book published, with PDF and ePub files available? You can upgrade to the eBook version at packt.com and as a print book customer, you are entitled to a discount on the eBook copy. Get in touch with us at customercare@packtpub.com for more details.

At www.packt.com, you can also read a collection of free technical articles, sign up for a range of free newsletters, and receive exclusive discounts and offers on Packt books and eBooks.

Other Books You May Enjoy

If you enjoyed this book, you may be interested in these other books by Packt:

Data Forecasting and Segmentation Using Microsoft Excel

Fernando Roque

ISBN: 9781803247731

- Understand why machine learning is important for classifying data segmentation
- Focus on basic statistics tests for regression variable dependency
- Test time series autocorrelation to build a useful forecast
- Use Excel add-ins to run K-means without programming
- Analyze segment outliers for possible data anomalies and fraud
- Build, train, and validate multiple regression models and time series forecasts

Packt is searching for authors like you

If you're interested in becoming an author for Packt, please visit `authors.packtpub.com` and apply today. We have worked with thousands of developers and tech professionals, just like you, to help them share their insight with the global tech community. You can make a general application, apply for a specific hot topic that we are recruiting an author for, or submit your own idea.

Share Your Thoughts

Now you've finished *Hands-On Financial Modeling with Excel for Microsoft 365*, we'd love to hear your thoughts! Scan the QR code below to go straight to the Amazon review page for this book and share your feedback or leave a review on the site that you purchased it from.

https://packt.link/r/1-803-23114-9

Your review is important to us and the tech community and will help us make sure we're delivering excellent quality content.

Made in the USA
Middletown, DE
14 January 2024

47853635R00192